REBOUND

THE ODYSSEY OF
MICHAEL JORDAN

REBOUND

THE ODYSSEY OF
MICHAEL JORDAN

BOB GREENE

MICHAEL JOSEPH
LONDON

MICHAEL JOSEPH LTD

Published by the Penguin Group
27 Wrights Lane, London W8 5TZ, England
Viking Penguin Inc., 375 Hudson Street, New York, New York 10014, USA
Penguin Books Australia Ltd, Ringwood, Victoria, Australia
Penguin Books Canada Ltd, 10 Alcorn Avenue, Toronto, Ontario, Canada M4V 3B2
Penguin Books (NZ) Ltd, 182–190 Wairau Road, Auckland 10, New Zealand

Penguin Books Ltd, Registered Offices: Harmondsworth, Middlesex, England

First published 1995

Printed in England by Clays Ltd, St Ives plc

A CIP catalogue record for this book is available from the British Library

ISBN 0 7181 4109 1

The moral right of the author has been asserted

FOR JACK ROTH AND CHUCK SHENK

REBOUND

CHAPTER 1

"One night," he said, "I was watching television—a movie or something—and they interrupted the show for a special report.

"Any time they do that, you get nervous because you think that war has broken out, or there's an earthquake somewhere—something bad.

"So I looked at the screen, and the newscaster came on, and behind his head there was a picture of me. The special report was about me.

"I'm not sure at what point this was—whether they were saying something about my father, or that I was going to retire from basketball, or play baseball, or come back to basketball—I'm not sure what this particular special report was about. Something in my life.

"What I do remember is watching the newscaster talk, and listening to him say that it had been learned that I was about to do this or that or the other thing. He said that the reports they were getting were unofficial, and that reporters were trying to contact me to find out what the real word was. He said that I was the only person who knew what I was about to do with my life.

"I remember sitting there watching him, and thinking: 'So you think so, do you? So you think I know what's coming next?' I was alone in the room, there was no one else with me, and the newscaster on the TV screen was saying that I was the one who had all the true answers, and I was thinking, 'If only you knew. If only you knew, you would never say that.'"

CHAPTER 2

"Are you sure you know where we're going?" Jordan said.

"Of course I'm sure," I said.

This was during that strange period in-between. He had retired from basketball, walked away from the Chicago Bulls and the three world championships. All the things that would come later—the decision to try to become a baseball player, then the decision to stop being a baseball player, then the decision to attempt a return to the National Basketball Association, and the madness that would ensue—all of that was yet to occur.

"Just stay on this freeway," I said.

"I know we're going the wrong way," he said.

He was behind the wheel of his Corvette. He had been at a factory on the far South Side of Chicago, fulfilling a business commitment; he had offered to drop me at work. We were on the Calumet Expressway, and he was convinced that we were headed in precisely the wrong direction.

"Look," he said. "There's 111th Street."

The exit flashed by.

"There's 115th Street," he said.

The street numbers should have been getting lower, not higher.

"I'm pretty sure we're OK," I said.

"There's 130th Street," he said, and steered the car sharply toward an exit ramp and off the expressway.

"I should have followed my own instincts," he said, driving down a quiet residential block.

"Michael, we love you!" a woman called from the curb.

"I think we can find the entrance ramp up here," he said.

We pulled up to a stop sign. No one had known that he would be in this neighborhood—now, or ever. There had been no announcement that he was coming, and with any luck in finding the on-ramp he was only going to be here for a matter of seconds. But already a crowd was forming, people were running out of houses and onto the sidewalks.

"Michael, come back," a man called.

Two others, across the street, yelled, "Come back to the Bulls!"

"I think it's up there," Jordan said.

Meaning the entrance ramp. That was his reaction to strangers screaming at him from the curbs: no reaction. It was as if he were wearing blinders, or as if soundproof curtains were hanging from the side windows of the car. As if having strangers calling to him was the most natural thing in the world.

Which in his world it was. Within a minute we were back on the expressway, heading downtown. "I was out in California," he said. "And some friends and I were riding bikes near the beach. There was a basketball game going on, on a court next to the beach—a pickup game.

"One of the guys I was with walked onto the court and asked if we could have the next game. My friend said that I was with them, and the guys on the court thought he was making a joke. Then they looked over.

"I got off the bike and walked onto the court and started playing. It was fun—the guys who had been there wanted to prove that they could take me on, so it was fun. But I guess the word started to spread about what was going on, and pretty soon about six thousand people had gathered. So I finished the game and left."

"Sounds like a nice moment," I said.

"Yeah, I think we're going to re-create it for a commercial," he said.

Of course. I think he said it with an ironic tone, but I couldn't be sure. Whatever the nice moments in his life, whatever the pure moments—whatever the twists and turns of the Michael Jordan Story—it eventually all gets fed into the machine. It's probably past the point where anyone can even do anything about it anymore. Good news, bad news, funny news, sad—it never seems to slow down, never seems to take a breath. In a way, he is watching the story unfold along with the rest of the world. Everyone assumes that he knows what the next chapter will hold. Yet a lot of the time, when you see all of this with him from up close, you understand that he is as much a captive of the story as everyone else. That he is in the audience, too.

We were on Wacker Drive, downtown. "Where do you want to be dropped off?" Jordan said.

"Take a left up here," I said.

We were stuck in traffic, which had come to a halt. There was a loud, startling banging on the driver's-side window.

He turned quickly toward the sound. This unexpected pounding on the car window was not necessarily what he needed to be hearing right now. It had been only a few months since the murder of his father, who had been approached by strangers while sleeping unawares in his automobile.

A man in a suit and tie was standing in the street. This was in the middle of heavy traffic, on one of the busiest roadways in downtown Chicago. Jordan rolled the window down. The man thrust a piece of paper into the car.

"For my son," the man said.

"Where is your car?" Jordan said.

The man gestured back in traffic, where he had left his car with the motor running.

It struck me at that moment: You can retire from the Chicago Bulls; you can retire from the National Basketball Association. You cannot retire from being Michael Jordan.

Jordan signed, and the man left. "Pretty weird," I said.

"I suppose," Jordan said, not much in his voice, stepping on the accelerator.

CHAPTER 3

What follows in these pages is the diary of a journey—a chronicle recorded from inside an odyssey that, I am convinced, Jordan had no true idea he was embarking upon.

The public aspects of the odyssey have been among the most scrutinized events in the recent history of big-time sports—indeed, in the recent history of America's mass culture. When Jordan declared at a press conference in October of 1993 that he was walking away from professional basketball, the event was televised live worldwide. In the months and years that have followed, there were times when it seemed that not mere cameras, but X-ray machines were trained on him whenever he appeared before crowds.

Yet those who considered this to be a basketball story, then a baseball story, then a basketball story again, may have been missing the essence of what was taking place. Even those who saw the relentless fascination with Jordan as a mirror of our madhouse culture were observing only part of the tale. For as large as the story became, and continues to become—as outsized, sometimes frighteningly so, as the public side of Jordan's life grew—the most compelling thing that was going on was composed of small and utterly private moments. The drama may have appeared to be played out on a world stage—except there is no world stage. Jordan may have seemed to loom huge on the international landscape—except he was, and is, merely the size of a man. As in all the most riveting stories, the lasting truths of this one occurred in quiet instants, with few people around.

More than anything, it has been the story of a man who had all that a person could ever want—or so it seemed—and then, having lost something that was so important to him that his pain was unfathomable, had to decide what to do. In plain sight, Jordan faltered, and then in his mourning abandoned one of the parts of his life that he cherished the most while the world wondered what he might be doing. The litany of events that ensued was so confusing and seemingly haphazard that some guessed he might be cracking up, falling into an unexpectedly deep spiral from which he would never emerge.

But what happened was at the same time much more complicated, and much simpler, than that. Overcome with grief and uncertainty, Jordan made the instinctive decision to do what few men and women in adult life ever do: to start over. He tried to turn himself into who he had been before all the renown and all the privilege and all the adulation—to find out, as a kind of medicine for his grief, if he could do it all over again.

On the sports pages the odyssey has been mostly measured in box scores and game results. But the contests themselves, although they have provided high drama, will soon enough, like all contests, be forgotten. For all the front-page coverage of these watershed years in Jordan's life, the most transfixing story of all was an inner story, painted with tiny brushstrokes, that had its core where no one could see it.

Hang Time, the book I wrote about Jordan's championship years with the Chicago Bulls, ended with Jordan and his teammates as the best basketball team in the world. I am not a sportswriter—*Hang Time* was the story of time spent with Jordan the person, not Jordan the shooting guard—and when the book was finished, I expected to inevitably be seeing much less of him than I had during the years when it was being reported.

Yet that didn't happen. In the months after the death of Jordan's father I found myself talking with him still, and perceiving in him just as much insight, but on a different and more profound level, than during those years at the Chicago Stadium. I had always felt that Jordan alone—Jordan in a hotel room with the door double-locked, the Do Not Disturb sign out, the phone off the hook, his feet up on a table, trying to make sense out of his life—was even more interesting than Jordan on the basketball court.

When his world changed—when he got the news about his father, when he made the choices that would alter his life—that private Jordan became no less fascinating. In the brief period after he left the NBA with no clear destination in sight, I didn't know what was going to become of him—who was Michael Jordan supposed to be, once he declared himself not to be an athlete?—but I found his quiet reflections, his constant self-questioning, his observations of his own life, to be every bit as acute as when each of his moves was greeted with the sound of cheers.

And then the sports journey began anew, and I went along. For whatever reasons, Jordan has long allowed me to spend private hours with him, to see parts of his life that he has chosen to shut off from the rest of the world. There is no shortage of people who enjoy analyzing Jordan from afar, and the picture you get of him varies depending on whose analysis you accept. Many admire him; some consider him to be a self-centered gambler, a spoiled multimillionaire; still others treat him as something close to a religious figure. Most of the world simply enjoys watching him do what he does on fields of play.

In my time with Jordan—the *Hang Time* years, and the years since—I've tried to pay close attention to what I was seeing with my own eyes, to what I was hearing with my own ears. In my years as a newspaperman, those are the only things I have ever been able to count on for sure—the things that I knew were true, because I had been there to watch and listen. Whatever the story—a crime story, a courtroom story, a story of human dignity or human cruelty—I have never felt confident passing on a version of events unless I was present.

So what you will find here is not an arm's-length analysis, gleaned from nameless sources and third-party observers. These pages are a succession of moments in the company of Jordan as he tried to reinvent his life. If *Hang Time* was a journey with Jordan as he pursued certain championships, this is a journey with him as he searched for a quite different kind of championship. The first championships came during a period when for Jordan the most important victories could be commemorated with trophies and champagne showers. As a man grows older, he often comes to realize that the most veracious triumphs are determined not by others, but by oneself; that the only lasting victories are won when a person defines his own goals. He need not announce what those goals are; sometimes, when the pursuit begins, he need not even know.

The story in these pages is a tale of a champion's journey in search of that separate championship. Thanks for choosing to come along.

We will start at the beginning—but first, before we do, a scene from near the end.

After all of this had taken place—the grieving for his father, the departure from the Bulls, the trip into baseball and back and everything that would follow as he returned to the NBA—Jordan and I were talking about his decision to play basketball again. With all the worldwide attention that rejoining the NBA had brought to him, we spoke about how he might be tempting fate.

After all, had he become a private citizen as he had originally announced—or at least sought a small measure of a conventional citizen's right to privacy—he would not be inviting the kind of scrutiny that was now, once again, destined to be constant. He had to know what lay ahead—people once again would be looking for his flaws great and small, fishing around for his failings and carting those failings off to market. It was the kind of thing that had driven him to near-despair the first time around—the kind of thing he had vowed that he never wanted to go through again.

And here he was.

"I know," Jordan said. "I thought a lot about it. It used to just about make me crazy—no matter what I was accomplishing, I was always afraid that I would do something to screw it up, to make people disappointed in me. I would achieve something that I felt was really pretty good, and I never let myself feel too good about it, because I was afraid that if I felt too good, that would bring on my downfall.

"I expected myself to be purer than pure—even though I knew that I wasn't pure, that no one can be completely pure. So I'd win something, or people would tell me that they thought highly of me, and I would smile and say 'Thank you,' and inside I was thinking: 'Uh-oh, if they only knew.'

"And finally I figured it out. I could never be as pure as I felt I needed to be. I could never be so perfect that no one could ever find something bad to say about me. And my only answer was to decide: OK, I'm going to do the best I can. But I'm human. Do I have flaws? Have I made mistakes, and will I make mistakes?

"Yep, I have and I will. So here I am, this time around—a human being. Before, every second of every day was devoted to living up to a certain image. Every second was built around being afraid of doing something that would destroy me. I'm not going to be afraid anymore. I can only do my best. I'm not going to be afraid that someone will find out when I've failed."

"Is it as easy as that?" I said. "Just saying you're not going to be afraid?"

"It's not easy at all," Jordan said. "But it's the only answer. Otherwise, I couldn't live."

But that was well along in the journey. The journey began on a somewhat less certain note.

CHAPTER 4

". . . And someone who said he was Michael Jordan called," the assistant at my newspaper office said.

I was standing in the corridor of a courthouse in McHenry County, Illinois. I was out in the mostly rural area covering the case of three children who were being treated horribly by a judge; during a break in the hearing, I had used a hallway pay phone to call back to Chicago for messages.

The assistant had gone through the phone calls that had come in. She told me about the Jordan call almost as an afterthought.

"He said he was Jordan?" I asked.

"Yeah," she said. "I asked him for his phone number, and he said you'd know."

"Do you think it was him?" I said.

"I highly doubt it," she said. "He sounded like someone who was trying to sound like Michael Jordan."

"All right," I said. I hung up, returned some of the calls she had told me about, then headed back into the courtroom. Since the publication of *Hang Time*, I had received a number of phone calls from people wanting to reach Jordan, pass messages to Jordan, request autographs from Jordan. I assumed this fit into that same category—figured it was someone screwing around.

I rode the train back to Chicago that night, wrote a story, and the next day was in my office. The assistant was fielding calls; she stuck her head in the door at one point and said, "It's that guy who says he's Jordan again."

I picked up the phone and said hello.

"What, you don't return your phone calls anymore?" Jordan said.

I laughed. "So that was really you yesterday?" I said.

"Who else is going to say he's me?" Jordan said.

Maybe he really didn't know. "You got a minute?" Jordan said.

"Sure," I said.

"Well, you kept your word about that Comiskey thing," he said. "So I'm keeping mine."

During the weeks after the murder of Jordan's father, and then the time after his sudden retirement from the Bulls, people had reacted in a variety of ways to what had happened. As always, the specifics of Jordan's life affected, in profound ways and slight, the specifics of the lives of people he knew, and of people he would never meet.

Carmen Villafane—the lovely young woman with cerebral palsy who, in her wheelchair, sat behind Jordan's seat on the Bulls' bench every game night—had been made distraught by the loss that Jordan had suffered. In her short life she had undergone more than twenty-four operations; because she was subject to violent spasms, her arms and legs were strapped to the wheelchair, and she spoke in a gasping voice, with great effort. Jordan had met her at the Stadium one night when she was a teenager and she had approached him to give him a Valentine's Day card; moved by her courage and her unending determination, he had become her friend, and had arranged for her to sit near him each evening. Her life had literally been changed because of Jordan; he had welcomed her into his life, and into the life of his family, and now she had completed school and was out making a living for herself, working steadily.

"I'm so devastated, and I can't get over it, and I don't know what I can do to help," Carmen said after the killing of James Jordan. "I feel so helpless. I try to think of something I can do to help him, and I can't. He has never asked me for a single thing. And now that he's the one who needs the help, I don't know how to give it to him."

When, in the midst of his mourning, Jordan decided to leave basketball, President Clinton said that he would be missed "in every small-town back yard and paved city lot where kids play one-on-one and dream of being like Mike." At Children's Memorial Hospital in Chicago, a microbiologist named Dr. Stanford Shulman paid tribute to Jordan in a somewhat different way. He named a new strain of salmonella in honor of him. "I haven't told many people about this because I thought that they might take it the wrong way," Dr. Shulman said. "Believe me, I meant this to be a high honor for him." He said that a patient with a high fever and a severe case of diarrhea had been found to be carrying an unknown salmonella organism; he submitted the bacterium to the official salmonella ruling body in Paris, and named it *Salmonella mjordan.*

Dr. Shulman kept this quiet at first; Jordan's restaurant was just opening in Chicago, and the doctor "didn't want anyone to see Jordan's restaurant and the word 'salmonella' mentioned in the same newspaper stories, and get the wrong idea." He wanted Jordan to know that this was meant as a lasting measure of esteem; Air Jordan shoes become frayed, Dr. Shulman pointed out, posters tear, basketballs deflate. "But this bacterium," he said, "will be around forever."

So people were reacting to the changes in Jordan's life with the entire range of emotions. Jordan himself wasn't saying much in those weeks after he retired. One of the things he had mentioned he wanted to do was to more closely observe his children grow up—specifically, to be there to watch his daughter, Jasmine, take her first steps.

It was a lovely sentiment, but already it wasn't sitting well with Bulls fans, who were just beginning to realize what the new season was going to be like without Jordan. On the October day he was driving me to my office, I had mentioned that a friend of mine named Paul Galloway had impatiently wanted to know: "Jazzy walking yet?" Meaning: OK, now that you've seen her take those steps, do you think you might come back to the Bulls?

Jordan laughed at hearing that. "Yes, she's walking," he said. "And yes, I'm going to start playing again. But not basketball."

We were driving past Comiskey Park, the home of the Chicago White Sox. Jordan nodded toward it. "That's what I'm going to do."

For a second I didn't understand.

"I'm going to start coming out here in December," he said. "They have an indoor facility. Because it's winter, no one will know I'm here. I'm going to work at it for a couple of months, and then I'm going to go down to spring training with the White Sox."

By the next March, of course, the entire world would know this. At the moment, though, I thought Jordan was joking. We were driving past the park, and he was saying this, and I thought he might be kidding around simply because he had caught sight of the ballpark.

"When people ask me what I'm doing at spring training, I'm going to say that Jerry Reinsdorf"—the owner of both the Bulls and the White Sox—"is just letting me use the facility to get in shape. But what no one will know is that I'm really trying out for the team. If I'm good enough, I'll go north with the White Sox after spring training. If I'm not good enough, no one will ever know that I was trying out."

I still couldn't tell if he was serious. "Does anyone know this?" I said.

"I've told my family and a couple of my friends," Jordan said. "Look—please don't write anything about it. Will you do me that favor? If people know I'm doing it, then I'll never get it done. I've got to have some privacy at Comiskey this winter to find out if I'm any good."

"All right," I said. "But you know it's going to get out." I kept waiting for him to tell me he was fooling around.

"I'll make you a deal," he had said. "If you keep this to yourself until I know whether or not I've got a chance, I'll let you know what I decide. I just don't want people around if I'm embarrassing myself."

And now, two and a half months later, in January, Jordan was on the phone.

"I'm going to do it," he said. "Everyone keeps asking, so if you want to let them know, it's OK."

"Baseball?" I said.

"Yep," he said. "It's for sure."

I wasn't exactly surprised. Jordan had, indeed, been out at Comiskey regularly since early December; sports reporters had gotten wind of his workouts, and had been speculating almost nonstop about what he was up to. Because the ballpark was closed for the winter, no one had seen him at work, and the guessing ranged from the idea that he was going to come back to the Bulls after all and was doing his weight work in privacy, to the thought that he was merely keeping in shape so that he didn't get fat, to the theory—this was still considered unlikely—that he harbored some fantasy of being a professional baseball player. Within months, millions of people around the world would accept this as a given—that Jordan was trying to change his life completely. At the time, though, the concept seemed so goofy that few were able to take it seriously.

"So what do you want to do?" I said.

"I'm getting sick of people guessing," Jordan said. "If you want to write it, go ahead."

"You're a hundred percent sure?" I said.

"Yep," he said. "I'm flying down to Sarasota on February ninth."

"OK," I said. "Do you want to talk now?"

"I don't have to talk," he said. "I'm tired of hearing myself talk. Just go ahead and put it in your own words."

"What do you mean?" I said.

"Put it any way you want," he said. "Just say that I'm doing it."

"I don't want to do that," I said. "If you're not going to say it yourself, I don't want to write it."

"You can say it any way you want," he said.

"I can't do that," I said. "If I'm going to say in the newspaper that you 'said something yesterday,' then it has to be something that you said yesterday. I don't want to put words in your mouth."

"But I told you it's OK," he said.

"Listen," I said. "If the time comes when you really want to talk about it, let's talk. But I don't want to be in a position of being the one to say you're going to play baseball unless the words are yours."

He paused for a few seconds. "Let me think about it," he said.

"Fine," I said. Then: "You're really doing this?"

"Yep," Jordan said. "This is going to be fun."

A day or two later I was getting ready to fly to Palm Springs, California, for a reporting trip I'd scheduled weeks before. As I was packing at home I called in for messages.

"Michael Jordan called again," the assistant at the newspaper said. "He said he's ready to talk."

She said he'd called from an office he maintained in downtown Chicago. I had to be on my way to O'Hare International Airport within five minutes. I called Jordan's office, and the office manager said that he had just walked out the door.

"He's going to be calling in from his car," she said. "He asked you to leave a number where he could reach you."

I couldn't miss the flight to California. I told her I'd call back within the hour. I headed for O'Hare, made a quick call to my editors at the *Tribune* to tell them what I might have, made sure there were phones on the plane, took my seat and sat back as we departed. Then, using the in-flight phone that was built into the seat, I called Jordan's office again.

"He's on his way home right now," the office manager said. "He said that you should call him there in fifteen minutes."

The man in the next seat apparently hadn't heard the phone conversation, but it turned out that he had read *Hang Time*. He introduced himself and gave me his business card. He said he was an advertising executive in Chicago. "Do you think the Bulls have a chance this year without Jordan?" he said.

This was verging on the comical; if you were going to write a movie about this, you'd be reluctant to put in a scene this silly. I told my seatmate that I had no idea how the Bulls might do in the coming season, that his guess was as good as mine, probably better. I unfolded the tray table, borrowed some airline stationery from the flight attendant, and in exactly fifteen minutes called Jordan at home.

His wife, Juanita, answered. "He's waiting for you," she said. The connection was fuzzy, filled with static, her voice fading in and out. Jordan got onto the line, sounding as if he were on Mars.

"All right," he said. "I want to be done with all this speculation."

I began to ask questions. Jordan went from his conversational voice to the stiffer, more formal wording he often shifted into when he was watching his words. I had seen that shift hundreds of times; one second he was talking like a person, the next like some kind of basketball statesman. There were occasions when, like a president or a foreign minister, he seemed to be envisioning his words in cold print even as they left his mouth.

"I want to go to spring training for one reason, and that's to make the team," he said. "This is no fantasy. I plan to be in Sarasota by mid-February."

I asked him if the White Sox knew he was saying this, and if they approved.

"If the White Sox were to tell me that they didn't think I was good enough to make the team, and that they don't want me at spring training, then I would accept their wishes and not go," he said. "But my enthusiasm for doing this is so great that if they wanted me to pay my own way, then I'd pay my own way down there just for the chance to show what I can do."

He had not played organized baseball since he was a teenager in Wilmington, North Carolina. I asked him if he was really convinced that by the end of spring training he would be good enough to be selected for the major-league team.

"I'm getting better every day," he said. "I'm out there at Comiskey five days a week, getting instructions and working on my batting. The team's management now knows what my goals are, and they tell me that they understand, and that they're behind my effort."

That formal language again; that press-release syntax. Five miles in the air, I asked Jordan about newspaper reports that the real reason he had been at Comiskey was to get in shape, and that his athletic aspirations did not extend beyond that. I heard Jordan laugh.

"I'm not out there sweating for three hours every day just to find out what it feels like to sweat," he said, and for the first time since the conversation started the words coming unevenly out of the airplane phone sounded like a human being, not a news bulletin.

I began to ask him another question, and he said, "Just a minute. I know these calls are expensive, but you're going to have to hold on." And there was silence on the line.

After a few seconds, his wife picked up the phone. "Bob?" she said softly. When I responded she said, "There's something on television about his dad. About a court hearing for the people who are charged with doing it. He's over at the TV set watching."

A few minutes later he returned to the phone. "It was my dad," he said, leaving it at that. I asked him if he wanted to continue, or would like me to call back later. "No, let's go ahead and get it done," he said.

I told him that many fans and sports experts—as he was fully aware—were scoffing at the idea of what he was about to try. As skilled as he was at playing basketball, they said, he would be unable to master hitting big-league fastballs and curves. All he was about to do, these people said, was to humiliate himself in public.

"I love to hear them say that," Jordan said. "My whole life, that's been the kind of thing that has driven me. You tell me that I can't do something, and I'm going to do it."

And the notion that some of the White Sox players would resent his presence at spring training—that they would consider him to be a sideshow and a distraction?

"I don't think so," he said. "I'm not going down there to distract anybody. I'm going down there to play baseball. A number of White Sox players have been helping me out at Comiskey—Frank Thomas, Mike Huff, Dan Pasqua, Julio Franco. I don't think I'm wasting their time.

"I don't know whether I actually will be good enough to make the team. But I feel my chances are better than fifty-fifty already. And I'm still learning."

But why even do this? Why even start?

"First of all, it's fun," he said. "I'm not doing this for a fantasy-camp experience. I can have a fantasy on the golf course. This is a better challenge. This ball is moving.

"And this is something my father always wanted me to do. He started me in baseball when I was six years old. Two years ago, he told me that I should go for it.

"I'm serious. My father thought I could be a major-league baseball player, and I'm sure that right now he can see me trying. He's watching every move that I make."

I reminded him of a conversation we'd had at the height of the Bulls' championship years. He had said that in the dreams he had when he was asleep at night, he heard cheers. But in those dreams, he was not a basketball star. He was a baseball player—in the dreams, he was a pitcher. He had said that the cheers he heard in his dreams were different from the cheers he heard in real life, in arenas around the NBA. The basketball cheers he heard in his waking hours, he said, were almost demands—the cheers he heard every NBA night were almost ordering him to be good. In those odd baseball dreams, he said, the cheers were cheers of hope. They sounded different to him. In the baseball dreams, the people in the stands didn't know anything about him, didn't know if he had the talent to succeed, but they were on his side anyway.

And now he was about to step into that dream.

"That's still how I feel," he said. "And now it's going to be real. I keep hearing on TV and on the radio how I'm not doing all that well at the Comiskey workouts. How do they know? None of them have seen me. I think a lot of people want me to fail. Good. Let them keep saying it. The person who is going to have to succeed or fail is me, not them."

But what about the things he had said at his press conference on the day he retired—that he needed time away from public scrutiny, time with his family?

"Baseball teams stay in a city for four or five days at a time," he said. "It's not like the NBA, where you fly out after every game. I'd like to take my wife and children with me on the road. There were certain things I was thinking about when I retired that I didn't want to express to anyone. I know this will put me back in front of people. But I hope they'll be looking at me in a different light."

And what if he did make the team—but his summer turned out to be endless days of sitting on the bench as a seldom-used reserve player?

"That's no problem," he said. "Sitting on the bench, I could learn every day. I'd be watching great baseball players close-up. I don't like sitting around, but that's not a bad way to spend the summer, is it? I think it sounds great."

To him, apparently, it did. But he had to know that many people were saying that he was going through some sort of early mid-life crisis, and that on a more serious level he was reacting erratically in the aftermath of the murder of his father.

"This is my life," Jordan said. "I'd like to lead it the way I choose to. Everyone else is free to watch it—but I have to live it."

I asked him if he was having any second thoughts about this being in the paper the next morning. "No, just go ahead and do it," he said. "It'll stop people asking questions." I said goodbye; I had not brought my portable computer along with me, so on the airline stationery I began writing, in longhand, the story based on the conversation I had just had with Jordan.

The advertising executive in the next seat was eating his meal. If he'd been eavesdropping, he gave no hint of it. What he did do was say to me:

"What do you make of all this talk that Michael Jordan's going to try to be a baseball player?"

At the hotel in Palm Springs, I called the *Chicago Tribune* and was connected with Paul Sullivan, a sportswriter who was going to take the dictation. I read the story off the airline stationery; it was two hours later in Chicago, getting close to deadline. When I was finished dictating, I called Jordan's house to let him know what to expect. The answering machine picked up. The voices of his two sons, giggling on the tape, said in unison: "We're not home right now . . ."

I fell asleep, and was awakened at 4:30 a.m.—6:30 in Chicago— by a radio host who had just picked up the morning *Tribune*. As soon as he hung up, a wire-service reporter called. Then the British Broadcasting Company. No one could reach Jordan, it seemed, and they didn't know quite what to make of this. There had been no official announcement from the White Sox.

At 7 a.m. I switched on the television set. On the "Today" show, Bryant Gumbel was talking with a photo of Jordan superimposed behind him: "The *Chicago Tribune* is reporting in this morning's editions . . ." I could hear the words I'd written on the airplane coming out of my TV set in Palm Springs.

Such a disorienting world he lives in. Wired and linked up, the hardware of international communications ready to take anything he says and disperse it across the globe in an instant. He takes it for granted—both the caution that must come with that knowledge, and the resignation that in the end there's not a thing he can do to alter it. I picked up the airline stationery from the nightstand. Outside the window, the sun was rising over a golf course. I looked at the scrawls on the pieces of paper. Right this second, people were talking about Jordan's words in Japan, people were talking about those words in China and Italy and France. Just because Jordan had decided he wanted to say them. I didn't even think he considered any of this all that peculiar.

If he had maintained any illusions that, having announced he wished to change his life, he could go about it in a low-key way, all of that exploded within days. In worldwide press and broadcasting circles, Jordan's deciding to be a baseball player was classic man-bites-dog. The commentary and analysis were endless; Jordan was the subject of late-night talk-show monologues, of network news reports, and of every sports program and call-in show in the country. You couldn't pick up a newspaper or turn on a car radio without reading or hearing about it—and if the rest of the world couldn't avoid it, neither could Jordan. Most of the voices were saying that he would be a flop.

"So?" he said as we talked one day during the weeks before he left Chicago for spring training. "Am I supposed to worry about what people will think if I drop a fly ball? That happens. People drop fly balls, and I'm sure I will. If people want to judge me on that, there's nothing I can do about it."

Even though he claimed not to care about all the voices that were making fun of him, it was clear that it stung. He had just left a sport in which he was considered so good that even the critics who found fault with other parts of his life had to concede they had never seen a basketball player who could do what he could do. After the murder of his father, he had been moved by the expressions of condolence from men and women he had never met. Now, all of a sudden, he sensed he was being snickered at—and it caught him by surprise.

"I am about to turn thirty-one years old," he said. "I am not a child. I know what I'm doing.

"Every day when I wake up and I get in the car to drive myself to my workouts, I'm happy during the drive. Sometimes I have the radio on, and I can hear the people saying that I don't have a chance. I don't care. I'm in a happy mood that whole drive.

"And when I'm out there throwing and catching and hitting, I can't even tell you how good it makes me feel. All of a sudden I'm a kid again. I'm a little kid, and I don't know if I'm good enough, but I have the will to try to do something. It's a sense of complete freedom. It's a feeling I haven't had in a long time. I'm not going to allow anyone to take that from me just because they want to make fun of what I'm trying."

The sports pages were full of stories about who would replace Jordan as the leading attraction in the National Basketball Association. The consensus was that it would be Shaquille O'Neal, the young Orlando Magic center who had come to the league with millions of dollars in product endorsements before he played a single minute of professional basketball. Many people were saying that O'Neal was taking marketing the logical next step, following in the pattern that Jordan and his agent, David Falk, had set. Jordan didn't see it that way.

"He's a nice kid," Jordan said of O'Neal. "But I don't know about this next-superstar-in-line thing. This is very different from when I came into the league. Then, you just assumed that if you did well on the basketball court, other opportunities might open up to you.

"Now, it's like there's a job opening to take over my marketing, and someone has to be chosen to fill it. What happened to proving you're a good basketball player first? It just seems sort of backward to me. The way it's supposed to be is that you achieve something on the basketball court, and then maybe you get some endorsements and commercials. Now it's the other way around. The sponsors need a superstar, so they decide who the superstar will be before the superstar has even done anything."

Not that he was in any danger of anyone deciding in advance that he would be a superstar in baseball. His workouts at Comiskey Park were showing him how far he had to go. "At the end of the session every day, I watch tapes of myself batting," he said. "And I compare what I see with tapes of other players batting. Really good players—Frank Thomas, Ellis Burks. I sit there and I watch very carefully, to try to understand what they're doing that I ought to do. I look at me and I look at them, and I look at me again and I look at them again, and the next day when I go out there I try to make myself better."

The White Sox had been deluged with requests from reporters and television stations around the globe, all of them wanting to go to Sarasota to cover Jordan at spring training. He had yet to be officially invited to training camp by the White Sox—the story about his desire to play had caught the team's management unawares—but even before the invitation, the team was facing the heaviest media turnout in its history. Jordan knew that every moment of every day, cameras would be trained on his every move. There would be nothing at all private about this pursuit. And he was nervous.

"Very nervous," he said. "In basketball, every time I got in a tense situation on the court, I would make my mind go back to a similar situation I'd been in before, and that would calm me. I would be able to tell myself: 'You've been here before, and you did all right.'

"I won't be able to do that in baseball, because there is no baseball situation where I've been before. So when I'm nervous on the baseball diamond, I suppose for a while I'll put my mind back in basketball situations, and remember what that felt like. Hopefully, before long I'll have some baseball situations to replace them with."

The one thing he did not want to deal with, he said, was the feelings of people who believed that, if he failed in baseball, he would tarnish the basketball legend. That he would somehow be robbing them of something.

"I know there are people who have said: 'You retired from the Bulls, so just go away and let us remember what used to be.' If those people are tired of hearing my name, then they ought to quit saying it so often. I wish they could understand the feeling I have when I walk out there every day to try to do this."

Many of those people, I said, seemed to want to protect Jordan from diminishing his own legacy.

"What legacy?" he said, the second word pronounced with something close to contempt.

The basketball legacy. The legacy of excellence at his craft, the legacy of championships.

"There is no legacy," he said. "I don't have a legacy. I only have my life."

CHAPTER 5

The machine—"Vitality Juices," the illuminated sign said—was fully stocked. Orange juice, apple juice, lemonade, cranberry juice, all chilled and free of cost for the major-league baseball players at the Chicago White Sox spring training complex in Sarasota.

Most of the men in the room clearly knew their way around. They wore shorts, T-shirts and spiked shoes as they maneuvered through the carpeted clubhouse. Jordan, sitting at his locker near the trainer's room, was the only person wearing a White Sox uniform. He looked less than comfortable, out-of-place, like a boy who has worn a suit and tie to the first day of school only to find that everyone else is wearing jeans and sweatshirts. He was the most famous person in the room—he was among the most famous people on the planet—and still he had the appearance of someone who wished he fit in.

Never mind that the satellite uplink trucks that had surrounded Ed Smith Stadium on the first day of workouts would not have been here if not for Jordan; never mind that all the other players in the room certainly, when they called home at night, were being asked by their wives, girlfriends and children what Jordan was like. The voices of the ballplayers who walked past him seemed to be changed slightly from whatever their usual register was; the place had the feel of a living room on a night when a family is talking not just to each other, but in the presence of a guest they can't quite figure out.

Jordan's voice, too, was different. "Do I look like a distraction?"

he said, smiling. I had just arrived in Sarasota; he was making a joke about all of the news stories that were describing him as a distraction at spring training, but his voice was quieter than the locker-room voice that had been heard around the National Basketball Association for so many years. "I don't feel like a distraction. I feel like I'm having a ball."

But the new-kid-in-school, new-kid-at-summer-camp aspect of this was unmistakable. It probably should have been expected—who wouldn't have trouble fitting in, stepping into a world he had never been a part of? Add to that the resentment that many of the players inevitably were feeling about all the attention being paid to Jordan— it should have been no surprise at all that in the Sox clubhouse he seemed like the answer to a what's-wrong-with-this-picture puzzle.

"I truthfully have no idea what is going to happen to me," he said. That voice again—lowered as if he didn't want to disturb any of the other conversations in the room. "But this is such a different feeling from anything I've ever gone through before. . . ."

Kirk McCaskill, a White Sox pitcher, called, "M.J.—come on."

There was a Ping-Pong table set up in the clubhouse; McCaskill was standing at one end of it, a paddle in his hand. He was in a T-shirt and shorts; Jordan, in his full uniform, turned, saw that he was being invited, and got up to play the game.

McCaskill served. "Oh, there it is," McCaskill said, as Jordan hit the ball harmlessly back into the net. "I think I've found his spot."

"My backhand?" Jordan said. "The whole world knows I have no backhand."

McCaskill hit it there again.

"I usually run around them," Jordan said, trying to hit the shot. "You have to put it right . . . there . . . to be sure you have a winner."

The two men kept playing—one of them the most recognizable athlete in the world, the other a journeyman pitcher who, if he walked through most American shopping malls, would go unnoticed. "What's that, 11–8?" Jordan asked.

"11–8," McCaskill said, slamming a ball past Jordan's outstretched paddle.

Alex Fernandez, a young star of the Sox pitching staff, standing and watching with some of the other players, giggled.

"Stop laughing at me, son, I'm not that bad," Jordan called to him, not taking his eyes off the table.

Lance Johnson, the starting center fielder, walked into the room and up to the table. "Time-out," Johnson said. Jordan held the ball. "Welcome to the club, man," Johnson said, shaking his hand. Even the friendly gesture felt a little strained, though; Johnson would not have done this for any other rookie. Jordan, by his presence, was altering the way the ballplayers behaved. Everyone had known it was going to happen. Knowing it in advance wasn't enough to stop it from happening. "You ready?" McCaskill called.

"You're not going to win this game," Jordan answered.

The atmosphere inside the clubhouse was in absolute contrast to the furor around Sarasota regarding Jordan's presence in town. If, inside the walls of the White Sox complex, he was the odd man out, to tourists and sports fans on the west coast of Florida he was the only reason to be at the ballpark. Early each morning people would line the streets leading to the Sox training camp; police officers stood behind barricades to keep the throngs in control. When Jordan went to a restaurant, crowds and television crews gathered outside; the sight of him walking onto the practice field in his new number 45 uniform brought screams and shrieks from the people in the stands.

The *Sarasota Herald-Tribune* had run a "countdown to Jordan" feature in the weeks before he came to town, ticking down the days until he was scheduled to arrive much as children mark off the days before Christmas. I had seen people's reactions to Jordan for years—it was almost a chemical response—so I wasn't surprised to see it in Florida, but his teammates seemed not to know whether to be amazed by it, to ignore it, or to mock it. The ballplayers would all walk together through an opening in the right-field wall of Ed Smith Stadium, to do stretching exercises in the outfield. A wail would go up like something in old Beatles newsreels; some people would holler, some would try to climb over the railings, a few would cry. The major-league veterans were unaccustomed to seeing strangers crying involuntarily, especially when nothing sad had happened; for them to accept that the person causing the tears was a man who had never played an inning of big-league baseball was perhaps expecting too much. His fellow White Sox would snicker and elbow each other at the sound of the screaming; Jordan, behind sunglasses, would pretend not to notice the ceaseless noise.

"Now when you're missing those balls—where are you missing them?"

Walt Hriniak, the White Sox's weathered, florid-faced batting coach, was asking the question. This was before 7 a.m.; the spring training complex was all but deserted, the grass still damp with dew.

"Underneath," Jordan said.

The two of them were in a covered batting shed—there was a sign on it saying that it was named in honor of Sox Hall of Famer Luke Appling—working before the rest of the team arrived for the day. Jordan had asked if he could have the extra instruction; Hriniak had agreed to come early each morning to work with him.

Hriniak, standing behind a protective cage, tossed a baseball to Jordan. Jordan swung, connected, drove the ball into netting.

"That too long?" Jordan said, referring to his swing.

"A little bit," Hriniak said. "Better that than under."

Jordan, grunting with exertion, perspiration streaming down his face, swung again, again, again.

"All right," Hriniak called. "I'm going to come down now. You've got to get that same feeling in your left hand. So you feel you can get on top of the ball."

"Standing like this, it *makes* me go down on the ball," Jordan said, breathing with some effort.

"It's hard," Hriniak called to him. "Remember—your foot is going *that* way. That's your natural move, your natural stride. I don't think you should allow that. If your head goes that way, you're fucked on that pitch."

Jordan stood there like a young boy, shifting his feet self-consciously in the dirt, trying to remember what he had been told.

"Two things now," Hriniak called to him. "Stay on top of the ball—and remember about your head. Think about those two things."

Hriniak threw another pitch. Jordan connected. "OK?" Hriniak called.

"Yep," Jordan answered, sounding uncertain. "Perfect."

"It wasn't perfect," Hriniak called. "But it was good."

Jordan grinned.

"That might have been your best one," Hriniak called. "OK, now I'm going to repeat myself. Then I want you to explain it to me—what I just said. Your own words. You tell me."

Jordan furrowed his brow and tried to give his teacher the correct response. He didn't have to be here—he didn't have to be here at all, he certainly didn't have to be here this early in the morning. He had numerous options, including the option of traveling the country and accepting the nightly rapturous ovations from basketball fans as he performed at a higher level than anyone ever had.

"Come on, keep throwing," Jordan, his voice raspy, said to Hriniak. "I'm waiting a split second before I hit."

"What's the difference here?" Hriniak called. "You tell me."

"I'm coming through too early," Jordan said, almost apologetic.

"Relax with the left hand," Hriniak called.

Out on the streets, the crowds were already gathering in the hopes of catching a glimpse of him. Some of the other members of the White Sox were arriving at the complex.

"I'm sorry," Jordan called to Hriniak. "Could you give me a couple more? I can't seem to get it. . . ."

"Sometimes I'll sit out here at night," Jordan said. "Just sit here and look up at the sky and think."

We were at the house he had rented for spring training—a house behind the security walls of a gated complex, adjacent to a country-club golf course. This was on a steaming afternoon after a full day of practice, which Jordan had begun before dawn. He had fixed himself some lunch; wearing a pair of red shorts and a T-shirt, and thick black socks with no shoes, he looked down toward a creek that separated the house from the fairways.

"I'll sit out here and think about how much my life has changed in the last year," he said. "The stars will be out, and it will be very quiet, and it's just so peaceful. I'm not afraid. Everything is changing, but I look at the sky and nothing scares me."

His bedroom—on the first floor of the house—was just a few feet away, its sliding glass doors open to the air. On the nightstand next to the bed was a framed photograph of his wife and children, the keepsake of a father on an extended business trip. With all the turmoil around him, all the camera crews at the ballpark staking out his every move, here there was absolute silence. The phone, with an unlisted number, didn't ring; his temporary neighbors, respecting his privacy, did not knock.

"Just being out there on the baseball field every day is a totally different feeling from what I've been used to," he said. "I've been cooped up indoors in gyms for so many years. Now at practice I stand out in right field, and the sun just beats down on me. Every moment is a warm moment. I used to catch a cold at the beginning of the basketball season and keep it all winter. Not down here. Knock on wood."

Sitting around in his shorts, he looked more like the Jordan that the world was used to seeing. The news photos of him wearing his White Sox uniform struck many people as jarring. Jordan in a pair of baggy shorts—that was the basketball player, the human logo, that's what Jordan the athlete was supposed to look like. I asked him if he looked funny to himself in his baseball uniform.

"I'm used to wearing the uniform by now," he said. "Hey, when I was a kid I wore a baseball uniform before I wore a basketball uniform. It's good to have one back on. The uniforms have changed a lot since I was young—there's a lot more tightness in the legs. Baseball players show their bodies a lot more than they used to. Remember how the pants on baseball uniforms used to be so loose?"

I asked him about those first days of training camp, when he was the only man in uniform. The other members of the Sox had gone through their drills in gym shorts and workout shirts. Why had Jordan chosen to dress so formally, in the game uniform?

He looked a little sheepish. "I didn't know," he said. "I wasn't sure what the norm was. They hung the uniform in my locker when I got here, so I assumed I was supposed to wear it. I wanted to go by the book, but I guess I wasn't quite right. It doesn't matter now. Now everybody is supposed to wear the uniform every day, so it's OK."

No one told him. No one told him what he was supposed to wear, and he didn't ask. He said that he was well aware of how harshly his baseball days were being judged; for that reason, he said, he didn't read the sports pages in Sarasota. He spent almost all of the hours away from the training camp here, at the rented house; his wife and children were up north in Chicago.

"You notice I keep a nice good distance from the pool," he said.

Jordan cannot swim. The view on the back terrace was lovely, but whenever Jordan came out here from his bedroom he tried not to walk within five feet of the water, and he avoided going down to the banks of the creek that separated his house from the golf course. The water was not the only aspect of Florida life whose charms were lost on him; a notoriously speedy driver, he was not in love with the way many of the Gulf Coast's elderly motorists maneuvered slowly in traffic.

"Everybody's 'Driving Miss Daisy' down here," he said. "But I'm liking this very much. More than anything that's happened in my life in a long time."

In quiet moments, it was easy to lose sight of how different his life was from the life the rest of us lead. But then something would happen. A Federal Express envelope had been delivered to the house; it was the daily packet from his agent's office.

"All my mail gets sent to them, and they decide what I should see," he said.

He opened the envelope. Inside was a letter from boxing promoter Dan Duva. Jordan read it, laughed briefly, and handed it to me.

The letter offered him $15 million if he would agree to box for the heavyweight championship of the world against the winner of a fight between Evander Holyfield and Michael Moorer. Accommodations and transportation for an entourage would be provided. The letter emphasized that the $15 million was merely the minimum guarantee, and that Jordan's take could go much higher: "It is possible that Mr. Jordan's proceeds in the event would exceed $25 million." It didn't matter if he won or lost, if he lasted twenty seconds or ten rounds. The money was his if he wanted it.

"Are you going to think about it?" I said.

"No," he said.

"It's hard to comprehend," I said. "You could go out there and lie down on the canvas, and they'd give you fifteen million dollars."

"Yeah, and be a joke for the rest of my life," he said.

A second envelope was from the White House. President and Mrs. Clinton wondered if he'd like to come to dinner.

He scanned it and then dropped it back into the Federal Express pack. He went into the kitchen, went through the cabinet and found a granola bar, then returned to the terrace. The multi-million-dollar boxing offer he had just thrown away, the invitation to the White House, were not what was on his mind. What he was thinking about was how people at the ballpark, every day, would cheer wildly for him, even when he did something utterly routine. "I'm embarrassed," he said. "I don't like it."

He would be taking fielding practice with the veteran White Sox players, he said, and he would catch an easy popup, and the crowd would cry out as if Willie Mays had just made the play of his life. An established Sox star would do the same thing to the sound of total silence.

"I was standing there in the outfield with Frank Thomas," Jordan said. "A ball was hit to me, and I caught it and as soon as it touched my glove I could hear the cheering starting. I didn't look over there, but I was thinking: Please, don't do this to me. Frank Thomas is the ultimate baseball player right now, he's a consummate pro, he's the most valuable player in the league. If I can hear the cheers, Frank Thomas can hear them, too.

"I'm in his arena. I didn't say anything to him, but we both knew what was going on. Those cheers started and I tried not to show anything on my face. But I was cringing. I was thinking: Not now. Please don't do this right now."

For a person who seemed aware that his progress was being judged as quite slow, he didn't seem to be lacking in confidence about his long-term prospects. I asked him what the ball looked like as the White Sox pitchers released it toward him.

"It looks like an object I can hit," he said. "I'm not nervous. I'm not scared like everyone was saying I would be. I just think I can hit it. You have to read it. It's just like a basketball situation, to a certain extent."

What about the famous Ted Williams line—the line about hitting a baseball being the most difficult single act in sports?

"He never played basketball," Jordan said. "He never played football. Has he played golf? I think, of the different games I play, the most difficult is golf. You have to play it with your mind more."

But the golf ball is just sitting there motionless, on the tee or on the grass. The speed with which a baseball approaches the plate . . .

Jordan got up from his chair. "Look," he said. He wound up like a pitcher, then stopped in the middle of his motion. He took his left hand and, with a pointed finger, drew an imaginary square over his right shoulder. "You watch that box over the pitcher's shoulder," he said. "The ball has to come out of that box. You can see it. They're hoping you don't have the eye coordination to do it, but you can learn that."

What about standing in the outfield? His whole athletic life had been spent on basketball courts; the outfield in a ballpark is so immense, there is so much more ground to cover . . .

"You don't think of the whole field," he said. "You divide it into sections. I'm learning to recognize the different sounds of the ball coming off the bat. As an instinct you take a step back when you hear it. . . ."

Yet he had never done this in a situation that counted. What if the White Sox were to decide that he did, indeed, possess the requisite athletic skills to play on their team—but that they just didn't want to depend on him when a ball was hit sharply over his head in an important game? That he simply didn't have the experience?

"What qualifications are you looking for?" Jordan said. "Are you looking for the type of person who has proved he can handle pressure? Are you looking for a person who has inner calmness—who has been in that kind of athletic situation, and who knows how to maintain the certain calmness that lets the good come out of him?

"Is there a big difference between being in Game 7 of the playoffs, and needing a basket to get to the next round, and knowing you can make it—is there a big difference between that, and making the catch in right field? No, I haven't made the catch in a baseball playoff game yet—but by the time the situation came up, I will have made it in a regular game in the season. So what's the difference? If I'm the manager? I'm taking a chance on me. I'm taking the chance that I can produce.

"I know, I know—I'm not the manager. But I will take the chance on me every time."

All of this talk about the mechanics of the game, all of the sports-page speculation about whether Jordan would ever be good enough to compete in the major leagues—it seemed to be missing some of the essential questions about why he was here. He either would or wouldn't turn into a big-leaguer—but the thing that was certain was that he would never be the best at this who ever lived. He had accomplished that in one sport; he would never accomplish it in this one.

"Don't they understand at all?" he said. "That's not what this is about. That's not even in the back of my mind—not even in the realm of possibility. I'm thirty-one years old. I don't even know how many years I have left to play sports on a professional level. But let's say that

I have two, three, maybe four years left where I could be a professional baseball player. Greatness doesn't come in that length of time. My standards are not set at that height.

"What I do hope I can do is be good. I hope I can be good enough to compete well at a professional level. This is not some competition against myself when I was a basketball player. This is a very different thing."

The close attention I was seeing him pay to the White Sox coaches, especially to Hriniak, the batting instructor—it was the kind of attention he never showed with the Bulls, when head coach Phil Jackson and his assistants were in charge. Now, at spring training, Jordan was taking in every word, often asking for more help when he wasn't satisfied with what he had heard.

"I've got to listen now," he said. "I haven't done this before. With Phil, he would talk and I would tune it in and tune it out. I knew that game. I knew what I was doing.

"Here, everyone in camp has a little bit I can learn from. I have to be a little careful about it—by being so open to learning, I don't want to confuse myself. My knowledge of professional sports, of what to do in pressure situations, is still valuable to me, and I don't want to lose that. If you try too hard to remember every detail that anyone tells you, it can end up being so confusing that it works against you. But I do have to take everything in and pay very close attention. With the Bulls, with basketball, I was on top of the game and I didn't need to be told much. Now I do."

And the answer to why such an immensely wealthy and successful man would be putting himself through this, would be walking away from everything safe and risking such public failure—the answer had little to do with the standard goals of traditional athletic contests.

"I set the alarm next to my bed for just after five a.m.," Jordan said. "I sleep pretty well. The buzzer on the alarm clock goes off, and it's pitch-black outside.

"I go into the kitchen. I pour myself a bowl of cereal and I have a couple of doughnuts. I'm in my car and out of the house by six a.m.

There aren't that many cars on the road at that hour. I have my head-lights on.

"It's about a twenty-five-minute drive from here at the house to the White Sox facility. I'm alone in the car, but my father is with me. I think about him every day. Every single day.

"I think about him when I'm worried, and I think about him when I have a decision to make. I think about him when I have a bad problem. I think about what advice he would give me, what he would say to me.

"So on my drive to practice in the dark every morning, he's with me, and I remember why I'm doing this. I remember why I'm here. I'm here for him.

"The sad days in your life you tend to forget. The happy days you remember. The happy days stay with you all of your life. You can always bring them back when things are not going that great.

"He's with me in that car. I look over at the next seat, and I think: We're doing this. We're doing this together. You and I, Pops. We're going to get this done. You watch. You and I are doing this. We're on our way."

The sun was getting low in the sky. He had grown silent after talking about his father; when he spoke again, it was of all the people who were guessing how the Chicago Bulls would have done had he stayed with them for the season.

"If?" he said. "If I would have played this year, I think we proba-bly would have won seventy games. But I don't believe in 'if.' I think there has always been a plan for my life, and that I don't really have any control over it. There is no 'if.' Everything that happens was de-termined in advance."

Did he really believe that? That his life was like some movie script, and that he was only following the directions and the di-alogue?

"Yes," he said. "It's beyond my control."

But every day, a person has to make so many decisions. Whatever decisions a person makes changes things one way or the other—sometimes changes those things drastically.

"But the decisions I make, someone has already planned which way I will make them," he said. "So it's not really my decision after all. I know that may sound strange to you, but I become more and more convinced of it as I grow older. There is no 'if.' It has all been determined."

The good and the bad?

"The bad turns into good."

But some things that happen are so terrible, there can be no good in them.

He was looking off toward something I could not see. "My father was here with me for almost thirty-one years," he said. "I had a dad for thirty-one years. Some children never have their fathers for any years, and I had mine for almost thirty-one. No one can convince me that I was unlucky."

In Sarasota, he was more than a little bit isolated, even with all the crowds that gathered to wait for him and, if they could get close enough, to stare at him and watch. Familiar faces and voices were few. He said that he talked to his mother on the telephone every other day.

"She always tells me the same thing," he said, smiling. "She says, 'Take care of your money, son.' She says, 'Keep your eyes open.' And she says, 'Don't trust anybody.' "

He started to say something: "I . . ."

He stopped, then waited a moment.

"Look, I have this thought," he said. "But I want you to know that it's just a thought. It's not serious."

More silence.

"So when I tell you this, it's just something I think about, OK?"

I waited.

"I make the team," he said. "I make it to the majors. And I come up to bat, and I stand at the plate and I realize that I've done it. I've gotten it done.

"So I'm standing at the plate, and the pitcher throws the ball, and

I knock it out of the park. Home run. I'm rounding the bases, and the ball goes out of the park, and the crowd is cheering. I head for home plate.

"And as I'm running toward home, I see that a gate is open. I cross home plate, but I don't stop. I run right out the gate, and through the tunnel and out of the stadium. I'm still in my uniform, and I'm running away, down the streets, as fast as I can. I can still hear the crowd back in the stadium, and I just keep on running. Keep on running forever."

Jordan, who had been up since before dawn, got up to go into another room. I was alone on the terrace; across the way, across the creek, golfers were moving down a fairway in steady succession. They were small enough, from that distance, that I couldn't make out their faces; I was quite sure that the golfers who had been playing during these last few hours, had they looked over, did not know that one of the men sitting behind the house by the creek was Michael Jordan.

Several minutes passed. He did not come back outside. I went into the kitchen, then walked through the house. Nothing. I heard the audio from a television set, and followed the sound into a small room off the front hallway.

On the TV set, the early-evening news was on. Jordan, on his back, was sound asleep on a couch. All the frenzy surrounding his being at spring training, all the noise and uproar all over town, all over the country, and here he was. His bare right leg draped off the side of the couch, bending onto the carpet; his eyes were closed, his mouth was wide open. He was breathing deeply, his head tossed back. He seemed as vulnerable, as absent of defenses, as a man could ever be.

He sighed, and took another breath, and other than that he was motionless on the couch. I looked at him there and then I let myself out of the house.

CHAPTER 6

The scenes would vary wildly. None of this was lost on Jordan; none of it was lost on his White Sox teammates.

One scene:

After a morning's practice session on the back diamonds—on this particular day he had been having trouble hitting the ball out of the infield, no matter how down-the-middle the batting-practice pitchers had tried to deliver their throws to him—Jordan headed back to the clubhouse. As always, fans were pressed against the low fences, hoping for an autograph.

Most of the players never stopped to sign; not only did they refuse to give their signatures to the customers, they did not even look at them—it was as if the fans were invisible. Jordan, most days, paused to sign autographs. Today, again, he did.

Immediately the people rushed forward. The waist-high fence was not sturdy—it began to sag and bend. As the people called to him and jammed against the fence, Jordan saw that a little boy—he appeared to be around six years old—was being crushed. The child had been fine, standing with his parents by the fence, where they had staked out their territory early that morning; it was only when Jordan walked by that the rows behind began to surge.

So there were dozens of arms reaching over the fence, thrusting baseballs and pieces of paper at Jordan. He was signing a ball for one boy when he noticed the child, terror on his face, smashed face-first against the metal webbing of the fence.

"Hey!" Jordan yelled. No response. "Hey! *Hey!*" He began to push the people back. "Stop it!" he yelled, trying to make himself heard. "There's kids up here!"

He glanced around, trying to summon security guards. The boy's parents—they had been so excited to see Jordan that they had ignored their son; Jordan had noticed that the boy was being smashed against the fence, but they hadn't—looked down, saw their boy weeping, and picked him up. The boy was sobbing now, gasping for breath.

Jordan shook his head. "That's all," he said, sounding disgusted. "This is ridiculous." The parents of the other boy—the boy whose ball Jordan had signed—were beaming at their son. "You're a good boy," they said to him. They examined the baseball, with Jordan's signature on it. "Look at that. You're a good boy." As Jordan walked toward the clubhouse, some of the other White Sox took this all in with amusement. "Hey, Jordan, come back here," a man in the crowd yelled angrily at Jordan's retreating figure. A woman in a halter top beckoned to Sox pitcher James Baldwin, and smiled invitingly toward him. When she caught his eye, she said, "Can you get me Michael Jordan's signature?" Jordan was alone as he entered the clubhouse door.

Another scene:

In the Luke Appling batting shed, Frank Thomas was working with Walt Hriniak. Thomas, the American League's leading home-run hitter, was swinging with his left arm only, clobbering the balls backhanded; his power was so great that, even hitting that way, the contact the bat made with the baseballs sounded like trees being hacked down by axes. The news had that day been announced that Jack McDowell, the Sox's star pitcher, had just lost an arbitration hearing with the team's management. McDowell had wanted $6.5 million to pitch during the new season; because the arbitrator had turned him down, he was going to be paid $5.3 million instead.

"Well, they got Jack again," Thomas said to Hriniak.

"Who?" Hriniak said.

"McDowell," Thomas said. "They beat him."

"So how much does he get?" Hriniak said.

"Five-point-three million," Thomas said.

"That's enough," Hriniak said.

Thomas smacked another ball backhanded, with enough force to knock it over a fence.

"So what's Jordan like?" Thomas said. He knew that Hriniak was having the early-morning sessions with Jordan.

"The guy is fucking outstanding," Hriniak said.

"He can hit?" Thomas said, doubting.

"I don't mean that," Hriniak said. "But he listens. I didn't know what to expect from him. This is one hardworking motherfucker. He can't hit yet. But I've never seen a guy willing to work so hard."

Thomas did not respond. He pounded another ball, not breaking a sweat.

"Hey, Frank," Hriniak said. "Before the season, you and I got to talk."

Meaning that Hriniak had some hitting advice for Thomas. Meaning that he wanted to analyze Thomas' swing, try to get him to refine it.

"You choose a time," Hriniak said. "Just a few things."

"OK," Thomas said, with a disinterested inflection that meant: No.

Another scene:

On the grass beside the dugout at the main diamond in Ed Smith Stadium, some of the Sox players were sitting, waiting their turn at bat during an intrasquad workout.

Jordan lay on the grass next to an outfielder named Dan Pasqua, talking quietly. It was a splendrous Florida day; the sun brought out all the colors in the outfield signboards: Jiffy Lube, Sarasota Kennel Club, Office Depot, Siesta Key Decor Inc., Bud Light. The day had a lazy, timeless feel to it, the kind of day that has lured kids to leave the house and play baseball for decades upon decades, before any of these players were yet born. So Jordan and Pasqua and the rest of the ballplayers were on the grass, just talking, just taking in the day, and the sound came out of the stands:

"I want to be like Mike!"

It was one voice, and then it was joined by others, and it became a chant: "I want to be like Mike!"

That stopped the conversation between the players lounging in the grass. Jordan didn't say a word; neither did his teammates. "I want to be like Mike!" the chant continued, and Brandon Wilson, an infielder, turned to outfielder Mike Huff and said, "Hey, they want to be like you, Mike."

Jordan was called to the plate. Another bad day; he was connecting, but there was no real pop as the bat met the ball, the sound conveyed no energy, no thrust. From the stands, some voices, unlike the ones before:

"Throw it underhand to him!"

"You stink! You stink!"

"Hey, he actually hit one—get it on film!"

Jordan finished his turn at bat, then walked back to join the players sitting and lying in the grass, not giving any indication he had heard the voices, or that he knew the other men had.

"Hey, Joe," Jordan called to Joe Hall, an outfielder.

Hall was eating sunflower seeds from a plastic bag.

"Over here," Jordan said.

Hall tossed the bag to him. Jordan poured himself a palmful of seeds, then tossed the bag back.

"Hot," Dan Pasqua said, looking at the still-rising sun.

"I've got nothing to lose," Jordan said. "What am I supposed to worry about—whether Jack McDowell will accept me into his locker room?"

We were talking about the coolness with which Jordan was still being greeted by many of the White Sox veterans. McDowell, the team's number one pitcher, was being the most distant—he had made it clear from the beginning that he didn't like the idea of Jordan's coming to spring training, and even though they dressed only ten or fifteen feet apart in the clubhouse, along the same row of cubicles, they seldom made eye contact, much less spoke.

One day early in spring training Jordan had seen that I had a White Sox media guide—a booklet that contained the names and photographs of every man at camp, not just the players, but the clubhouse personnel, the equipment handlers, the support staff. He had asked if he could borrow it. I had seen him studying it, matching names and faces, closing the book and quizzing himself and opening it up again to make sure he had it right. I figured out what he was doing. He wanted to walk into the clubhouse every morning and be able to greet every person by name. He knew from his days in the NBA that often people who met him for the first time were nervous around him, shy; I used to notice all the time that when people met Jordan, they would inadvertently speed their voices up—it was if they subconsciously felt that if they didn't speak very quickly and say what they had to say, Jordan might walk away.

He was accustomed to that; in light of it, and with the undercurrent of discontent he faced in the locker room, he determined to make the effort to approach the people and let them know there was no need to be hesitant about approaching him. So every morning it was "Hey, Rod." "What's up, Darrin?" "Hey, Ozzie." Like a greeter at a nightclub, he almost manically worked to let them know that he accepted his role as the interloper, and was willing to adapt, to be the low man.

And meanwhile, before any of the others arrived, he pulled into the parking lot each day as the sun was coming up. He was aware how far he had to go to be good enough—and how little time he had.

"I don't know," he said early one morning. "I don't know. I don't know what these guys go through in a season. What the hundred sixty-two games feel like. The things they all take for granted, I have no idea about. The pacing, the feel of it. I have to figure it out."

Frank Thomas, arriving for the day, saw Jordan coming out of the batting shed, saw how somber Jordan looked.

"Hey, Mike," Thomas called. "Quit trying to memorize the fundamentals. Just hit the damn ball."

"Easy for you to say," Jordan said.

· · · · ·

There is an old line: If you saw how they made sausages, you'd never want to eat one.

That might apply to baseball cards, too.

Pitcher Alex Fernandez, cursing and impatient, was near the front of the line. "Let's fucking go," he demanded. "Let's fucking go."

Inside a room at the spring training complex, and snaking out the door and onto a practice diamond, photographers had been set up and waiting for the ballplayers since dawn. Every Sox player was being asked to move from photographer to photographer, in assembly-line fashion. The purpose of this was to have photos taken for use on baseball trading cards.

It resembled nothing if not an Army physical—except the major-league baseball players were reacting with even more antipathy than if this were the military. The entire process was going to take each player fifteen minutes at the most—probably less. Yet they appeared annoyed, angry, full of resentment.

"Way down there?" catcher Ron Karkovice complained to Doug Abel, the head of public relations for the White Sox, after Abel had told him that he would have to walk the entire distance from third base to home plate to start the outdoor-photo portion of this exercise.

"Way down there," Abel said. "Then work your way back up this way."

"Picture day is getting longer and longer every year," pitcher Dennis Cook said in an unhappy voice to Scott Reifert, another member of the Sox front-office staff.

"You'll like it when you get your licensing check," Reifert said.

Indeed the players would. The sports-trading-card business had grown into an enormously profitable industry; adults and children had somehow become convinced that the trading cards had inherent monetary value. All of the cash that the trading-card companies paid to the athletes was put into a pool, administered by the players' union. According to sources inside the trading-card business, each player who made a major-league roster—it didn't matter if the player was a superstar or a substitute—received a check for about $90,000 at the end of the season.

Ninety thousand dollars—for walking through a line on a sunny morning. Upper Deck had a photo station set up, as did Fleer and Donruss and Pinnacle and Topps, and companies from Japan and Canada.

"Are you a pitcher?" the photographer from Pinnacle said to pitcher Steve Schrenk, handing him an ID card to hold in front of his chest. All of the players were required to hold up these placards bearing their names. They might be idols to boys and girls around America, but in some photo lab somewhere, they were just faces to the technicians. "All right," a trading-card photographer ordered infielder Craig Grebeck. "Now one without your hat."

Catcher Doug Lindsey and outfielder Darrin Jackson were attempting heroic expressions for side-by-side photographers working for different card companies. A Sox regular stood behind the cameras, removed his pants, and struck a genuinely nauseating pose, attempting to distract Lindsey and Jackson. During the summer ahead, when the cards were released, observers of Lindsey's and Jackson's Olympian likenesses would have no idea of what the two men had been looking at as the camera lenses clicked.

"Hey, man," shortstop Ozzie Guillen barked at a card photographer on the outside diamond. "You took forty-five pictures of *Michael Jordan*— I play every fucking day, and you took four shots of me. I know what you're doing—you want to go home and tell your wife, 'I met *Michael*.' "

Frank Thomas was about to pose with a bat that had a splinter sticking out of it; a Sox staff member rushed to warn him, so that he would not snag the material of his uniform. All around the diamond, pitchers were affecting windup poses, and batters were pretending to swing, and players of every position were calling out that this $90,000 stroll was taking too long.

On a stool atop a motor-driven turntable set up by a company endeavoring to market holographic baseball cards, outfielder Tim Raines revolved around and around and around. "Don't move a mus-

cle in your face," a photo assistant called to Raines as a waiting outfielder spat, a catcher belched, here at the sausage factory on a warm
Florida day.

Rick Gano, assigned to cover the White Sox by the Associated Press,
was on the phone in the press room, calling his office.

"Yeah, he was asking for four-point-seven million," Gano said
into the phone. "He got four-point-three."

He hung up, turned to some of his fellow sportswriters, and said,
"You know, every day I write about one of these guys making six-
point-one million, or another making five-point-eight million. I
become numb to it.

"Man, I would give anything just to make the point. Forget the
number in front of the point—how I wish I just could make the number that comes after the point."

Jordan came into the clubhouse one day and saw that Gene Lamont,
the manager of the White Sox, had posted on the wall the starting
lineup for an intrasquad scrimmage. He walked over to see if he had
made the first team. He hadn't.

I saw him reading the list, then saw him walk to his locker and sit
down. "How long's it been?" I said.

"I guess fifteen years," he said. Meaning: It had been that long
since he had felt compelled to even look at any coach's lineup sheet.
It's a drill every kid in the world has gone through—that fluttery feeling when the list goes up, hoping that you've been chosen, that it will
be there for you to see and for everyone else to see: the proof that
you're good enough. If everyone knows the feeling, most people, at
one time or another, know the disappointment on those days when
they're left off the list. When it's official: that they are lacking.

He was lacking here; his name was not on the board. The last
time this happened—the time when he was fifteen, a high school
sophomore, cut from the school's basketball team—he turned it into
one of the great stories in sports history. You say I'm not good
enough? I'm going to become the best who ever played.

Here it was again, only now he was thirty-one. Frank Thomas came into the clubhouse and didn't look at the list; he didn't have to. Ozzie Guillen didn't look at the list, and Tim Raines didn't look at the list, and Julio Franco didn't look at the list. Why should they? They knew they were going to be on it, that's what the White Sox paid them all that money for. I asked Jordan if he had been nervous, looking at the list.

"I'm nervous every day down here," he said.

"Mrs. Jordan?"

A woman behind the low fence by the back practice diamonds saw Juanita Jordan and, calling to her, shoved a piece of paper in her direction for her to sign.

"I'm sorry," she said, with courtesy but leaving no question about it. "I'd rather not. But thank you."

She didn't like signing autographs; she knew that people really would have preferred to have her husband sign, and it's something she avoided when she could. She had flown down to watch him practice. She took a seat on a wooden bench in the back complex.

Jordan himself was annoyed when people said that he was breaking his word to his family—that, because he had announced he was going to spend more time with them, he was letting them down by playing baseball.

"The people who say that don't know me, and they don't know my family," he said. "Do they think I'd be here if I hadn't discussed this with my wife and children? Do they have any idea what an important decision this was? It's the greatest support my family could give me—the encouragement to try this. It's the nicest thing they could ever do for me at this point in my life. It's a gift they've given me."

On this day, as Jordan finished batting practice, he worked the fence, signing autographs, dressed in his full Sox uniform. Security guards flanked him on either side—he had spoken with them after the incident with the young boy who had been pushed against the fence, and now every time he signed they were there, scanning the crowd.

Twenty-five feet away, Juanita Jordan stood and watched him from behind, watched the man in the uniform being grabbed at by the screaming, squealing people. I was standing next to her; I looked over, and just for a second I got the impression that there were times when Michael Jordan—whoever that might be—seemed a million miles removed from her, too. When she might as well be looking at him from the farthest row in the highest deck of the biggest stadium in the world.

Late one morning a great chill came out of nowhere.

In Ed Smith Stadium, the nonstarters—including Jordan—were being put through conditioning drills. Jordan was working in the batting cage; other players were running sprints in the outfield.

One of these men was a player named Norberto Martin. I could see that, out near center field, he was fooling around with something. At first—seeing it from across the expanse of grass—it was difficult to believe.

He had a toy gun in his hand. A black toy handgun, which he had concealed in a pocket of his uniform. He kept pulling it out and aiming it at his teammates. He appeared to be amusing himself.

The wisdom, in our current era, of flashing anything that even has the appearance of a gun is more than a little questionable. Major-league baseball, though, sometimes seems to pride itself on being disconnected from the outside world. But there couldn't have been a player on the team who was unaware that Jordan's father had recently been shot to death with a handgun, and that part of Jordan's reason for being here was to ward off his despair. The coach who was in charge of the practice session told all the players to run the basepaths as part of their workout.

Jordan was right in front of Norberto Martin. The way the drill was set up, the players were supposed to run the basepaths in reverse order. So Jordan was heading from first base toward home plate.

Martin stepped up behind him—and shoved the barrel of the toy gun into Jordan's back. Right on the numeral of his uniform shirt.

Jordan involuntarily stiffened. And Martin pulled the trigger.

Click.

He pulled it again. He pulled it a third time.

The stands were virtually empty; this practice was not open to the public. Jordan reached behind him and pushed the toy gun away.

Still an outsider, still trying to fit in, he said nothing about what Martin had done. He kept running the basepaths. A bright and lovely Sarasota morning with not a hint of darkness.

Click. Click. Click.

For the fans who came out to the practice sessions, there was always this confusion. You could see it in their faces. Most of them had come to the spring training complex for one reason: to look at Jordan.

But Jordan playing baseball was not what they expected—and this had little to do with his skills, or his lack of them. Rather, there was this unspoken feeling that something was out of proper balance. They would cheer—they would cheer every time he so much as moved—but eventually all the cheers began to end in question marks.

It was because of this: Jordan playing baseball—even if he were to succeed and meet his own highest goals—simply did not have the potential of providing the audience with the same sense of electricity that Jordan playing basketball did. It was a function of the difference between the two games, and there was nothing that either Jordan or the game of baseball would ever be able to do about it. In the National Basketball Association, something stirring had to happen every twenty-four seconds. In baseball, a shot clock would be a sacrilege. Long minutes go by, and the game proceeds at its own pace. That languorous texture is what many people find beautiful about the sport.

Jordan, too: "I don't find it tedious at all, standing in right field. I like the way the game feels—waiting to see if the ball is going to come off the bat." The fans at the ballpark, though, would see him come onto the practice field, and some of them would shriek. Ten minutes later—when he was still standing there in the outfield—the shrieks would have subsided. The people would still be looking at him, not saying the words, but almost certainly thinking them: So this is it?

To use the Elvis Presley analogy: Had Presley for some reason decided to quit his singing career, to become, say, a percussionist with a symphony orchestra, one question would have been: Can he do it? But even if he had proved himself talented enough to be a good percussionist—a great percussionist—Elvis Presley as a member of a symphony would have been unable to provide audiences what Elvis Presley behind a microphone did. He would still be a musician. But he would be in a completely different line of work.

"It's proving day, isn't it?" Jordan said.

This was the morning of the first game that really counted—a regulation contest, in home and away uniforms, in front of paying customers: the White Sox playing each other, with the team's executives, coaches and managers evaluating them in deadly seriousness. Now it was beginning: From here on, every mistake would count against a player, every big play would be a step toward making the club.

His mistakes were many. He struck out the first two times he came to the plate; in the outfield, with cameras from news organizations all over the world trained on him like sniperscopes, he appeared ill at ease, stiff, even ungainly. The most photographed of all athletes suddenly seemed skittish about the cameras, seemed to be pulling back from them ever so slightly. A perfectly understandable reaction for most people—to recoil from all those heartless glass eyes—but for years he had lived among them without showing even a sliver of concern. Now he avoided making eye contact with the glass eyes, as if by his not looking at them, they might be persuaded to look away from him.

After one of his strikeouts, the Bob Seger song "Still the Same" blasted out of the ballpark's loudspeakers:

> *You always won, every time you placed a bet,*
> *you're still damn good, no one's gotten to you yet. . . .*

He went to the outfield, and the worst moment arrived.

A batter hit a high, lazy fly in Jordan's direction. It was a fly ball that any journeyman major-leaguer would have had no trouble with.

Jordan hesitated a moment, then took off after it. Those dozens of glass eyes were on him every step of the way. He ran slowly, then quickly, then slowly, then quickly. He extended his glove. The ball hit it, then popped out onto the grass by his feet, sitting there like a taunt. He bent low to look for it, to try to pick it up. The glass eyes sucked it all in, recorded every faltering gesture. The television cameras, with the almost silent whir of their videotape, and the still cameras, too. Click. Click. Click.

There was a dumpy little white van with an open back door, sent to Ed Smith Stadium by the Nike sporting-goods company to sell its line of Jordan gear at the workouts and games. On the day of the dropped ball it was parked behind the right-field stands, at the end of the row of concession booths. It was a low-rent touch—with newspaper clippings about Jordan taped to its exterior sides, it was something from a sad carnival midway, as far from the sleek commercial grandeur of the big-city Nike Towns as Jordan's melancholy day at the ballpark was from those championship games in NBA arenas.

As the game ended, the stadium announcer intoned: "Fans, Michael Jordan items and other sports memorabilia are for sale in the special van just outside the . . ." Jordan heard it; all of the other White Sox players heard it. He, and they, ran windsprints on the field before going back to the clubhouse. He peered straight down as he ran, not looking at his teammates.

"I thought I could put it out of my mind," Jordan said when we talked the next morning. "Walt Hriniak had told me that my swing was OK, and I thought I could just forget about dropping the ball.

"I went to bed around nine o'clock. But I kept waking up and replaying it."

"You and every TV station in the world," I said.

"I know it," he said. "Damn! I couldn't quit seeing it. Easy! I fell asleep again, and then I woke up at three-thirty, and I was still seeing it. Still thinking about it."

"Did anything feel right out there?" I said.

"There's so much little stuff I don't know about," he said. "When I was coming in from the outfield, I realized that I wasn't sure what I was supposed to do with my glove. Where to put it. Stuff the rest of them don't even have to think about."

"There was probably a time when they didn't know, either," I said.

"None of them would have dropped that ball," he said. "Damn! I hardly slept at all. I kept seeing that ball coming down toward me, even though I didn't want to."

One Sunday, after a morning at the ballpark during which Jordan had done poorly again, I went back to my hotel. There was a professional basketball game being telecast on NBC; the Chicago Bulls were being defeated badly by the New York Knicks. On the screen Scottie Pippen looked like he was out of answers; Horace Grant and Scott Williams were wandering around the court as if they had lost their map; John Paxson seemed like a visitor. Marv Albert and Matt Goukas were calling the action. "Last year, Michael Jordan could take over a game by himself," Goukas said.

That evening I had a sandwich at an outdoor restaurant over-looking the Gulf of Mexico. There was a guitarist singing old Beatles and Gordon Lightfoot tunes, but in the warm night air I kept hearing Matt Goukas' voice: "Last year, Michael Jordan could take over a game by himself. . . ."

That's what Jordan had rejected; that's what he had decided meant nothing. It was as if, every day at baseball practice, he was living with the decision he had made: the decision to will himself to be ordinary, to be that fifteen-year-old boy who was left off the team, who was told he was no good. To see if he could start from nothing and do it all again.

On a back practice diamond Jordan was finishing batting drills with the other substitutes. The team's big stars—Frank Thomas, Robin Ventura, Tim Raines—were over on the big field in the company of each other.

The coach back on the reserves' diamond ended the session and told the men to retrieve the stray baseballs. That was a part of this—to pick up the balls and put them into a wire basket that had been placed directly on the pitcher's mound.

Jordan, as if by instinct, began to shoot the balls toward the receptacle as if they were not baseballs, but basketballs. A fan who stood behind one of the low fences called to him: "Three points, Mike!" If Jordan heard the man, he did not look over. But neither did he stop shooting. On a broiling and humid Florida afternoon he took aim, lofted the next baseball into the air, and watched as it settled into the wire basket. "Nothing but net," another man behind the fence called to him. Jordan bent to pick up more balls, cleaning up the field.

The games against other big-league teams began. Jordan was getting in, and failing every time. He couldn't get a hit.

He was working so hard at this; even the ballplayers who had resented his presence, even the sportswriters who had thought this was some gimmick, found themselves shaking their heads at the ferocity of his effort to better himself. First man on the premises, often the last man to leave, he was working himself to near-exhaustion, and it seemed to be doing him no good at all.

After yet another dismal day for Jordan, Alan Solomon, the *Chicago Tribune* baseball writer assigned to cover the Sox and travel with the team all season, approached Jordan at his locker. The job of a beat writer at spring training is to be a cold-eyed evaluator of the players; only twenty-five men would be selected to go north each spring, and the beat writer was supposed to let the readers back home know just who held promise, and who didn't. Solomon, like many of the writers, had been skeptical about Jordan when all of this began.

On this day he approached Jordan and, in a genuinely soft tone, said, "I wish you were an asshole."

Jordan looked at him. "Why?" Jordan said.

"So I could rip you apart in the paper and not feel bad about it," Solomon said.

This was not a joking exchange. It was a serious, even emotional, thing for one man to say to another.

Jordan smiled slightly and nodded his head. He understood. Then he headed for the showers.

CHAPTER 7

In a way no one could have predicted, it was the cover of *Sports Illustrated* that began to turn things around.

Jordan had been on the magazine's cover more than any other person in sports history, with the exception of Muhammad Ali. During his basketball career, *Sports Illustrated* did not just report on Jordan as a news story—it quite openly and unapologetically used him to generate money. To boost its circulation, the magazine ran television commercials informing viewers that, if they would agree to subscribe, they would get a free Jordan videotape. The marketing assumption was that some sports fans might not feel the overriding need to have the publication in their home every week—but that they might indeed be persuaded if they were given the Jordan highlights tape. For many who called the toll-free 800 number to order, the magazine was undoubtedly an afterthought—they'd take it, as long as they received what they really wanted, which was the Jordan tape.

It was a curious position for a news-related publication to be in—using, as a subscription come-on, promotional videotapes of an athlete whose performances the magazine's reporters had to cover, presumably objectively, every basketball season. Now that Jordan was attempting to play baseball, though, and it was clear that he was struggling, the magazine decided to mock him.

After a reporter and photographer had visited spring training camp, *Sports Illustrated* devoted its cover and a color spread inside to a story and pictures ridiculing Jordan. The coverline was: "Bag It, Michael! Jordan and the White Sox Are Embarrassing Baseball." Having used Jordan to sell magazines when his skills in one sport were superb, *Sports Illustrated* was attempting to sell a few more issues by making fun of his failings. Two years before, *SI* had lauded him as its Sportsman of the Year; now the editors saw fit to jeer at him—not because they suddenly disapproved of his sportsmanship, but because he was committing the ultimate and unforgivable transgression in the world of sports: He wasn't good enough.

His teammates read the story, saw the cover—and knew that it wasn't fair. Jordan may have been a lot of things, but he wasn't a joke—his baseball teammates saw how hard he worked, how he wasn't afraid to look foolish in front of them when he couldn't achieve something, how he acknowledged that he wasn't as talented as they were. They still might not quite have understood what he was doing down here—but most of them were beginning to respect the honesty of his effort. The *Sports Illustrated* cover, more than anything else, put them on his side.

"All right," a coach named Terry Bevington called out on the Billy Pierce practice diamond. "A base hit to right field—runners on first and second, we got a cutoff man." Bevington was setting up an imaginary game situation, to check the players' instincts and reflexes. Half an instant after shouting the instructions, he tossed a ball into the air, knocked it toward the right fielder—and watched as the baserunners and fielders did what they were supposed to do.

Jordan, who had been told to be the runner at first base, dashed for second. He was thinking too much—his concentration threw him off, he was neither quick enough to get where he was going nor slow enough that he could have returned to first, and Ozzie Guillen, playing shortstop, ran after him for the tag. Jordan pirouetted like a gangly novice ballerina, trying to avoid Guillen and the baseball, looking almost dainty, if a six-foot-six-inch baseball player can ever be said to be dainty. Guillen wasn't fooled; Jordan contorted his body, tried to levitate out of Guillen's space, and fell into the dirt. He grinned and pulled himself up, panting.

The others would not have made the baserunning error—they had been doing this forever, it was their only job, playing baseball in the sun was all they did. On an adjacent practice diamond Jack McDowell, the Cy Young Award winner from the season before, was throwing fastballs, working his arm into shape, and the sight of it—the speed and accuracy with which he threw the ball, the precision and the zip—were astonishing to behold. Days like this, moments like this, spring training seemed like the only place in the world anyone would want to be—like a place to run away to, a haven from both the dreariness and the pain of the world outside the fences.

The regulation games against other major-league teams were beginning. Scott Reifert of the Sox public relations staff sat in the press box and, as the first pitch left the hand of the man on the mound and smacked into the padding of the catcher's glove, announced with authority to the sportswriters in the box: "One-oh-six p.m., eighty-seven degrees, winds are calm." Time and weather conditions as the game began, the environment of a closed and controlled universe.

"Grebeck! Come over here!"

Walt Hriniak, in the batting shed with Jordan at the end of an afternoon—most of the White Sox had gone home, but Jordan had asked for extra instruction—was summoning infielder Craig Grebeck, who had gotten a solid hit on a day that Jordan had gotten nothing.

"When you got that base hit this afternoon," Hriniak said to Grebeck, "what was the difference between that being a hit, and being an out?"

Hriniak knew the answer; Grebeck knew that Hriniak knew the answer. This was for Jordan's benefit. Grebeck picked up a bat and showed Jordan how he snapped his wrists as he made contact with the ball. Grebeck was a little guy, but he consistently peppered the ball with cold assuredness. "This," he said to Jordan, teaching him the wrist motion. "This." Jordan, with his own bat, tried to imitate. "Like that?" Jordan said. "Sort of," Grebeck said. "Look. This. Like this."

When the session was done, and Hriniak and Grebeck had left, Jordan said, "This was one of those days when I didn't feel like I deserved to be a part of the team. I was just bad."

"Are you starting to doubt your decision to come here?" I said.

"I'm not saying I'm going to be bad forever," he said. "I'm saying I had a bad day today. Today's not tomorrow."

The team traveled down to Port Charlotte for a game against the Texas Rangers. Sox manager Gene Lamont was giving Jordan plenty of playing time; Lamont hadn't wanted Jordan at spring training in the first place—he had said Jordan's presence would bring too many "non-baseball-people" (Lamont's phrase) to the ballpark. Now he figured that the quicker Jordan was allowed to fail, the quicker he'd be gone.

In a pretty little ballpark, with senior citizens working as vendors and ticket takers and old Beach Boys songs sounding on the P.A. system between innings, Jordan played right field hesitatingly; in the second inning a ball came screaming toward him, and instead of charging it he waited for it to bounce, and in the press box the voices were saying, "He's playing it safe." Jose Canseco, the Rangers' star slugger, smashed a double into Jordan's part of the field and when Jordan reached the ball he was so eager to pick it up and fire it to the infield that he bobbled it, had to retrieve it twice.

"Ladies and gentlemen," the public address announcer said during one break between innings, "come up with the correct answer to our quiz, and win a free video. In the movie *Blue Chips*, Shaquille O'Neal has a starring role. Our question is: Name the fictional college that Shaquille attends in the movie, and his fictional college coach." The NBA's star-building machinery was moving on; Jordan, in the dugout, fooled with his glove and watched the game.

The statistics sheet in the press box gave the averages for each player on each of the two teams. Jordan was the only man whose batting average was .000. The miserly little Nike van with the clippings and pictures taped to it had been driven over from Sarasota, and it was parked outside the field, its windows covered with a dust film from the trip down side roads, its driver assigned to stand in the sun and sell Jordan souvenirs.

In the seventh inning, he got on base. It wasn't an official hit—he made contact with the ball, and reached first on a fielder's choice—but for the first time of the spring he was on the basepaths after his time at bat. Later, in the compact visitors' dressing room near the end of the left-field line of Charlotte County Stadium, he was ebullient—in the same kind of wired, almost manic mood he'd been in after the Chicago Bulls had won their second NBA championship, when he and his teammates had danced on the scorer's table in Chicago Stadium.

"I'm really trying," he said. "I'm really trying to learn this." Gene Lamont had taken Jordan and a few others out of the game for the final innings; to speed things up so the team could get back to Sarasota as quickly as possible, Lamont had told them they should get their things ready for the bus ride back—he sent them to the locker room while the game was still on.

Jordan was replaying every moment of the game—the game that meant nothing—with catcher Ron Karkovice. In the visitors' clubhouse, a sign was tacked to the wall: "Remember—Your Worst Day at the Ballpark Is Better Than Your Best Day at Work."

"You want another card game on the way back?" Jordan said to Karkovice. "I want to win my money back." Karkovice was finding it hard to disguise his amusement at this—he'd been playing pro baseball since he was little more than a kid, this was just another day in a another spring training park for him, and here was Jordan, snapping out of his gloom, excited and in overdrive because he'd finally reached first base.

"Is this thing about over?" Karkovice said to Doug Abel of the Sox staff.

"Not for a while," Abel said. "I think it's 13 to 6."

"We're losing?" Karkovice said, knowing it didn't matter.

"No, we're up," Jordan said to him. "We're ahead—we're *winning* 13 to 6."

I sat with him and asked him what the best part of the day had been for him.

"Just the feel of the bag under my foot," he said, keeping his voice low so that the others in the room would not hear how important it had been to him. "I stepped on first base after getting on, and there was that bag under my foot, and I could feel it through my shoe—and I knew I was there."

Three sheriff's deputies came into the clubhouse. They were carrying baseballs. "We're here to escort you to the bus, sir," one of them said to Jordan. "There's a large crowd gathered."

The other ballplayers exchanged glances; a few shook their heads. The deputies wordlessly handed the balls to Jordan to sign. Making sure this wasn't their second time through seeking signatures, he said to them, "Have I seen you guys before?"

"No, sir," one of them said.

"All right," Jordan said, signing. "As long as you get me out of here."

"We will, sir," a deputy said. The game had ended; the other Sox were entering the clubhouse. Jordan, deputies flanking him, left the structure for the short walk to the team bus. The other White Sox players in the room could hear the sound of screams.

Those other Sox never seemed quite sure of how they really felt. In the confines of their own spring training complex, the ballplayers, day by day, drew closer to Jordan, accepted him as a person, put the iconography out of their minds. But the screams from the public always appeared to bring out something else in them.

In Bradenton, after an away game with the Pittsburgh Pirates, the Sox were in the visitors' clubhouse getting ready for the short ride back to Sarasota. Fans had rushed to the left-field railing, and were hanging over it, begging Jordan to stop.

Which he did, signing autographs for them as he slowly worked his way to the clubhouse door. I was inside the clubhouse; I saw that Frank Thomas and Ozzie Guillen were standing at an open window, watching Jordan with the fans.

"All right, that's enough," Thomas said quietly in Jordan's direction. "Get the fuck in here. You've signed enough."

"Look at him," Guillen said to Thomas.

Hundreds of fans who couldn't get close enough to touch him were chanting: *We want Michael, we want Michael.* . . .

Guillen laughed and began a nasal chant: "We want *Michael.* . . ."

Jack McDowell walked over to join Thomas and Guillen. He shook his head at what he saw through the window.

"We want *Michael* . . ." Guillen continued.

"Get the fuck in here," Thomas said.

Another day, at practice at the White Sox complex, Guillen was walking from the back diamonds to the clubhouse. A fan behind the low fence—all the fans had read about how badly Jordan was doing—pointed to Jordan on the field, and said to Guillen, "Hey, Ozzie—Michael's not a baseball player, is he?"

It was one of the few times Guillen stopped to talk with the customers. He looked at Jordan, laughed, and said to the man: "He's wearing a baseball uniform, isn't he?"

I saw Eddie Einhorn, one of the owners of the Sox, one afternoon. At this point Jordan was 0-for-10 in regulation games.

"I know, I know, he's 0-for-10," Einhorn said. "But keep in mind that we pay two million dollars a year to some guys who spend the season hitting two out of every ten."

"Follow me," the Sarasota police officer said.

"Same route as yesterday?" Jordan said.

"Same route," the police officer said.

We were in the parking lot of the White Sox complex, after practice. Jordan was ready for the twenty-five-minute drive to his rented home. He had climbed behind the wheel of his red Corvette—the car he had been driving all during spring training.

Inside the clubhouse, he knew where he stood—at or near the

bottom of the list of all the men who were trying to win a spot on the team. When the others left each afternoon, though, he stepped back into his separate world, the world the rest of them—regardless of how successful they were in professional sports—would never be a part of. That world was waiting for Jordan daily whether he felt like re-entering it or not.

The police car steered slowly through the parking lot, with Jordan in the Corvette following close behind. The police car, then Jordan's car, moved between the security guards at the gate leading to the street. There were the screams at the sight of Jordan's car; the police car's siren was switched on, and it raced its engine and turned sharply to its right and the officer stepped on the accelerator and Jordan stepped on his and they hurtled at emergency speed down the side street.

"He'll pull off at this main street up here," Jordan called out, his voice raised to be heard above the rush of the wind in the convertible. Sure enough, once the two cars had turned onto a main thoroughfare, the police officer waved goodbye and Jordan roared away.

Immediately people began rushing off the sidewalks and toward the car. This was no special occasion; there had been no announcement about when he would be departing the baseball complex for the day, no publicity on which route he would take.

But here came a boy, running right in front of a sanitation truck, which slammed on its brakes. Jordan was at a red light.

The boy ran to the driver's-side window and shoved a basketball at Jordan. "Don't you know it's not safe to run into the street like that?" Jordan said.

"I know it," the boy said.

"No, you don't," Jordan said. "If you knew it, you wouldn't have done it."

He signed the basketball. The light turned green. He stepped on the accelerator, and on both sidewalks, on either side of the street, men and women were calling his name, bellowing, applauding. On every block it happened, block after block—this is what a presidential motorcade would feel like, if Americans still automatically cheered their president on sight. But this was no motorcade, this was one man driving home from the office.

In a car in the next lane, a man tried frantically to roll down his window. Jordan looked over at the man, which seemed to make him even more excited. He could not get his window down.

As we had gotten into the car, I had noticed that the license plates were from Michigan. I asked Jordan why.

"I wanted to get a car like this to drive while I'm down here," he said, his voice still loud against the wind. "They didn't have the right car in Florida. So I called the Chevy dealers in Chicago, and they called their headquarters in Detroit, and they brought this down for me."

"It's free?" I said.

"They're lending it to me," he said. "They take it back when spring training is over."

On the sidewalk, a man was waiting for a bus.

"It shows you how backward this country is, doesn't it?" Jordan said. "That guy over there, he may not have a ride and no way to get a ride. No one would ever help him get a car, no matter how badly he needed it. I don't need a car, and they drive one down for me."

"Why'd they do it?" I said.

"I told them I had a new Porsche back home," Jordan said. "But they wanted to get the Corvette in all the camera shots of me leaving practice. I know—you don't know whether to laugh or to cry."

The entire way to his house, the cheers and the sound of clapping hands continued. At a light, the fellow who had not been able to roll down his window appeared at Jordan's own window. He had caught up with Jordan's car and run over to it.

"I don't want an autograph," the man said, out of breath. "Just please pay a visit to these children."

He handed Jordan a piece of paper with the names of some children and the address of Sarasota Memorial Hospital. Jordan accepted it and stuck it in his pocket. I could not read anything in his expression. Across the street, people shrieked and waved their arms and shouted indecipherable exhortations. The light changed and he drove on, heading for a night's rest before returning in the morning to the ballpark where he would once again be insufficient.

The thing that meant the most to Jordan came out of nowhere, and began with a moment of failure.

During a game against the Detroit Tigers, he sat on the dugout steps while the White Sox were at bat, his face in the sun, not joining the others on the bench. He was starting to do this more—sit a few feet closer to the game than anyone else, as if watching from a nearer vantage point would allow him to see a secret he had somehow missed, something that would help.

Several times during spring training games, when he had hit infield grounders, he had come close to beating them out for singles. Each time, the first-base umpire had ruled that the ball arrived at the bag before Jordan did: Out. "I don't have any history," he'd told me after one of these calls. "In the NBA, I'd probably have gotten the benefit of a close call like that. Here, I have no weight."

Today, against Detroit, he watched and attempted to learn, and in the bottom of the eighth inning, with two outs, Glenn DiSarcina, trying to make the White Sox main squad, came to the plate and hit a long triple. So with DiSarcina on third, Jordan came to bat.

He hit a hard ground ball toward the shortstop, and ran toward first base with all the energy he had. It looked as if he might beat the ball—and when he touched the bag it looked as if he had, indeed, beaten it, for his first hit.

The umpire called him out.

And before Jordan could say a thing, a White Sox outfielder named Dann Howitt—another man who, like Jordan, was in camp trying to make the team—came running out of the dugout, screaming at the umpire, yelling that Jordan had been cheated, that he'd beaten the throw and that he had reached first safely and that he had earned his hit. The umpire, surprised to see Howitt—so was Jordan, he hardly knew Howitt—just stood there. Howitt kept yelling, and the umpire ejected him from the game, sent him to the clubhouse.

Where, later, Jordan and the rest of the White Sox changed from their uniforms into their street clothes. I saw Jordan look across the room at Howitt's locker, and when the two men's eyes met, Jordan nodded in thanks. Howitt nodded back. It was the one thing Jordan had never needed from any teammate in the NBA—he had never needed someone to stand up for him, never needed someone to be the big brother. After all that had gone on at spring training, there was Howitt, without being asked, treating Jordan like a teammate who could use some help. Getting tossed out for him. Some moments stick.

"On the days that I go 0-for-4, I try to tell myself that there are other guys who go 0-for-4 or 0-for-5," Jordan said.

We were talking one afternoon about how he was dealing with the fact that he still could not get a hit.

"But I can't really tell myself that, because I know there's a difference," Jordan said. "The difference is that the other guys may go 0-for-4 once in a while, but the day before they were 2-for-3 or 3-for-4. Frank Thomas may go 0-for-4, and he can tell himself that will never happen again. I can't tell myself that, because I don't know. I don't know whether I'll ever get a hit."

Jerry Reinsdorf, the principal owner of the White Sox, was at one of the spring games, and I walked up to him as he was leaving the ballpark after it ended. He saw his players striding by the waiting fans without stopping to sign autographs, to say hello, to return the fans' greetings with as much as a wave.

"It wouldn't kill them," Reinsdorf said.

I asked if he ever thought about possible ways to persuade the players to treat the fans a little better, just as a public relations gesture.

"We can't make them do anything," Reinsdorf said. "Their union would be all over us."

Had anyone ever tried to explain to the players that treating the customers like that could end up hurting them?

"We've tried," he said. "They don't understand that it's the fans who pay their salaries. We've suggested that they take one day a week to sign some autographs. They don't want to be bothered."

Couldn't Reinsdorf, as the employer of the players, assign his employees to do certain things?

"We can only ask," he said. "This year, we've written into all the contracts that the players have to sign a certain number of balls and other items for the team each year. For the team to give to charity. We had to negotiate it."

"What's it like to pay someone forty million dollars?" I said.

That's what published reports said that Frank Thomas was getting in a multi-year deal. "What's it feel like to sign those checks?" I said.

"I don't actually sign the check," he said.

"But you sign the contract," I said. "Do you ever wake up in the middle of the night and think: 'I have to pay someone forty million dollars, and he's only one of my twenty-five players'?"

"It's not forty million every year," he said. "It's only seven million a year."

"Still," I said.

"After I sign the contract I don't worry," Reinsdorf said.

"Would you ever not be able to honor a contract like that?" I said.

"If the people stopped coming to the games," he said. "If the television money went away. That's why I don't like to sign long-term contracts with pitchers. It's one thing to pay a pitcher five million dollars a year. But what if the guy can't play?"

"Who does sign those checks?" I said.

"Not me," he said.

"But someone has to," I said.

"I don't know who it is," he said. "Someone in the organization. I think Howard Pizer actually signs them."

"Most people get nervous every month when their American Express bill comes in the mail," I said. "I think it might be a little scary to think about the size of the checks you're committed to handing out every month."

"Yeah," Reinsdorf said. He lit a cigar.

"I guess it is scary," he said, sounding like he didn't mean it.

The first night game of spring training was on a Monday, against the Minnesota Twins. The ballpark felt wonderful—the heat of the day had gone away, the Florida dusk was intoxicating, and the field had a different feel than in the sunlight; it had the feel of a movie set with a baseball script yet to be written, the feel of the game of baseball at its most enticing, luring people to it tonight as baseball has always lured Americans out of their houses.

It was apparent to everyone that Jordan was not going to make the major-league team—there had been no announcement, but it was obvious that he would not be going north with the White Sox. With two outs in the sixth inning, with Jordan playing right field, a Minnesota batter sliced a hard drive down the line, and Jordan, under the lights, sprinted right to it and grabbed it before it hit the ground, a genuinely fine catch. As he ran with the ball to the dugout, Ozzie Guillen ran with him and patted him on the back, and it was not for show, and it was not patronizing, it meant what it looked like, which was: Good work.

The public address announcer intoned the license plate of a car to the crowd and said, "Your car is locked . . . your engine is running . . . and you're running out of gas." Children were laughing all over the ballpark—the P.A. man said these same words every day, and children always laughed—and so they were laughing as usual tonight, laughing and enjoying themselves at the game.

The next inning, Jordan got his hit.

It was a solid single down the third-base line, a real hit, not a dribbler that he managed to beat out but a hit that any major-leaguer would take pride in, and as the fans rose to salute him he was fighting to keep the smile off his face, he didn't want to seem to be celebrating something that any of his other teammates would take for granted, but this was it, this was what he had worked for.

Dann Howitt came to the plate and hit a home run, driving Jordan in. Jordan's teammates met him and Howitt at home plate, and for a second or two they all seemed like children having fun on the nicest night of spring.

When the game ended Jordan entered the clubhouse through a side door; his teammates, waiting for him and putting their fingers to their mouths, silenced each other, and when he came into view they jumped all over him, dousing him with cans and bottles of beer. "Is this a tradition?" Jordan said, laughing. "You didn't tell me about it." They were all congratulating him, and he was saying, "Now, if I can keep it up—if I can develop it into something, keep doing it . . ."

The celebration lasted for a few minutes, and almost all of the players soon left the clubhouse to go home. I asked Jordan if he thought playing at night had anything to do with his change of luck— after all, playing games at night, in the NBA, was what he had done for so long.

He looked as if he hadn't thought about it, but he immediately seemed to want to buy it. Anything to keep this going: "You know, that's right, I'm used to playing at night. Night is my game. This is when I play." Ozzie Guillen, overhearing this, gave Jordan an "Oh, shut up" look, but he meant it to be good-natured and funny, this was not another dig. All baseball nights might not be Jordan's night, but this one was.

Frank Thomas, having gotten dressed, made the walk across the room to Jordan's locker.

"Now you can relax," Thomas said.

"I've been relaxed," Jordan said.

"No, you haven't," Thomas said.

"I have too," Jordan said.

"It's not hard," Thomas said. "This game's not hard. I told you."

"I know," Jordan said. "Now I've got to keep building."

"None of this minor-league shit," Thomas said to him. "I've been hearing you talk about that. None of this minor-league shit for you."

"I just started something," Jordan said.

"You keep this up tomorrow," Thomas said. "None of this minor-league shit."

Thomas left; Jordan seemed almost drunk with pleasure. "My family's waiting outside for me," he said. "They're leaving tomorrow. They're going to . . . what's the name of that amusement park in Orlando?"

"An amusement park?" I said.

"Yeah," he said. "In Orlando. Big amusement park."

"Are you talking about Disney World?" I said.

"Yeah," he said. "Disney World."

I couldn't tell, the way he said it, whether forgetting the name was a joke. I asked him what he thought about tomorrow.

"What's tomorrow?" he said.

"A game," I said.

"Who are we playing?" he said.

"Who are you playing?" I said. "You're playing the New York Yankees."

"Oh," he said, no more impressed than if I'd said the Main Street Marauders. But of course he was a man who had known the feeling of being the '27 Yankees all by himself, a man who had known the feeling of being as big as Mickey Mouse, a character over at that amusement park in Orlando.

I ran into Eddie Einhorn on the way out.

"This doesn't change anything, does it?" I said.

"No," Einhorn said.

"He's going to the minors?" I said.

"Yes," Einhorn said.

Jordan's wife and children were waiting for him on a little walkway right outside the clubhouse. He came out carrying the ball—the baseball he had gotten his first hit with. It was impossible to even estimate how much that ball would be worth on the sports memorabilia market.

Jordan handed it to his younger son, Marcus, who was three years old. "Don't lose this," Jordan said to him.

Jordan turned to talk with his wife, and Marcus turned, threw the ball onto the grass, where it rolled under a bush and remained.

There were bursts of cockiness from Jordan in the days that followed. "Hey, J.B.," he called to White Sox pitcher James Baldwin one afternoon, after Baldwin had pitched to him and Jordan had hit the ball well. "Were you nervous out there, throwing to me? Yeah, you were. Yeah, you were." It fell a little flat—Jordan had hit well, but not that well, not well enough to kid a pitcher.

Still, there was a sense of relaxation between him and the other players, the kind of looseness that hadn't been there before. Jordan had brought a couple of McDonald's hamburgers with him to the clubhouse one day; Gold Glove third baseman Robin Ventura slipped around behind him while he was putting on his uniform, swiped the burgers from between two of Jordan's bats on the floor, and took them into the trainer's room to eat them—he finished them by the time Jordan discovered they were gone.

It was as though, if Jordan could pretend this was going to last forever, then it somehow would. "JoJo!" Jordan called in right field to fellow aspiring outfielder Joe Hall after Hall had made a good catch during practice. "That's it, JoJo. That's the way to do it." Hall looked over at Jordan, pleased by the compliment but wondering why Jordan should be the one to offer it.

Meanwhile this all had the feel of something ending. The shadows would creep across the outfield late in the afternoon, and the stars of the White Sox would look better and better as the weeks wore on, and Jordan would continue to arrive early and stay late, trying to get good enough so that he could reproduce that first hit at will, and this had the feel of something finite.

The hits did come once in a while. "A rope," a sportswriter said to Jordan after he had hit a legitimate line drive one day, and Jordan, more sheepish than proud, said, "I can't dribble the ball out of the infield every time." As his at-bats got fewer, and the regular players were given more innings, he was beginning to understand that he was heading for the minors. He would arrive at 6 a.m., and by 3 or 3:30, accepting that he would not be getting in the game, he would sit on that top step of the dugout, one man in the waning sunshine.

I asked him how Gene Lamont would tell him that he was going to get to go into a game. "He doesn't," Jordan said. "He has someone do it for him."

"He doesn't even talk to you?" I said.

"He'll send someone over to me and the person will say, 'Right field,' or 'D.H.,' " Jordan said. "It'll be toward the end of the game. I'm going to the minors. I know they're sending me down."

One Tuesday—this was on one of the many days he would not get a hit—the White Sox were playing in Ed Smith Stadium. Jordan was several hundred yards away, off behind the stadium on the Nellie Fox practice diamond. Jordan had left the dugout of the real stadium during the game, and had departed through the opening in the right-field fence. Some who had seen him leave assumed he was headed for the showers—that he had been told that he would not play at all this day.

That wasn't it. On the practice diamond, Walt Hriniak was down on one knee in the dirt, directly next to Jordan. "Come through like this, Michael," Hriniak said. He motioned as if he had a bat in his hand. "Watch me. Like this."

Jordan, frustration in his face, watched. There were no other players on the infield of the practice diamond. A minor-league coach named Roger LaFrancois was on the pitcher's mound. Jordan had been told that he would be inserted in the lineup soon. Rather than wait in the dugout, he had come back here, while the game in the real stadium was in progress, to work some more. To try, at the last minute, to learn something that might help him.

You could turn away from Jordan and look across the distance at the stadium. It was filled with people in the harsh sunlight, virtually all of them wondering if they would see Jordan play today. "Ladies and gentlemen," a disembodied voice echoed from over there, "at bat, number 28, Joey . . . Cora." Applause from the faraway stadium. "Watch me, Michael," Walt Hriniak said here. "Watch me."

LaFrancois threw pitch after pitch to Jordan. Jordan swung, almost always making contact, but visibly unhappy with what was happening to the ball, what he was feeling in his hands. "Take a step back," Hriniak said to Jordan. "If you don't take a step back you'll be too wide."

Something was going on in the game in the big stadium. You could tell from the sound. From over here, it was like the sound of every stadium you've ever remembered from your whole life, every stadium whose noise you have heard from afar, where something was happening and you were not there. That delicious, taunting stadium sound that makes you want to be inside, that makes you feel you're missing out on something by not being present. "Now batting for the White Sox," the echo announced, "number 35, Frank . . . Thomas."

"Michael," Walt Hriniak said.

"Yes, sir," Jordan said.

"Another way," Hriniak said. "Another way. You don't have to do it this way. It's just a suggestion." Hriniak stood next to Jordan, the imaginary bat in his hand. "Wind up," Hriniak said. "Take a step back. Then . . ." Hriniak swung through. "Go."

Jordan imitated Hriniak's swing. All the colors visible across the way, in the real stadium; all the sounds. In the other direction, from property contiguous to the White Sox facility, a tree trimmer could be heard cutting through bark, metal on wood.

Hriniak seemed to become aware of something. He and Jordan had worked too long; it was past time for Jordan to go over to the real field and into the game. "Michael," Hriniak said, with an edge in his voice. "You've got to get over there."

Jordan, a bat in his hand, looked over at the filled stadium. He was sweating and a little out of breath. The echoes kept coming, and the noise of the baseball game, the voices of the crowd.

"Now, Michael," Hriniak said.

Jordan started running. Clutching the bat, the colors of the stadium in front of him, he ran by himself across the expanse of grass. In the newspapers the next day the sports stories would say that in his first at-bat of the game he fouled out weakly along the first-base line. That would come in a few minutes, though. Right now it hadn't happened. Right now he was running as fast as he could, running across an open field, a solitary figure sprinting toward the sound of distant joy.

He was sent down—assigned to the Birmingham Barons of the Class Double-A Southern League. He spent the final weeks of spring training working out with the minor-leaguers on the outlying diamonds, while the real White Sox continued to play against other major-league teams.

The White Sox left camp to go north for the season. Jordan remained behind. The clubhouse looked desolate, with the twenty-five best players gone. Remaining were the young men, many of them just a year or two out of high school, who would be sent to the various Sox farm clubs. Those young men, and Michael Jordan.

"I've lived high on the hog, and I can live not high on the hog," Jordan said.

So he was going to take up the Sox management's invitation? He was going to do it—report to the minors?

"This is going to be one fun summer," he said. "Riding the bus all summer . . . Do you remember how much fun it was to miss sixth-period and seventh-period classes, and ride to an away baseball game on the school bus? Eating peanut butter and jelly sandwiches? And you can't play around and laugh on the way back if you lost?

"This is going to be a great summer. The only thing that will make it bad is if I go 0-for-2,000."

Some of the minor-leaguers asked Jordan if he was really going to buy a luxury bus for the Birmingham team. That had been in the newspapers—that Jordan didn't want to ride on the rickety old bus the team owned.

"Yeah, and I'm going to charge my teammates twenty-five cents a trip for seats," Jordan said.

"No, really," one of the minor-leaguers said, standing in front of a locker where Frank Thomas used to dress.

"I don't want to be on some creaky old bus that's going to break down on some back road at night," Jordan said.

The young men in the room didn't seem to pick up on it.

"In the South," Jordan said.

"What, you afraid of seeing some guys in white hoods?" an eighteen-year-old second baseman said, joking. But it wasn't the Klan that Jordan had on his mind.

"I'm serious," Jordan said, and for an instant you could see James Jordan behind his son's eyes. "I don't want to be in some bus that breaks down by the side of the road."

He looked around the clubhouse, then followed the young ballplayers outside for fielding practice, the last of spring training, the last before the summer.

CHAPTER 8

The bright and insistent strains of a country music song were coming out of the loudspeakers at Greenville Municipal Stadium in Greenville, South Carolina:

Life's a dance, you learn as you go. . . .

I saw Jordan in the outfield, chasing down fly balls. It was a brutally hot Carolina afternoon; the heat was almost visible, it made the air distort the shapes of objects in the distance, made the objects seem a little wavy, a little misshapen. Something that wasn't a heavy-aired illusion was that Jordan appeared to be the one thing even his severest critics had never called him: slow. Soaked with perspiration, taking fielding practice before the gates would open for the night, he ran at about half-speed: He wouldn't have been able to catch himself on a basketball court.

I had just arrived in town. Jordan and the Birmingham Barons had pulled into Greenville the night before on the now-famous bus; he had, indeed, chartered it for the team, and it had been reported on in the newspapers, photographed as it cruised down the highway, televised, although no one but team members and staff had been inside it. In the first weeks of the Southern League season Jordan had been playing unexpectedly well, hitting over .300, and the ballparks around the league were standing-room-only each night.

"Do you believe this?" Jordan said, gesturing up toward the relentless, unshielded sun. He was gasping for breath.

"It's only April," I said.

"I know," he said. "I can't even imagine August."

A batter hit a popup toward him. He circled under it, blocked the sun with his glove, pulled it in. There were no sounds in the ballpark, save for the music echoing off the empty seats. The customers would not be allowed in for several more hours.

"I should have remembered this," Jordan said, mopping the sweat from his face. "I did grow up down here."

"You're sure this is fun?" I said.

"More fun at night," he said. "More fun once the sun goes away."

He was on an eleven-game hitting streak as the Barons got ready for a three-game series against the Greenville Braves, an Atlanta farm club. The night before, playing in this same stadium against another Southern League team, the Greenville club had drawn barely over 1,000 fans, a generous estimate at that; tonight against the Barons the paid attendance would be 8,026—the place was only supposed to hold 7,027, the rest would stand and squeeze into the aisles—and now the person who was the reason for the surge in sales scratched at his arms, slapped at mosquitoes, and at the signal of Birmingham manager Terry Francona went with his teammates into the clubhouse.

The place was cramped beyond all reason—this locker room was as modest as the facilities some junior-high school teams are provided with. Jordan attempted to get to his locker. His jersey, with his name and the numeral 45 sewn onto the back, was hanging on a nail. A pitcher named Luis Andujar dropped his duffel bag directly in front of Jordan's locker.

"Yo, Lu," Jordan said.

Andujar was eating a powdered doughnut, slowly consuming it bite by bite, standing right at the spot where Jordan wanted to sit.

"Lu, do you mind?" Jordan said.

Andujar held his doughnut up. "Bueno," he said.

"Bueno," Jordan muttered beneath his breath. "Hey, Lu—let me sit down, OK?"

On a table a few feet away was the team's meal for the day—industrial-sized tins of Peter Pan peanut butter, Honey Buns sticky to meltdown point inside their plastic wrappers, white bread, grape jelly. Some of Jordan's teammates—these were guys who were young enough that more than a few of them, three or four years ago when they were in high school, surely had Michael Jordan posters on their bedroom walls at home—were glancing at a hard-core magazine left behind by last night's visiting team.

"They always wear that shit," a youthful-looking infielder, staring at a photograph of a woman in a black garter belt, said.

"How great is that?" an outfielder said.

A tape player boomed rap music throughout the dank, wooden-walled room.

"Someone want to turn that down?" Jordan said.

No one did. A pitcher, peering at the woman in the magazine, said, "Look at the expression on her face."

"You're looking at her face?" the infielder said.

"Yeah," the pitcher said. "Look how cold her expression is. She's sort of frightening."

"Someone!" Jordan called out again, a little louder this time. "Is someone listening to this?"

Apparently someone was. The music continued.

He started to change into his game uniform. He grabbed the last half-cookie off the table.

"Now, don't go knocking minor-league food," Jordan said as I looked at his meal. "I like the food down here. Steak and eggs, everywhere I go. I'm eating more grits than I ever ate in my life. Tell me where I'd get grits in Cleveland."

He could have picked any city as an example. Cleveland happened to be the city that was the home of the Chicago Bulls' first-round opponents in the National Basketball Association playoffs that were getting under way. Jordan's old teammates were scheduled to play the Cavaliers, in a game that would be seen nationwide. He claimed not to be all that interested.

"Like old times," he said. "Like how your world once was. You don't really know it anymore. It's something that used to be."

But of all the cities in the world he could have brought up this afternoon, Cleveland was the one he chose.

"I don't even think about it much anymore," he said.

He never found himself watching the Bulls on television?

"Not much," he said. "Really. Not too much."

"Come on, man," Jordan called teasingly to Kerry Valrie, a Birmingham outfielder who was taking swings in the batting cage as Jordan waited his turn. "You can't go deep."

Valrie took a furious cut that sent the ball far into left field, back toward the fence. Valrie pointed his bat at Jordan, a few feet away from him, and started hooting and laughing. "I can't go deep?" Valrie said.

"That's right," Jordan said. "You . . . can't . . . go . . . deep. You think that was deep? You didn't even get it to the warning track."

Valrie, still laughing, came out of the batting cage, pretended to wrestle Jordan toward the ground, then embraced him. The two men insulted each other with great playfulness in bright but dying sunlight at ten minutes after six. The fans were arriving now; taking their seats, they looked toward the field, ready for their first glimpse of Jordan.

It was the paradox that he was beginning to find he could do nothing about. If his goal in the minor leagues was to be nothing special—to be one of the boys once again (although the oldest of the boys, to be sure)—then it was a goal he would never be able to reach. Whether he hit .400 or .125 didn't matter. He was on full-time display.

"I feel a little bit like a fish," he said. "Like I'm in an aquarium. It's OK. This is my choice."

As the teams took to the field at the beginning of the first inning, the ballpark's public address announcer—aware that there were customers present tonight who would not be here on any other night—

said into his press-box microphone: "Ladies and gentlemen, if this is your first visit to a G-Braves game, we invite you to come back many times. We hope you will have an enjoyable evening. Thank you for supporting your G-Braves!"

The man they were really here to support struck out looking in the second inning. The press box, sealed in by closed windows from the sounds of the park, was silent and claustrophobic; I left my seat there and worked my way down to the field and into the photo pen next to the first-base dugout. The oppressive heat was gone from the early-evening air. This was a gorgeous setting: the little ballpark with its diamond lower than the surrounding land, the voices of the small-town baseball crowd like an old familiar tune at dusk, the seats along the right-field line adjacent to a steeply sloping hill, with a forest deep in the background beyond the outfield fence. At 7:49 on this resplendent Monday night in South Carolina, in the bottom of the second inning, no one out, with Jordan playing right field, he sprinted to his right in pursuit of a sharply hit ball. It looked for a moment as if it would fall safely to the grass, but at the last second he dove in its direction, speared it with his glove, came up showing ball, and the cheers from the crowd—the crowd that should have been cheering its own team—reminded me of something, and it took me a second to realize what it was. The sounds from the dream—the dream he had told me about so long ago:

"In the baseball dream, everyone has been saying that I can't do it—that I'm not good enough. . . . In the baseball dream, they're more cheers of hope than cheers of expecting me to be good. They're cheering for me even though they don't know that I'll be good. No one knows if I'll do well, but they hope that I might. . . . The crowd is on my side because they don't know much about me, but they hope I'll do OK. . . ."

I watched him as he waved the ball toward the umpires to make sure they knew he had caught it cleanly, I heard the cheers, and somehow he had done it, he had summoned that dream out of his nights and he had made it happen, right here in a little ballpark in Greenville. He acknowledged the cheers with a slight nod of his head, but if he was acknowledging the fans he was acknowledging himself, too, for willing himself to change the sounds that he heard, for stepping into his own dream and pulling that dream into his waking life.

In the top of the fifth, with runners on second and third, Jordan, at bat, leaned into a curveball and placed it neatly into an empty part of left field, driving in two runs, extending his hitting streak to twelve games and building the Barons' lead in this game to 6–0. But the Greenville team came back, winning the game 7–6, and the next morning in the *Greenville News* the headline in the sports section was "G-Braves Win Sixth Straight," and Greenville manager Bruce Benedict was quoted:

"We talked a lot before the game about playing the Birmingham Barons—not Michael Jordan. We knew it could be a distraction, but I think our guys maintained their concentration. It always feels good to win."

Richard Nixon had died.

"Maybe, when you die, people forget the adversities in your life," Jordan said as we watched television coverage of the preparations for Nixon's funeral. "Maybe when you die they are willing to remember the good things. . . ."

He stopped.

"I don't know," he said. "There's still only one death I can think about."

The van driver from the hotel where I was staying, giving me a ride to the game one night, said pleasantly:

"Do you have gum?"

At least that's what I thought he said. When I offered him a piece, he said, "No—do you have a *gun*."

"Why would you ask that?" I said.

"Everyone needs a gun these days," he said. "People are *bold*."

I was in Greenville for three days. It was a lovely way to spend time— the feel of the minor-league ballpark every game was welcoming and quickly familiar, a good place to look forward to visiting. Each night—not just for this Braves–Barons stand, but each night of the summer—a local high school girl had the job of taking a blue grease pen and, on an erasable board near the ticket window, filling in the starting lineups for both teams.

She would first carefully write the names of the players on the home team, in the correct batting order—O'Connor, the left fielder; Wollenburg, the second baseman; Gillis, the first baseman . . . and when she had finished that list, she would start on the Barons.

Brady, the second baseman; Coughlin, the center fielder; Tedder, the designated hitter . . . She would get to the seventh spot, and write the name: Jordan—and she would turn around to find forty or so people, every night, watching and applauding and taking photographs. Of the name.

It would have been nice if he had been able to wander around the grounds and take in some of this soft and pleasant peacefulness; after all, that's what he was doing here—trying to give himself some of this. But he couldn't. The top level of the Greenville stadium, where the fans entered, above the sunken playing field, was lined with food stands—Sub Station II, Tacos & Burritos & More, TCBY Yogurt, Hot Wings—you could stand among the stadium seats near the diamond and look up at the lighted signs, and it was like a county fair on top of a baseball game, it was summer nights the way they are supposed to be.

He, on the other hand, when he wasn't practicing, sat in the laundry room of the visitors' clubhouse, playing dominoes for money. It was called the trainer's room, but all it was was an area with a big washing machine, a big dryer—for the uniforms to be tossed into after each game—and a table. Jordan would round up a few players and coaches, break out the dominoes, and pass the hours until it was time for the baseball game to begin.

"You're playing dominoes with him and you start thinking that he's just like any other guy," said Dallas Williams, an outfield coach. "And then it's time to throw a few dollars onto the table, and he opens up his wallet and there's ten thousand dollars in there. Two stacks of hundreds, each of them with five thousand dollars in them. And you remember again that he's not any other guy."

Meanwhile, outside, the ballpark was inviting. There was a picnic grove behind the third-base-line stands; you could reach it by walking down a wood-chip path that led through some trees, and you could sit and have a barbecue sandwich and a cup of lemonade, waiting for the game to begin. Jordan might possibly have liked it out there in the shaded grove, had sitting quietly among a bunch of strangers been one of the options life had made available to him. The bus he had chartered for the team—it had taken on a meaning of its own in the minor leagues, it had received such extensive publicity that the bus itself was a celebrity by now—was parked within yards of the picnic grove. Chris Pika, the Barons' young public relations man, answered questions about it for people in the grove.

"No, there's no wet bar," he said to a woman from Greenville. "No dancing girls, either." The bus was like Elvis' jacket on the old "Saturday Night Live." The premise of that skit was that Elvis' jacket was an attraction all on its own, the gold jacket could tour the country and draw a crowd. It was funny then; funny and absurd. "There are no slot machines on the bus," Chris Pika said, as the people in the picnic grove stared at it, as if by looking at Michael Jordan's bus for long enough, they might come to understand certain secrets.

During the long bus rides from city to city, the ballplayers and coaches said, Jordan had been made the butt of jokes. "Sit the fuck down, rookie," the young ballplayers would yell at Jordan every time he rose from his seat. "You're blocking the TV." But the jokes stopped after the first week or so—it was Jordan's bus, he was paying for it, and soon enough everyone accepted that and the laughter ceased. "It's not like we had such a bad bus last year," Chris Pika said.

You could walk all over the ballpark, buy a hot dog and a Dr Pepper, stand next to an outfield signboard—Greenville Rubber and Gasket Company—and notice that the signboard must have been freshly painted, it had a pungent, acrid smell to it, a smell that you wouldn't notice from a distance—and you could listen to another country song coming out of the stadium P.A. system, a deep, male, crooning voice: *I wouldn't have it any other way.* . . .

Over in that little clubhouse, with security men guarding the door, the domino game was in progress, nestled away next to the washing machine.

"It's a streak, yeah, but it's a nervous streak," Jordan said. "I don't take this game for granted. It's not like in basketball, when I thought I could do everything. Here, with this hitting streak, I'm nervous every night. All I hope is that people might notice I'm getting hits every night and say to themselves—'Hmm, maybe he's not that bad.' "

We were talking about the twelve consecutive games in which he had gotten hits. When he had decided to go to spring training, many baseball experts had said with confidence that he would never even be able to make decent contact with the ball, much less get on base. When he was assigned to the Southern League, those same experts said that Double A pitching was the sort that would frustrate him and leave him bewildered at the plate. Yet here he was, heading into May, still over .300, reaching base with a hit at least once every game.

"For me, it's more a feeling of, 'See, I told you so,' " he said. "I don't say it out loud, but it's like proving to people, 'I told you I could learn to do this. I may not be great, but I can learn this.' "

"When did it occur to you that this was working?" I said.

"It really hasn't," he said. "If you asked me if it was working, I would tell you I don't know. The numbers say it is, but I don't feel that it really is. I know I'm more relaxed than I was. But you get your-self to a certain place as a hitter, and you realize it's only going to get harder and harder after that. I can hit the fastball now, but everyone tells me that doesn't mean anything—once they figure out that I can hit the fastball, the word will get around the league not to throw me that pitch. This is such a mental game."

It was sort of an otherworldly discussion to be having. There hadn't been that great a span of time between the conversation in Jordan's car as we passed Comiskey Park—the conversation during which he'd mentioned, almost casually, that he thought he might like to become a baseball player—to this night in South Carolina, where we were talking, as if it were the most unremarkable thing in the world, about his *hitting streak*.

Nevertheless, here he was, in full baseball uniform. . . .

"I'm more or less doing now what Dean Smith"—Jordan's college basketball coach—"got me ready to do when I was at North Carolina," he said. "Dean Smith gave me the fundamentals of playing basketball. It was up to me to take it from there. Down at spring training, Walt Hriniak gave me the fundamentals of hitting a baseball. Now I have to build on it, like I did with the game of basketball."

And those NBA playoffs that were just getting started, even as the Barons were playing the minor-league Braves here in Greenville?

"This is a lot more fun than where I was last year," he said. "Last year, we were trying to win a championship again for the Bulls. And we did it. If I was with the Bulls right now? We'd be trying again—but what would we be trying to do? We'd be trying to duplicate—duplicate something we'd already accomplished. There's nothing in that for me. If I were to succeed at that—so what? I'd be proving that my team could win the NBA championship—and I don't have to prove that. That's been proven, three times in a row. This, down here—this is something for me to prove."

The notion of reinventing himself—had it yet begun to strike him as a rather eccentric thing to be doing? Was it more confusing for him in the fulfillment than in the planning?

"This is it, isn't it?" he said. "Talking about it doesn't mean anything. If you're going to change your life, whatever you may say about it is basically meaningless unless and until you do it. Here I am, right here, tonight. I guess maybe people believe me now, huh?"

Is that what this was about—making people believe that he was actually willing to go through with this?

"It's up to you to decide what you ought to do with the time you have in your life," he said in this little ballpark on the border of the backwoods. "You're the only one."

· · · · ·

Every ballplayer in the Southern League was here because he hoped to have a career in professional baseball; from Jordan, to much lesser-known Birmingham prospects such as pitcher Steve Olsen and third baseman Chris Snopek, what they were looking for was a steady job in the game.

And it extended beyond the diamond itself. Whatever the lure of baseball, it also touched men and women who lacked the athletic skills of the men who were good enough to play the sport—it brought those men and women, too, to the ballparks and made them, too, want to be a part of this, every day and every night. In Greenville Municipal Stadium late one afternoon, I met a man named Sean O'Connor—he was twenty-seven, with two college degrees—who had been hired for the summer as an assistant in the team's front office.

"Last year I had a job with the Elmira Pioneers, in the Class A New York–Penn League," he said. "It was a good enough job, being around baseball every day, but in addition to working in the office I had to pick up all the garbage."

"What do you mean?" I said.

"Well, after every night game, I'd have to come to the stadium the next morning and clean up the stands," he said. "I had to blow all the peanut shells out of the stands, sweep up all the paper cups and nacho boxes and nacho shells, get the stands clean. Then if there was an away game I'd leave straight from there, drive to Auburn or Utica, and do the color on the radio broadcasts of our team's games."

O'Connor said he knew that picking up the stadium trash in Elmira was the price he was paying for a life in baseball, but "I found myself hoping for small crowds. I'd feel good inside when the seats weren't packed—I knew I could enjoy the ballgame, and that the next day there would be less garbage I'd have to collect."

His dream, he said, was to make this a full-time job, either in the minors or—he knew this was unlikely—in the big leagues. He liked this job in Greenville, he said: "I applied for it at the winter baseball meetings, and Steve DeSalvo, the general manager of the G-Braves, told me, 'Now, your job is technically a front-office job, but you should know that you're going to have to pull tarp once in a while.' When it rains—help the ground crews pull the tarps onto the field.

"And I'm like, 'I'll pull tarp. I'll be happy to pull tarp.' I was just worried that the job would include having to pick up the stadium again. But it doesn't—I don't have to come in and pick up the garbage this year. I like this summer a lot better than last. They have people whose job it is to clean up the ballpark."

We looked down toward the bright grass and soft dirt of the diamond.

"This is such a beautiful game," he said.

In Chicago, a new basketball arena was going up. The old Chicago Stadium, where Jordan and the Bulls had won their three championships, was going to be replaced by an extravagant new structure with skyboxes and luxury suites and gift shops. The word was that as soon as the new place was up, the old Stadium would be torn down to make room for a parking lot.

"I'm not sure if I'll ever see it again," Jordan said. "I wanted to, but I don't know if it's going to happen. Are they going to tear it down this summer? I don't know if I'll get back before it's gone."

It seemed like a million miles, a thousand years, away—that huge, gray old building on a cold stretch of Chicago's crumbling West Side, the building where everything that Jordan had become had taken place, the building where on so many winter nights Jordan had, game by game, transformed himself from a young man straight out of college to one of the most famous people in the world. It had been his unlikely stage—the northern stage where a kid from North Carolina had somehow managed to do what he'd done.

Now, on another sweltering baseball day, he was back in the Carolinas, sitting around in a pair of shorts and a T-shirt, waiting for the evening's game.

"I do kind of wish I could get to see it once more," he said. "If I get back to town before they tear it down, I think that some of the guys who work there would let me in. I'd just like to walk around in there by myself. Just walk around and think. One more time."

. . . . .

Being around Jordan so much, it was possible to fleetingly forget just what he meant to people who might have only one opportunity in their lives to see him.

On the third night of the Birmingham team's road trip to Greenville, the skies began to turn slate gray, then black, two hours and fifteen minutes before game time. Greenville Municipal Stadium had been sold out for weeks in advance. Around 5 p.m. the rain began, accompanied by lightning that could be seen over the center-field fence. The rain, hard and cold in the still-warm air, pounded hard against the stadium, pouring from the sky in fierce torrents.

And the people came anyway. They arrived first by the dozens, then by the hundreds, then by the thousands. In the driving rain, which showed no indication of letting up, they went to their seats and sat in the downpour. The two baseball teams were inside their clubhouses. The thousands of fans sat in the storm.

And as the storm continued, the crowd grew instead of diminished. What a sight it was, a moment that felt like it should be pressed between the pages of a scrapbook—those thousands of people on a South Carolina evening, sitting in the rain, waiting to see one man. The game was delayed, then delayed again, and they didn't leave. They were soaked, their clothes were sopping, their hair and their faces covered with water, and then, with the stadium lights on, after eight o'clock in full nighttime—some of the people had been out there in the rain for three hours—the Birmingham team began to appear from that visitors' clubhouse down the left-field line. The ballplayers rounded a corner, one by one, and you could hear the sound before you saw anything.

The people in the left-field seats caught sight of him first. The noise spread throughout the little ballpark—there was still a drizzle visible through the lights from the towers—and here came Jordan, a minor-leaguer, carrying three bats, walking down the third-base path toward the dugout. The sound was amazing—it became louder by the second, it moved from one end of the ballpark to the other, growing and growing, section by section, from left field to right as the fans got their first glimpse of him.

People still need something to believe in; people still need something to hold on to. How else do you explain it? On this night, Jordan's hitting streak would end; on this night he would begin a descent into a batting slump that would last virtually the entire season. That would come later, though. Right now he was walking in the drizzle, toward his team's dugout, and the people in the seats were drenched, they were on their feet and shouting, and you could see that some of them were crying, too, and who would have believed this? Who would have conceived of such a scene? The noise filled the little ballpark, deep in the Southern woods, and who would have dared to dream up a night such as this?

I left in the sixth inning. Jordan had said he would be departing town right after the game; immediately after he and his teammates had showered, they would be getting on the bus for an all-night ride to Huntsville, Alabama, arriving at 5 a.m., sleeping all day, then playing the Huntsville Stars that evening.

So I called a cab to pick me up at the stadium and take me back to my hotel. I asked the cabdriver if the Greenville games were broadcast on local radio; he said that he thought a station that usually featured gospel music carried the games. The roads were still slick from the storm, and not well lighted; he turned the knob on his car radio, shifting through music stations and talk stations, some of them coming in strong, some barely coming in at all, and then, faded and soft and full of static, there was the sound of a ballpark.

"Michael Jordan is on deck," the voice of the radio announcer said. "But now he's going back into the dugout."

The announcer's partner in the Greenville press box said, "Will manager Terry Francona pinch-hit a left-handed batter?"

"No," the play-by-play man said, "Jordan's just putting some pine tar on his bat. Always good on a humid night like this."

It was difficult to make out their voices. Whatever the wattage of the radio station, we were having trouble pulling the signal into this cab. It was pitch-dark on the road outside; the sound of the voices from the ballpark was the only noise as we drove, the low murmur of the crowd and the hum of the static and the men in the broadcast booth back in the stadium I had just left.

"The G-Braves' front-office assistant, Sean O'Connor, has just given us tonight's results from around the Southern League," the play-by-play announcer said.

So there he was—Sean O'Connor, not having to sweep up the stadium this summer, not having to collect the peanut shells, was a figure on the airwaves tonight, he was coming into this cab via the radio broadcast, just like Michael Jordan, two men trying to hang on in the baseball world they so coveted. "Jordan is kneeling in the on-deck circle now," the broadcaster's voice intoned. "The score is 1–1. . . ."

The air coming through the open windows of the cab was still heavy, the night all but windless, and there was baseball coming out of the sky. "This will be Jordan's fourth at-bat of the game," the announcer said, his voice fading in and out. "He's without a hit so far. . . ."

Television satellites had carried his basketball image live to every corner of the globe; when he was playing the game he was best at, the most advanced communications technology in existence had been used to bring pictures of his NBA performances to tens of millions of people at a time. Tonight the one radio station was carrying the game, the station whose signal was scarcely making it into this cab, ten minutes away from the ballpark. He was hiding in plain sight down here; he was doing what he was doing out in the open, but there was an invisible aspect to it, also, a knowledge that few were watching, fewer still paying close attention.

"Jordan is looking at the pitcher," the announcer said, "studying his moves from the on-deck circle for when he comes to bat. . . ." The road dipped, and as we drove down toward the bottom of a small incline we lost the signal completely, until a few seconds later when we were heading upward again, rubber tires on wet blacktop, and

DETAIL; COURTESY OF
CAPE FEAR MUSEUM, WILMINGTON, N.C., IA 3457

DETAIL; COURTESY OF CAPE FEAR MUSEUM, WILMINGTON, N.C., IA 3459

Soaring toward the basket, as he is seen on the preceding page, is how most people think of Michael Jordan. But as a child growing up in Wilmington, North Carolina, he tried baseball (here at age twelve) and (at age fifteen) football. That same year, Jordan was a member of the E. A. Laney High School JV basketball team (front row, second from right), having been cut from the varsity.

DETAIL; COURTESY OF CAPE FEAR MUSEUM, WILMINGTON, N.C., IA 3460

At the University of
North Carolina,
Jordan, shown here
gliding by Clemson
defenders, was a star
from the beginning.
In his junior year,
1983–84, he was pre-
sented with a trophy
(BELOW) naming him
college basketball
player of the year.

Soon after, with his
coach, Dean Smith,
at his side, Jordan
announced he would
forgo his senior year
of eligibility to enter
the National Basket-
ball Association
draft.

Wearing number 9, Jordan led the 1984 United States Olympic team to a gold medal. When he signed with the Chicago Bulls, he was given number 23. He was the only rookie starter in the 1985 NBA All-Star game, playing for an East squad coached by K. C. Jones (BELOW). At the end of the season he was named NBA Rookie of the Year.

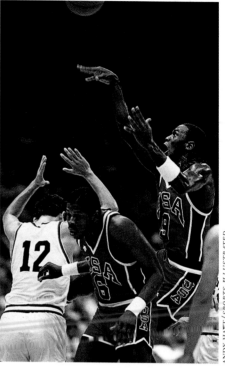

In his early NBA years, the Michael Jordan–Magic Johnson show captivated basketball fans.

The Jordan family at home during the years of his ascent to worldwide fame. "My own heroes," he once said, "are and were my parents."

Carmen Villafane met Jordan when she gave him a Valentine's Day card at the Chicago Stadium. They have been friends ever since.

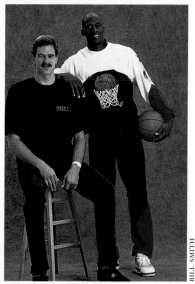

Chicago Bulls coach Phil Jackson and his starting guard.

In 1991, 1992, and 1993, Jordan and the Bulls won three consecutive NBA championships, first defeating the Los Angeles Lakers in the Finals, then the Portland Trail Blazers, then the Phoenix Suns and their star forward Charles Barkley.

JONATHAN DANIEL/ALLSPORT

FOCUS ON SPORTS

JONATHAN DANIEL/ALLSPORT

Jordan was named Most Valuable Player in the Finals each of the three years. No one else ever won the honor three times in a row. Here, he and his wife, Juanita, celebrate the 1991 victory.

JONATHAN DANIEL/ALLSPORT

JONATHAN DANIEL/ALLSPORT

Jordan accepted that the eyes of the world would be on him during his public moments. In his private life, he and Juanita began to raise a family. He often seemed most at ease with children, or when trying to relax by playing sports at which he was not guaranteed to succeed, including football, golf, and pool. He saw his father and mother often.

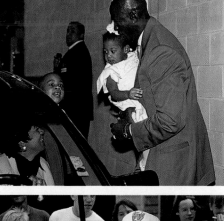

His second Olympic gold medal came at the 1992 games in Spain. LEFT: Jordan led his team in a quarterfinal win over Puerto Rico. BELOW: Jordan savors victory with Scottie Pippen and Clyde Drexler.

there was the sound. "Jordan at the plate now," the voice said, "looking out toward the mound," and other than that, in this car on this night, there was nothing, no sound at all, just the dwindling innings of a baseball game from back down the road.

CHAPTER 9

"I find myself watching the White Sox on TV more than I find myself watching basketball," Jordan said.

As his batting average went into decline, as the young minor-leaguers he played with saw their skills increasing while, deeply fatigued, he struggled to keep his own skills at an acceptable plateau even as those skills began to dwindle away, the National Basketball Association playoffs moved steadily toward the Finals. The Bulls had dropped out of contention, defeated by the New York Knicks; Jordan said that when switching around the channels on his hotel-room TV sets, he would often zap right through a basketball game in search of a major-league baseball game.

"Isn't that wild?" he said. "When I see the White Sox on TV, I know those guys, and I want to be with them again. It's the same for all of us on the Barons—everyone wants to make it to the White Sox—but with me, I watch them on TV, and it's like a goal, to earn the right to be with them again."

I asked him if he figured any of the White Sox regulars were giving him much thought—if, now that he was down here, the big-leaguers he'd spent spring training with were following his progress.

"Oh, probably not," he said. "I'd have to say no. I don't hear from them."

. . . . .

At an old Holiday Inn on a commercial street near a medical center in Memphis, the famous bus—with paint of purples and pinks on the exterior—sat waiting outside for Jordan and the Barons to emerge. Jordan's batting average continued to drop sharply—it was at .207 as Birmingham prepared to begin this mid-season road series with the Memphis Chicks—and in the lobby on a sultry late afternoon, Kirk Champion, a pitching coach for the Barons, asked if I'd seen the White Sox broadcast on television the night before.

I told him I'd seen part of it. "How was Jack?" Champion asked.

He was referring to McDowell, who had pitched. "Was he getting the split-finger over?"

I said that I didn't know enough about the intricacies of pitching to give him a proper answer. "The reason I was asking is that if he's missing the split-finger . . ." He proceeded to give me a short lesson on the mechanics of throwing a baseball, and as he talked I thought about Jordan and McDowell at spring training, and about how their worlds had by now diverged—how McDowell, who hadn't wanted Jordan around in the first place, was in the midst of a pennant race, while Jordan was upstairs at this Holiday Inn, waiting for the bus ride to Tim McCarver Field on the state fairgrounds.

"You going over to Graceland while you're here?" I said to Jordan when I saw him.

"It wouldn't be worth all the trouble it would cause to get it done," he said, Elvis in the outfield.

"I'm your birth twin, Michael," a man shouted from the first row of seats. The man was white and about forty-five years old.

If Jordan heard, he didn't let on. At 4:46 p.m., he and his fellow Barons—he was a head taller than any of the others—were doing stretching exercises in the Memphis ballpark. "I'm your birth twin," the man in the stands yelled, louder now, and Jordan moved away from the sound.

It seemed to be an instinctive thing; I was noticing that, in these small ballparks that put the early-arriving customers in close proximity to the players in the hours before the games, Jordan was careful to do his calisthenics in the middle of the field, putting as much distance as he could between strangers and himself. As I watched the warmups a man, not the same one, approached me and, as if continuing some conversation he imagined we had begun years ago, said, "I was a drug addict. I played football in high school, and then I got locked up in rehab. Me and Michael are going to be best friends."

Out there in right-center in front of a Kodiak Smokeless Tobacco signboard, Jordan picked up a grounder. "Me and Michael are going to play golf every day," the man said. "I'm off the drugs now, and Michael doesn't know it, but me and him are going to be really friendly."

I moved away and found Mike Barnett, the batting instructor who was working with Jordan down here. He'd taken over from Walt Hriniak, who was up north with the White Sox. "I didn't know what to expect," Barnett said. "You know—you're told you're going to be working with Michael Jordan. What I can't get over is that he cares so much. That's something you can't fool people about. The guy just cares so much about trying to do well."

I asked how Jordan was reacting to his recent hitting failures.

"He knows that he's not going to conquer this game by just showing up," Barnett said. "The word's gotten around the league that he has trouble with hanging curves, breaking balls and sliders, so that's all they're giving him now. He'll call me in my room early in the morning and ask me if we can come to the park before the rest of the team, so that he can learn. I don't know whether he'll ever make it to the big leagues or not, but it's as if he believes that if he tries hard enough, then that will make up for everything."

"I'm your birth twin, Michael," the man was calling, screaming now.

"I don't know how he puts up with some of this stuff," Mike Barnett said.

"Jordan!" the man yelled, sounding, for the first time, a little angry. "Jordan! I'm your birth twin."

. . . . .

In the bottom of the second inning, with the Chicks at bat with a 1–0 lead, a Memphis player named Hugh Walker came to the plate.

Walker laid a dead-wood bunt down the third-base line. It rolled lethargically—it might as well have been in slow motion—toward the base, and it appeared to be about to go foul. The Barons' pitcher and third baseman made the determination to wait until it rolled outside the line, rather than try to field it.

So they, and one of the umpires, and the shortstop, walked toward the ball and gathered to observe it. This was the opposite of action, the antithesis of excitement, this was like a tepid moment out of croquet. The players and the umpire stood there, and finally the ball reached third base, and bumped dully into the bag. The umpire motioned energetically that it was fair. The man who had bunted— he was already standing on first base, he'd gotten there without challenge long seconds ago—was credited with a base hit, and the next Chick moved into the batter's box.

I looked out at right field, where Jordan, his right hand on his hip, stood so far away in the grass. Every time I had asked him how he was dealing with the often-listless pace of baseball—this was a man whose whole athletic career had been based upon ceaseless, top-speed, furious physical action—he had said that it was just fine with him: "That's when I figure the game out, standing in right field and watching. You can't learn it from a book. I watch every move that every player makes, and I try to take it all in so that whenever a ball is hit, I know what everyone on the field is going to be doing, and what I'm supposed to be doing."

Although he seemed to mean it, he never said the words with much conviction, and on this night, after the ball had eventually touched the third-base bag and the play had been officially placed in the scorebook as a hit, he was too far away for anyone to see the expression on his face. That hand on the hip looked a little like impatience, and as the next Chick stepped up to bat Jordan pounded his fist into his baseball glove, like a child on a playground.

. . . . . .

In the ninth inning that night, with two outs and his team behind 2–1, Jordan came to bat with runners on first and third. The evening had turned impossibly muggy; he was 0-for-3 up to this point, with two strikeouts. In fact, in his last forty-four at-bats in the Southern League, he had gotten only four hits.

On this night he was the final hope for his team. A single would drive in the runner and tie the game; an out would end it. This was one of those moments around which National Basketball Association marketeers had grown accustomed to building highlights packages and home-video fortunes. Jordan with the game on the line—Jordan as a symbol for hope that is never dimmed and that will never fail. Many of the fans in Memphis had gone home—the "Is this all there is?" feeling usually set in by the third or fourth inning of these games, as the customers began to realize that baseball was inevitably baseball, and no one could ever change that, that Jordan would not be sailing through the air—so the ballpark was dotted with empty seats, and those fans who remained leaned toward home plate, watching him. Roller rink–style music wafted from the stadium's speakers. Jordan stared at Memphis pitcher Jimmy Myers.

Strike one. Strike two. Strike three. There was a fireworks display scheduled for after the game, so within a second or two of Jordan's third strike the ballpark's lights were switched off. I saw him there in the blackness—standing at the plate, having lost, the game over and gone and all the illumination extinguished. His teammates were already walking down the right-field line toward the visitors' clubhouse, but he remained in the batter's box, alone in the midst of darkness, not leaving, not moving, looking toward the pitcher's mound on which there was no longer a pitcher, looking toward the ground, waiting for something, one more pitch, one more chance, waiting for something that was not going to come.

"He should be arriving in just a few minutes."

An official of the Memphis Chicks made the announcement to a group of local reporters, and to four television cameras, including one sent to the game by ESPN. Nearly an hour had passed since Jordan's last strikeout. The reporters were waiting in the team's offices, with a portrait of the stadium behind the desk where Jordan was to sit, and color photographs of previous Chicks teams, the photos faded by the sun, mounted on the wall.

The routine, as Jordan and the Barons traveled around the league, was for him to hold a press conference following the first game of the road stand, to give the town's sportswriters the chance to ask him questions. This was usually done away from the locker room, so that his teammates did not have to put up with the affront of the reporters being interested in only one player. Tonight, though, as the minutes dragged on, and the last fans left the stadium, it became apparent that Jordan was very late. The Chicks official, looking at his watch, addressed all of the reporters half-jokingly: "Anybody notice how good the drainage system was tonight?" Their deadlines were approaching.

Finally, more than an hour after the end of the game, Barons public relations director Chris Pika entered the room and said that Jordan would not be coming. Jordan felt bad because of the team's loss, Pika said, and didn't want to hold a news conference.

The reporters in Memphis were understandably less than pleased. I had no ride back to the hotel; I asked Pika if he could give me a lift. There was a golf cart waiting outside the Chicks' business offices, and Pika motioned for me to come with him. We rode the golf cart across the outfield of the stadium, making a direct line for the visitors' clubhouse. "He's really upset about how he did tonight," Pika said. "I haven't seen him this down on himself before."

Pika went into the clubhouse. The rest of the team had already gone back to the Holiday Inn in the bus; the bus had dropped them off and returned to bring Jordan and manager Terry Francona to the hotel when they were ready. Pika was in the clubhouse for a few minutes, and when he emerged he said that Francona and Jordan were still talking. "They said that we should take the bus," Pika said. "They've got a car they can use to get back later."

So we walked over to the famous bus, where the driver was waiting. I had not been on it before—for all of the television and newspaper reports about the bus, it had been declared off-limits to outsiders, and so the mystique about the "luxury bus" Jordan had provided for his teammates had grown. It was supposed to be like a cross-Atlantic ocean liner in there, lavish and full of frills, high-tech and extravagant. It was supposed to be the most amazing bus any baseball team ever had.

It was just a bus, the seats arranged two-by-two, pillows on some of them, that closed-in motor-exhaust-and-Lysol smell that long-haul buses always have. It was clean and intact, but nothing special—it was not a vehicle in which you would want to spend eight hours if you had any other way of getting somewhere distant. Now, after ten o'clock at night, the driver pulled slowly out of the stadium gate, and we were on the streets of Memphis, passing pizza places and parking lots and a fruit stand lit up so brilliantly that the apples and bananas and pears, behind mesh screens, looked in the pure white light as if they were ready to star in a motion picture. I looked out my window, and Chris Pika, two rows ahead of me, looked out of his, and we didn't talk, and soon enough the famous bus was at the hotel, where about a dozen autograph seekers waited for Michael Jordan. The driver pulled the lever to open the door, and we got out, the people on the street trying to get a glimpse inside as if the interior of the bus was the Land of Oz, which in a way it was, illusion built upon illusion.

"I keep waiting for myself not to be a sideshow," Jordan said. "I keep saying to myself, well, tomorrow may be the day—tomorrow may be the day that people figure out that I'm just down here to try to accomplish something, and that I'm not all that good yet, and that I'm just here to play baseball, there is no sideshow."

"And?" I said.

"And I guess tomorrow hasn't come yet," Jordan said. "Because the sideshow never ends."

He was accustomed to it in basketball; well before the Bulls won their three consecutive championships, the Jordan sideshow was an expected part of the NBA experience. It didn't matter whether the Bulls won or lost on a given night—everyone knew that when the

Michael Jordan Show was in town, that was the place toward which to gravitate, that was the ticket to covet.

Now, though, it was as if the man who was paid to swallow the sword couldn't do it, as if the human pretzel couldn't bend his legs behind his neck, and yet the throngs lined up outside the canvas midway tent anyway. The sideshow was unending, in fact thriving, even though there was seldom a payoff—even though once the people got inside the tent, the person they found sitting on the stage was merely a man.

"I come to the plate at our night games, and I see all those flashbulbs going off all over the stadiums," Jordan said. "It's not a good sight for me. I don't deserve that kind of adulation here. It makes me feel like they've wasted their money, going out and buying the cameras and the film. I try to block out the sight of the flashes."

"It's the same kind of thing you used to see at the free-throw line," I said.

Which was a fact: Every time Jordan stepped to the line in an NBA game, the interiors of the urban arenas would twinkle like suburban front-yard Christmas-season displays. It was always a remarkable thing to observe: a man poised to toss a ball toward a hoop, and eighteen or twenty thousand seats looking as if they were short-circuited.

"At the free-throw line, I was deserving of the attention," he said. "I knew why the lenses were aimed at me from the seats. These days, I feel sort of foolish in front of the other players. They can see the flashbulbs, too."

"The flashes start up before you're even settled in at the plate," I said. "They're taking your picture before you've even done anything."

"Exactly the point," Jordan said.

At the Holiday Inn one night, after the game was over, I went down to the bar and found three of the Barons players having beers and watching TV.

They were Kevin Coughlin, a twenty-three-year-old center fielder; Glenn DiSarcina, a twenty-four-year-old shortstop; and

Randy Hood, a twenty-five-year-old outfielder. I didn't want to interrupt their conversation; I knew that there were many things that they might want to talk about without a reporter present. But they motioned me over and invited me to join them.

"No food, no ESPN," Hood said, the melancholy mantra of a minor-leaguer at a tavern's closing time.

They looked like ballplayers always seemed to look back in pre–Jackie Robinson America: short haircuts, sunburned forearms, stocky legs in baggy shorts. They said that even though they had been traveling with Jordan all summer, they didn't know him; they asked me what I could tell them about him.

I said that there were many times I was convinced that I didn't know, either; I'd tried my best for a long time to learn, but on so many occasions it struck me that maybe no one knew him. They said they agreed; they said they couldn't figure him out. Their words blended in with each other's; they said that when they called home to talk to family and friends, all they were asked about was Jordan, and what he was like. They couldn't very well tell the truth, which was that they had no idea.

"He doesn't ask our opinions about anything."

"On the bus rides, he doesn't talk at all. He just sits there by himself, like he's thinking."

"Tell you one thing—every pitcher in this league is figuring out he can't hit curveballs."

DiSarcina said that if Jordan were to leave the team—either by a promotion to Triple-A or the White Sox, or a demotion to Class A —he would be relieved.

"I'm so sick of all those cameras pointing into the dugout," DiSarcina said. "I wish they'd just throw all the cameras out. We tell that to the manager, but he tells us that we ought to get used to it, that cameras pointing into the dugout is what the majors are like. That's not true—my brother's in the majors, and he says that the cameras don't stick into his dugout like that."

His brother was Gary DiSarcina, shortstop for California in the

American League. As the three of them talked, it wasn't as if they disliked Jordan, or even particularly resented him. It was as if he were simply from another planet.

"I don't know what he thinks—he doesn't tell me. He's *Michael Jordan*."

"He's always in his room. That's what he does—he checks into the hotel and locks himself in his room."

"If he goes to the majors before any of us, we'll just keep our mouths closed. Hey, we understand. It's our jobs on the line."

"He doesn't belong in the majors. He can't pinch-hit, he can't field, he can't base-run—not on the major-league level."

"He'd be picked off every time."

"I don't know why he's doing this."

The thing that confused them the most, they said, was that even though they didn't feel they knew Jordan, they liked him.

"That's the strangest thing—he's really a good guy. I just don't know why he's down here with us."

"The sportswriters come into the clubhouse, and the only time they talk to us is to ask us how it feels to play with Michael Jordan."

"Fuck them."

"Fuck all of them."

"Next year, if he hits .185 this year, he won't be here."

"Yeah, but you watch—he'll be in the starting lineup for the White Sox in September."

"This September."

I asked DiSarcina what the happy ending would be here. If Jordan didn't have the baseball ability, what would be the best way to end this that sent everyone—them, Jordan, the Barons, the White Sox—away feeling good?

"A happy ending?" DiSarcina said. "I don't know if there is one."

They said they were hungry. The bartender reiterated that the kitchen was closed. They said they had heard there was a place to get a sandwich—they thought it was called Huey's—three or four blocks away.

This wasn't the nicest area of Memphis, and it was late. They went to the front desk and asked if the hotel's van driver could give them a ride. But the van driver was finished for the evening.

They asked me if I wanted to come along, and I said I'd better get some sleep. They headed out the door and up the block, walking in the middle of the street as a gesture toward safety.

For a person with such a seemingly grand design for his life—he might downplay the audacity of what he was attempting, but he was, after all, endeavoring to go from being a person who had not played organized baseball since high school to a person claiming a spot on a major-league roster—Jordan took things in small steps. However voluminous his vision might be, he had trained himself to go after it in bite-sized increments.

The night he had stayed behind in the locker room with Terry Francona, for instance—the night he had loaned Chris Pika and me the bus—would turn out to be a key evening in his summer. He would admit later that he had thought about quitting after the game that night—that he had asked Francona to tell him whether he was wasting his time and the team's, whether he was taking up a spot that another minor-league ballplayer might deserve more. "If Terry had told me that I had no chance, I would have walked away that night," Jordan would say later. "I wanted to know. I didn't want to be a joke in front of the other players."

Francona had persuaded Jordan that evening that baseball came slowly—that his athletic skills were so exceptional that if he continued to show patience, there was a chance he could develop into something. Francona wasn't guaranteeing it—he was merely saying that it was too early for Jordan to quit.

Yet when Jordan thought and spoke about such things, that kind of extensive self-evaluation was the exception—he didn't usually think of things in terms of the big picture. Rather, it was as if he believed that if he could take apart his game—his life—and lay out the tiny portions, that might help him find a solution.

For example: When he talked about his batting slump, it wasn't as if he was looking down at himself at the plate from a panoramic camera high above the ballpark; it was as if he was studying a close-up videotape of his swing, slowing it down frame-by-frame, looking for the answer in the details.

"What I need to do is to get the feeling of what a hit feels like, and store it in my mind," he said.

"How do you do that?" I said.

"It's not enough to get the hit," he said. "If I just get the hit, that doesn't do me any good. But if somehow I can absorb inside of me everything that happened when I was at the plate when I got the hit—what my arms were doing, what my legs were doing, how I was standing, what I was thinking, how I was looking at the pitcher—if I can put that in my mind, then the next time maybe I can call all of that information up without having to consciously think about it. That's how I can get hits."

"But you're not getting many of them," I said.

"I know," he said. "And that means that storing the information isn't working yet. It doesn't mean that I can't hit—look, I've gotten hits, right? I got a lot of them at the beginning of the season. So the trouble isn't a physical one. The trouble is that I'm failing to store all the information so that it comes back to me without my thinking about it."

"So how do you plan to accomplish that?" I said.

"That's what I don't know," Jordan said. "Obviously, I did it in basketball. I never had to think on the court. There was never a situation where I had to stop and think. I had had the successes in the various situations before, and they just came back to me at the right times. Now I have to do it in baseball—get that information so that it's always ready to come back to me."

The idea that the challenge might be much greater than that—that the trouble might not be in calling forth the information, but in a basic lack of the physical skills necessary—did not seem to be something Jordan wanted to consider. Talking about going after difficult plays in the outfield, he was the same way. It was never a question of whether he could actually get to the ball:

"I can get there. At first, when I would see a ball come off the bat, I would spend too much time—even if it was fractions of a second—deciding how to chase it down. Should I run right at it? Should I watch it and then determine what to do? Should I look to see what the other outfielders were doing?

"Now it's just a question of going all out. The ball comes off the bat and I go after it. If I miss it, I miss it. I don't think about how embarrassing it will be if I go for it and don't get it—I don't worry about diving for a ball and having it bounce past me to the fence. That's the worst thing you can do—slow down because you're afraid you'll make a mistake. You have to tell yourself that if you make a mistake, it's not the end of the world. Just go all out for the ball, and chances are that you'll get it."

There it was again. For all his struggles down here, he was telling himself that his physical ability to do these things was not even a factor—that he was good enough to do everything he was being asked to do. And using that as a basis—the absolute belief that he had the talent to do these things—he had narrowed down the possible reasons for his failings to one essential point: He had to train himself mentally to succeed. If it wasn't a question of his body not being able to do it, then the only place to look was in his mind.

But what if that wasn't true? What if his willpower and understanding of what was needed were just fine—what if his weaknesses were, understandably and forgivably, basic physical weaknesses?

"But they're not," he said.

"How do you know?" I said.

"I just know," he said. "I can do these things. I just have to make myself."

Michael Bolton, the singer who is very popular with women fans, played in a softball game before the Barons–Chicks game one night.

Bolton and his band had been in town for a concert. He and his road crew considered themselves to be top-quality softball players, so as a special promotion they had agreed to put on an exhibition at Tim McCarver Field. It wasn't the most logical evening to have Bolton here—of all the nights during the season when the Chicks might need a lure to draw extra customers, a night when Michael Jordan was in town didn't seem to be the one to select—but the Chicks' management had no choice, because Bolton happened to be in Memphis at the same time Jordan was.

So there was Bolton, his dark-blond ponytail hanging out from behind his baseball cap, striding down the third-base line in a skin-tight tailored white uniform, waving to his fans. "Michael!" they called. *"Michael!"*

The other Michael was in the visitors' clubhouse, thinking about his slump. Bolton and his road crew played an abbreviated game—he really was pretty good—as the sounds of his hit "Love Is a Wonderful Thing" came out of the stadium's speaker system. When the night's real game began, Bolton coached first base for the Chicks for a few innings.

As Bolton stood next to first with the Chicks at bat, Jordan manned his position for the Barons in deep right field. The overlapping screams of "Michael!" competed with each other; after a minute or two, each group of fans customized their cheers: Michael! . . . *Bolton!"* "Michael! . . . *Jordan!"* "Michael! . . ." The security guards who had been assigned to the railing nearest the first-base line, to keep Bolton's admirers from climbing over, shook their heads and muttered to one another. Looking at Bolton, then at the fans, then at one of his fellow guards, a security man said, "This is so stupid."

But was it any odder—keeping fans at a minor-league park away from a crooner—than the presence of Michael Jordan in right field? Bolton, in his snow-white baseball uniform, played to the crowd as if he belonged in the stadium; whenever they called his name, he would turn immediately toward the sound, beam a bright smile in their direction, wave to them and favor them with long, warm glances. He was like a political candidate in his element.

Jordan, on the other hand, stood in right field and looked at no one. In his black Barons jersey and gray uniform pants, he peered across the hundreds of feet toward the batter, and when the people in the stands screamed "We love you, Michael . . . *Jordan!"* he did not turn even an inch toward them. It was as if what he was feeling was totally different from what Bolton was feeling. Jordan was the real athlete here tonight, but every move he made was as if he were trying to make himself invisible, as if on some level he believed he didn't deserve to be where he was, as if he were asking himself: What am I doing here?

I saw Kevin Coughlin, Randy Hood and Glenn DiSarcina, the young ballplayers from the hotel bar, checking out Bolton and Jordan. Here they were—central-casting ballplayers from a 1955 John R. Tunis novel, the farmboy-as-athlete visual paradigm—and they were taking in the new American ideals of male beauty: Jordan with his dark shaved head, Bolton with his ponytail hanging down the back of his uniform shirt. The three young Barons moved their jaws up and down, each of them chewing on something with great energy.

"Michael! . . ."

Newspapers around the country were reporting on the big crowds Jordan was attracting to the minor-league ballparks, which was true—thousands more people came to games in which Jordan and the Barons were playing than came to regular Southern League games. But, as the season wore on, by the third night of most Barons road series—and, increasingly, at most of the home games in Birmingham—seats were easily available. Fans were finding that the difference between watching Jordan play basketball and watching Jordan play baseball was that when you saw him play basketball, you wanted to come back the next night.

So in Memphis one evening, with empty seats plentiful, I walked out to the left-field bleachers late in the game. Seats there were only ninety-six cents—part of a radio station promotion—and even at that price, there was only a scattering of fans. I settled in to watch the end of the game.

Earlier that night, there had been an announcement over the P.A. system: "Attention, fans: Jeff Granger is now signing autographs in the Future Stars Booth. The Future Stars Booth is located by the left-field line. Come meet Jeff Granger and he'll be happy to give you an autograph." Granger, a left-handed pitcher for the Chicks, might very well end up a star in some tomorrow, or day after tomorrow. The man in right field for the Barons was, it increasingly seemed, not so certain a prospect.

On the Memphis scoreboard there was a nightly between-innings "turtle race" in lights—a variation of the racing-dots promotions that are a staple in many sports venues these days. For some reason, in an effort to honor Jordan—as if this might please him—tonight's edition was a "special NBA turtle race." The dots, according to the stadium announcer, were supposed to be Larry Bird, Charles Barkley and Michael Jordan.

The people in the crowd cheered when they heard this. "And they're off," the announcer called. "Larry Bird is in the lead, but Michael Jordan is catching up . . ."

As this was going on, Jordan walked slowly from the Barons' dugout toward his position in right. "Jordan and Bird are fighting for first place," the announcer yelled. The infield in the ballpark was made of Astroturf, but the outfield was real grass—the word was that the Kansas City Royals, parent club of the Chicks, wanted their Double-A infielders to play on the same surface that the big-league club played on in Missouri, but weren't so concerned about the outfielders—so as the turtle race concluded, Jordan stepped off the artificial surface and onto the real one, looking at the manufactured ground, then the genuine ground, as he walked. The electric light representing Charles Barkley won the race, which shouldn't have been the plan.

One fun summer, he had said. That's what this baseball time was going to be for him—one fun summer.

Was it?

"The fun part will be when I see the results," he said. He corrected himself: "If I see the results."

But how enjoyable was it for him, really? This was no longer some romantic concept of his—no longer an alluring and fanciful story he could weave for himself about recapturing lost simplicity and innocent hopes. He was riding that bus all night after each series against another team ended, waking up in second- and third-rate hotel rooms with only the television and the air conditioner to get him through the long days until game time, living hundreds and hundreds of miles away from the people he loved and the people who truly loved him. His batting average was going nowhere good, he was beginning to be seen as utterly life-sized by a public that was accustomed to gazing up at him, and even those among the baseball people who wanted to encourage him were telling him that this could take years, if it ever paid off at all. Did he want to be here?

"It's fine," he said. "I like the camaraderie—the guys. I'm tired a lot, and I have my down days, but if I weren't doing this, then I'd never know, would I? I'm here—and I'm here because I want to be here. I'll take the bad with the good. If I accomplish my goals, then the good will be very good. And if I don't—no one can say that I didn't try my best."

He didn't sound as if this was unfolding exactly as he'd planned it.

"What ever does?" he said. "If you knew what everything was going to be like going in, then why would you do it? You do it so that you can find out."

He was a man who for so long was accustomed to having every answer. Now often he seemed a little lost—lost and looking for something. If basketball was what he had needed to get away from, to flee from the trapped life he had been leading—the life that had consumed him until the day of his father's death—then this didn't necessarily seem to be the place where he was supposed to end up, either. Whatever grief, whatever hidden pain that being here was supposed to heal, it didn't seem to quite be working.

"Nothing's fun all the time," he said.

No one would think less of him if he were to quit. No one would accuse him of weakness if he were to gracefully walk away before the season ended.

"Not a chance," he said. "When I say I'm going to do something, I do it. As long as they'll have me here, I'm here."

. . . . .

In the lobby of the Holiday Inn in Memphis one night, I saw a little boy breathing through a mask.

It was placed over his mouth and his nose, held by a strap that was tight against the back of his head. The mask was attached to an oxygen tank that rested on the floor, a tank that seemed bigger than the boy.

I had seen this kind of thing so often in hotels where Jordan was staying—sick or disabled children in the lobbies, brought there by parents who wanted them to meet Jordan—that the sight of this boy made me not only sad, but a little angry. If that's what this was—if the boy had been left on the couch because his parents knew that Jordan would probably not walk by him without stopping—then where were the adults? Why was he here by himself?

The clerk at the front desk told me that the boy in the lobby had nothing to do with Jordan. He was here all the time, she said; he was undergoing treatment at one of the hospitals in the medical center, and the hospital always sent a van to pick him up. That's what he was doing—waiting for the van.

I could hardly see the features of his face beneath the mask. I didn't know where the parents or other adults in his life were. He sat there patiently, breathing in and out, trusting the mask and the tube and the tank by his side. He looked straight out the door, in anticipation of the van's arrival. There are many measures of courage in this world, few of which are ever posted on a scoreboard.

CHAPTER 10

Jordan stood near the half-court line of the Chicago Stadium. Dribbling the basketball waist-high, almost like a taunt, the ball bouncing just far enough above the floor for a defender to be tempted to try to steal it, he looked not at the five players on the opposing team, nor at his four teammates. His eyes were on the basket downcourt.

More than eighteen thousand people were on their feet and screaming, as they had been for most of the evening. The massive old scoreboard was gone, having been removed in preparation for the building's demolition; so were the pipe organ and the world-championship banners. The place had the feel of a house where a family had lived all of its life, where the family had shared all of its good times and bad—the Stadium had the feeling of a house like that on the night before the family moved out. A house with suitcases and boxes packed up and placed in the front hallway, ready for the movers to pull their trucks up the street.

Suddenly, as he had so many times before, Jordan crouched lower, dribbled closer to the polished wood, dipped one shoulder and started to drive. Now the screams were even louder, now this had the feel of something between an early Rolling Stones concert only half remembered from some grainy black-and-white kinescope and a revival meeting on a dusty county fairgrounds, the screams were screams of excitement but they were screams of gratitude, also, and Jordan slipped between two defenders—they, too, were watching him as if this were a newsreel—and as he passed the foul circle he put additional pressure on his right leg, shifting all of his weight onto that leg so that when he lifted himself into the air it would be with a force that was an answer to the weight, would be all of that weight springing back, and then he was sailing toward the hoop, as he had been doing all night, and the sound had passed the point at which sounds are able to register, either on an electronic meter or in the human ear, it had flatlined out into a roar that was dense and palpable and like low-lying thunder, and Jordan, the orange basketball flat against his palm, was reaching toward the metal and the twine.

He had ended the Southern League season batting .202. There had been some encouraging moments, the most memorable of which was his first home run; as he rounded the bases and headed toward home plate, he gestured toward the sky in tribute to his father. He would hit two more home runs before the season was over, and after the ball had cleared the fence each time he would point to the sky again.

No one was pretending that his batting average was good enough to get him to the major leagues. But some of his statistics were more encouraging. In the final month of the Birmingham Barons' season, he had hit .260. He had thirty stolen bases for the season, tying him for fifth in the league. Rather than just go home for the winter and decide whether he wished to keep trying this, he told the White Sox organization that he wanted to play in the Arizona Fall League, a six-team alliance composed of prospects from throughout the minors.

The major-leaguers had gone on strike in August. Although no one knew it yet, there would be no baseball playoffs, no World Series. Jordan—the man who had made the cover of *Sports Illustrated* for "embarrassing baseball"—was still playing the game while all the big-leaguers who had scorned him were sitting around waiting for their attorneys to tell them when they should play again.

In Chicago, Scottie Pippen announced that he was lending his name to a charity basketball game that would be the last to be played in the old Stadium. The game, underwritten by Ameritech, would benefit children's charities. Members of the Bulls' championship teams—B.J. Armstrong, Horace Grant—had accepted Pippen's invitation to play in the game, as had veterans from around the NBA such as John Starks, Ron Harper and Gary Payton, and young stars on the rise such as Anfernee Hardaway and Jason Kidd.

Pippen said he wanted to invite Jordan, but was having trouble reaching him on the phone. He hoped that his messages were being delivered.

Jordan soon let it be known that he would not be able to play in Pippen's game because of his baseball commitments. Pippen, hearing that Jordan would not play, said, "It's great to know that so many of my friends and so many great players want to come."

"Part of me felt like an old man when I was twenty-three or twenty-four," Jordan said. "When I think about it, it seems that I was never truly a young man. I never felt young."

We were talking about his age. I had asked him whether he felt like he was thirty-one; as autumn came and another new basketball season was getting ready to begin, the inevitable speculation was appearing in the press: If Jordan ever did decide to return to basketball, would his body be too old? Was Jordan at thirty-one a different person physically than the Jordan who had left the NBA? I had asked him what thirty-one felt like.

"I don't even know what age I am," he said. "Thirty-one going on thirty-two, in reality—but it seems like I was just eighteen, and it seems at the same time that I've never had an age."

"You're not feeling it at all?" I said.

"You'd think I would be," he said. "All of the guys I play with in the minors are younger than me, and they kid me about it, but I've always felt that I was older than everyone else my same age, anyway. Whatever you're supposed to feel that makes you feel youthful, I've never experienced that."

I said that the reason people were bringing it up, of course, was that they were thinking about what he might be like as a basketball player again.

"I know that Phil Jackson thinks I can still come back when I'm forty-five or forty-six," he said, smiling. "I think he says stuff like that just to try to get inside my head. Just to get me thinking. Whenever I see any of the guys or coaches on the Bulls, it's 'Come on back, come on back.' Tex Winter says it every time I see him."

Winter, in his seventies, was one of Phil Jackson's assistants. A softspoken man with encyclopedic basketball knowledge—he was the creator of the Bulls' complicated "triangle offense"—he had always been appreciative of what Jordan brought to the Bulls just by being there for intrasquad scrimmages.

"Tex tells me to come back for practices," Jordan said. "He tells me that even if I don't want to play in the NBA anymore, that if I want to I should just be a member of the practice team."

"He's kidding, right?" I said.

"Well, he's kidding," Jordan said. "He's just trying to entice me. But he knows me—he knows what to say. I always have had more fun at practice than in games."

"Why?" I said.

"At practice it was just me and the guys," he said. "The doors were closed. No one else was watching. It was play."

The day before Pippen's game—ticket sales for the charity event were said to be going slowly—Jordan announced that he would play.

If the mechanics of the announcement were stilted—at a press conference where Pippen was to read off the names of the players on a "red team" and a "white team," he picked up a cellular phone bearing the logo of the event's sponsor, told the gathered reporters that it was Jordan calling, and added his name to the starting lineup for the white team—the results were immediate. The news that Jordan would be playing basketball again, on the last night the old building would ever be open, suddenly made tickets for the event the most valuable sports commodity in Chicago. The game would not be televised—if you weren't there, you would not see it.

Three hours before game time, the building felt like some lost and lovely memory of your hometown—a place where you knew every corner and byway, but a place you always assumed was destined to exist only in the recesses of your mind and heart. This wasn't supposed to be happening, was it? The old Chicago Stadium open for business again, Michael Jordan playing basketball inside these walls—everyone had abandoned all such thoughts. But here were the yellow-jacketed Chicago cops, waiting inside Gate 3½ for Jordan to show up, just like always; here was that floor upon which all the victories had been won, the painted Bulls head in the middle, the scuffs in the varnish just where they had always been, the lights glaring down from up near the roof, the interior cold beyond reason, even in September, a Stadium coldness that had brought so much warmth to so many people on so many winter nights.

Being there felt like visitation without the depth of sorrow. Like paying last respects, and having no regrets. A young uniformed police officer in those hours before the game walked to the center of the floor, his cap in his hands, and asked an usher to take a snapshot of him there. A little boy stood in the seats with his father, just looking—looking toward the court as if the court were a ghost. Before the players even began to arrive at the Stadium, this felt like sports as sports are meant to be—sports as a relief from the troubles of life, sports as an answer that is good for at least the course of an evening. The baseball players might still be on strike, but here the lights were on. Horace Grant—who had signed a contract with the Orlando Magic, and who would be leaving Chicago—arrived through the door he had always come in, wearing a brightly patterned shirt and carrying a utilitarian gym bag, and as he was surrounded by reporters and cameras he said, "Are you here for the Michael Jordan Farewell Tour?" Someone brought up a story that had appeared in the papers—a story that had quoted Jordan as disparaging Grant and Pippen—and Grant, having heard this all before, smiled and said, "Garbage," his genial expression and the acrid word somehow not in conflict; this was a place for games, not debate, and he, too, took a long look around the arena.

I ran into Ray Clay, the public address announcer from all those Stadium nights. He showed me the script he had been given for the player introductions. "Look at this," he said. "Look how they want me to introduce him."

On the script, next to Jordan's name, it called for Clay to say:

"From the Birmingham Barons, and not a bad basketball player, either . . ."

"Are you going to do that?" I said.

Clay made a face. "Not a chance," he said. "You know what I'm going to say."

He paused a beat, then, softly, said the words he had said in this building so many times before, said them quietly tonight as if rehearsing and remembering at the same time:

"From North *Carolina* . . ."

Jordan was assigned to the visitors' locker room in the Stadium—the first time in his basketball life he had been asked to dress there. Pippen, Armstrong, Toni Kukoc and Grant—the Bulls—were all, along with an assortment of other NBA players, assigned to the red team, which got the Bulls' home locker room.

When Jordan came up to the court from the basement, the reaction from the people in the seats seemed to startle even him. After all the cheers and all the frenzy on all those old Stadium nights, no level of excitement would seem to have the power to be new or unexpected, but this was a shock—it was the sound of yearning, the sound of release, the sound of thousands of people setting eyes on something they had been told to accept was dead. If the analogy was visitation, then this was as if the loved one had suddenly stood up and walked across the room to greet the mourners. There was even a clergyman present; the Reverend Jesse Jackson, who was affiliated with one of the charities that would benefit from tonight's game, strode onto the court in a dark business suit to greet Jordan, who did not seem to be prepared for this, he had merely come out here to warm up.

Amid the din the photographers and camera crews, although they had been told not to do it, streamed onto the floor and surrounded him; he turned around and around, looking for space to walk. The other players converged on him, reaching for his hand, touching him on the back, trying to have a word with him, all of them at once. He looked confused, he looked as if he was seeking someone to provide some order here. But no one seemed to be in charge.

Pippen, whose game it was, was supposed to have the honor of coming upstairs from the basement last. Which he did—virtually unnoticed by the crowd. Horace Grant was with him, both men wearing the shirts of the red team, and as they came from the stairway and onto the court they were talking to each other with half-amused, half-resigned expressions on their faces, as they had in so many hotel lobbies and so many NBA arenas over the years with Jordan, accustomed to being in the same buildings with him, accustomed to being pushed aside as soon as he was in a room, knowing the realities of life with him, not even fighting it anymore, aware there are some things a man cannot control. Jordan, at his own end of the court, took a warmup shot to the roars of the crowd, missed it, then took another and made it—a shot by Michael Jordan had gone into the basket in the Chicago Stadium, something that had happened thousands and thousands of times before, and this one was merely during a pre-game shoot-around—but it was a sight that no one in attendance had ever thought they would see again, and the sound in the building was as if the Bulls had just won a fourth championship. Pippen and Grant watched from their own end of the court, then proceeded with their own warmups, no eyes on them.

The referee laughed out loud.

It was an understandable reaction. Jordan had just taken the ball all the way down the court and dunked it, and the referee's laugh was one of appreciation, a can-you-believe-this response to being here, on this court, watching this. Something felt both right and wrong from the opening tip—he was playing marvelously, but there was just about no defense being attempted in this game, you couldn't really tell how good anyone was because most efforts to stop drives and lay-ups were muted ones, and, observing Jordan, there was no true way to decide if this was supposed to be some new beginning for him, or just an early-warning edition of an old-timers' game.

Many of the NBA players on the court, with their shaved heads and baggy shorts, looked like not-so-inadvertent echoes of Jordan; they had followed his style every step of the way, and now that he was back among them it was as if he himself were an echo of an echo, with no chance ever to be one of them on any level. The score at the end of the first quarter—an absurd score—was 52–50, and there was something off-kilter about that, the contest was fun but it was close to a joke; the thought occurred that this kind of game was probably not the way he should be seen playing basketball for the final time.

The discordance came out of the Stadium's loudspeakers, too. A second P.A. announcer had taken over for Ray Clay, and he was jazzing it up. Every time Jordan touched the ball the announcer would call, "Do you *love* it, Chicago?" or "He's ba-a-a-a-ck!" During the Jordan years in the Stadium, overstatement had never been necessary—whenever Jordan scored a basket during those years Ray Clay would merely say, "Michael Jordan," which was not only enough, it was just right—and tonight's P.A. system histrionics only made the real Jordan basketball nights seem farther away.

Not that he wasn't trying to get past that. Little moments:

Ron Harper, playing for Pippen's team, the red team, took an extra step, and Jordan, as if by instinct, only had to look at the nearest referee and flash the smallest smile with a rise of his eyebrows—not a word was needed—to persuade the referee to make the call. He had gotten used to this during his Bulls years—other players around the league might shout and gesticulate at the refs in hopes of making their arguments stick, but Jordan came to know that he could win the officials over with a glance, a widened eye, he knew they didn't want to be his adversary, they were just as pleased to be on his team.

And:

Corie Blount, a young forward who had joined the Bulls as Jordan was leaving, was playing on Pippen's team tonight, and he tried a fancy move that was designed to show Jordan up. Jordan, his hands on his hips, gave Blount the kind of stare he used to give at Bulls practices to teammates with whom he was displeased—the stare said: Don't even think about having fun at my expense, it is only by my sufferance that you are permitted the illusion that we are playing the same game—and Blount, like a deflated student being singled out by a teacher whom he had wanted to impress but had succeeded only in annoying, looked away. Seconds later Jordan dunked over him, in effect chastising him in front of eighteen thousand, and after the dunk Jordan yelled something at him, as if he were back in a playoff game against the Knicks and as if Blount were the reincarnation of Xavier McDaniel in some angry confrontation long past. "Lookin' good, M.J.!" the out-of-place P.A. man screamed, but Jordan did not react, he just turned from Blount to run upcourt.

Ernie Banks was in attendance—the honorary coach for one of the teams. Before Jordan came to town Banks was probably the most famous and beloved athlete in Chicago sports history—all those summers with the Chicago Cubs, no pennants, no World Series, just a superlative player perpetually frustrated as the seasons ended—and the question tonight was, was the Jordan on this court merely Ernie Banks thirty years younger, taking the first step toward returning regularly to Chicago sports arenas as a warm, friendly spectator, an unthreatening and nostalgic presence? Or was Jordan fighting that— was he laying the groundwork tonight to push that day away? Was he deciding that he hated the idea of being anyone's fuzzy and clawless memory?

Certainly the two men with whom Jordan seemed to be having the most fun on the court were Anfernee Hardaway and Jason Kidd, the young NBA sharpshooters who were on his white team. He bantered with them, spoke energetically in their ears, encouraged them and coached them and whipped precision-sharp passes to them, celebrated baskets with them—he was giving much more of his attention and his energy to them than to any of the veteran NBA stars on the floor, minute-by-minute he was separating himself from those older players and setting up a team-within-a-team, a game-within-a-game, with Hardaway and Kidd. Before all of the things that had happened to Jordan—the riches, the endorsements, the magazine covers, the screams—he had willed himself to become better than anyone else who had ever tried to do these same things on a basketball court. With Hardaway and Kidd, he seemed to be sending the signal: I can still do this. Help me prove it to myself.

"Ladies and gentlemen," the P.A. man said in the fourth quarter. "Let's have a big hand for the man who put this whole evening to-gether—Scottie Pippen!" Paul Sullivan of the *Chicago Tribune*, cover-ing the game and sitting next to me at the press table, said, "That reminds me. I'd better put Scottie's name in the story." Joking but not joking—understanding that Jordan had once again made Pippen all but disappear.

And yet the interplay between Pippen and Jordan was the most interesting facet of the game. The contest between the two teams meant nothing—the final score would be of no consequence. But Jor-dan and Pippen went at each other ferociously, trying to block each other's shots, trying to take the ball to the basket on each other, not giving an inch, not letting up for a fraction of an instant. It was not a case of insolence on the part of either man, or of arrogance—it was the opposite, it was the height of respect. They were very different men—Pippen with his trouble expressing himself, his painful lack of social polish, his not-easily-hidden surliness, Jordan with his smooth-ness in front of strangers, his knowledge of the human marketplace, his knack for putting people at ease. On the court, none of those things mattered. On the court, outsiders and outside concerns had no place. Jordan had once told me that, for him, the basketball court during an NBA game was the only place he felt true sanctuary—that the boundary lines were like invisible walls, keeping the world away until the clock ran out:

"The basketball court for me, during a game, is the most peaceful place I can imagine. I truly feel less pressure there than anyplace I go. On the basketball court, I worry about nothing. When I'm out there, no one can bother me. Being out there is one of the most private parts of my life.

"No one bothers me at all, even the other players on the court, except when I get fouled. Being on the court is very much like medi tation for me. If something is on my mind, I can think about it on the court. If my wife and I have had a disagreement at home, I know that if we have a game that night, I'll be out there on the court by myself for a few hours, and by the time I get home again at the end of the evening, all of that will have passed.

"The basketball court is the one place where the rules say that no one can talk to me or walk up to me when I'm playing. During the game, for one of the few times in my life, I feel like I'm untouchable. I'm not untouchable anywhere else. . . . Sometimes, even in the middle of a game, I'm able to think about things. As loud as it is, it's almost a quiet time for me. I know that basketball games can be very exciting, but for me the game is one of the calmest parts of my life. No one can come onto the court. No one can cross those lines. It's a very calm place."

I watched him and Pippen, inside those invisible walls, and thought about the calmness in there.

He scored 52 points, the most of any player on either team. His white team won, 187–150, and with six seconds left and the clock stopped he embraced Pippen and then began to walk away.

As he got to the center of the court he suddenly dropped to the floor. For just a second it seemed as if he might have tripped, or even collapsed. But it was quickly evident what he was doing: He was kissing the painted Bull at center court. On his hands and knees, in his white uniform, alone in a place where he had always, in essence, been alone, he lowered his face to the wood, kissed the floor, then stood up and ran to the stairs and down to the locker room. It was an electric moment—more than a few people in the stands were weeping through their cheers—and it was widely reported that it was something he had thought up on the spur of the moment, on his way off the court.

But, he told me when we talked about it later, he had in fact decided to do it on the way to the game late that afternoon—during his drive from his home to the Stadium.

"I was on the expressway, listening to the radio," he said. "I was sort of stuck in traffic. And I was thinking about how this would be it—that it would be the last time I ever saw the Stadium.

"And I was thinking about what that building had meant to me, and I realized that it's not just a building to me—it's a friend. It really is—in a way, it's one of my best friends. So I was thinking about what you do when you know it's time to say goodbye to a good friend, and I knew that words are not good enough. You can't say goodbye in words. I thought how I would express what I felt to a friend who meant that much to me, and I knew that I would say it with a kiss.

"So I knew by the time I got to the building what I would do. I didn't tell anyone. I just kept it to myself. All during the game I kept looking around the building, and I had this feeling like it was really close to me—like how it was a member of my family, and I wasn't going to get to see it again. I knew I didn't want to cry when I left the floor—I don't cry very easily anyway, even when I feel like it. But I wanted to show how I felt in the way that felt right to me.

"So I said goodbye as if the building was a person. I didn't think about people watching me—I knew they would be, but when I was down on my knees I wasn't aware of them. It was private. I was on the floor, and I looked down and I kissed it, and I really wasn't hearing anything. And then I was up and gone, and I felt that I'd done what I should have done."

There was a press conference scheduled afterward in the basement of the Stadium. Pippen came out first and thanked all the reporters for covering the charity game. When he opened the session to questions, every question—every single one of them—was about Jordan.

What was it like to play with Jordan again?

Did Jordan still have what it takes?

Did Pippen think Jordan would come back to the Bulls?

Some men might have deeply resented this—on Pippen's big night, the entire focus was on Jordan. Yet not only did he seem unresentful, he appeared to like this, to be relieved by it. For the last year, ever since Jordan had left the team, Pippen had been number one—he had been cast in the role he'd never had before. It had seemed to make him edgy, apprehensive. Tonight all that was gone—Jordan was back in the building, the focus of all the eyes, all the lenses. This is what Pippen had left behind, and in a way, this was what he might have missed: having Jordan there as the world's constant target. A reporter asked Pippen what it had felt like to have to guard Jordan tonight when Jordan had really been driving on him, trying to score over him. In a soft voice with a hint of a smile in it, Pippen said:

"I've been checking him for seven years, behind the curtain."

Checking him: trying to guard him closely. Behind the curtain: in practice, where no one from the outside could see. For the rest of the people in the Stadium this night, the sight of Jordan and Pippen competing— and meaning it—was something they'd never observed; they had seen the two only as teammates. To Pippen, though, what had happened tonight was nothing new. He had gone through seven years of it, every practice, every day.

Another sportswriter asked him if Jordan had told him anything about any future NBA plans.

"He says he likes baseball," Pippen said. Not trying to evade the question; not trying to keep a confidence. He said the words a little awkwardly, and they were the truth, as far as he knew it. That's what Jordan had told him: that he liked baseball. Pippen, like the rest of the world, got only the official version from Jordan.

As Pippen was finishing his talk with the press, Jordan appeared in the basement hallway, in a business suit. Jesse Jackson was standing next to him, one arm on Jordan's arm, whispering in Jordan's ear. As Reverend Jackson continued to talk, Jordan's eyes began to glaze over. He was in the one place he liked being the least: hemmed in, nowhere to go, cornered with no outlet. This was no particular reflection on Reverend Jackson—the look in Jordan's eyes was no different from what I'd seen on many occasions when he was with, say, a Nike executive or a Gatorade official, someone who had a legitimate claim to his time and his attention, but who did not understand Jordan's almost chemical need to pull free after some invisible inner alarm clock had gone off.

Reverend Jackson followed Pippen to the lectern and made an

eloquent speech about the desperate need for help felt by so many impoverished young American men. That was the goal of the charities that were the recipients of tonight's fund-raising, he said—to help those young men. He said that there were young men to whom jail was actually a relief—it was the only place they had ever known where they could be sure of food, of shelter, of supervised recreation; the tragedy was that prison, which to most Americans was the lowest possible place to where a person could fall, to these young men was something close to a refuge.

As moving as the speech was, it was past ten o'clock at night and the Chicago television news broadcasts were on the air live, and the reporters needed for Reverend Jackson to be gone and for Jordan to be standing in his place. Jordan, even as Reverend Jackson was completing his speech, nodded toward George Koehler, his friend and driver; it was an all-but-imperceptible movement of his head, a motion Jordan had made thousands of times before. It meant: Get the car ready.

Jordan was inexplicably hostile to the reporters as he stood behind the lectern. He said that because most of the press was "sportswriters here," those reporters "probably don't understand what Reverend Jackson was talking about. I'm sure you have a lot of stupid questions." It was a rather remarkable thing—especially in light of Jordan's own evident inattention to Reverend Jackson's speech—for him to say to a roomful of journalists who had just watched him score 52 points, and were poised to celebrate him in their stories.

Maybe it was simply that this evening had reminded him of what he had left, and why he had left it, and what might face him were he to return; maybe he was just in sour spirits over something else in his life. But his session with the reporters was brief, his words showed little pleasure with what he had accomplished on the court during the game, and down the hallway in the basement his black Porsche had its engine running, as he had directed, and within minutes, guarded by police officers, he walked to it, climbed behind the wheel, sped up the ramp and into the night and, for the last time, away from the Stadium.

. . . . .

"I'm hoping I do well in Arizona," Jordan said. "If I don't, that's when I have some decisions to make. There's always the movie thing."

He had told me, a year or so before, that a deal was in place for him to make a feature film in which he would co-star with the Warner Brothers cartoon characters. Bugs Bunny, Elmer Fudd, all the rest—Jordan would appear as himself, a live human figure at play among the cartoons.

"It's done," he said. "The contract is in place. All I've got to do is tell them when I want to do it."

It seemed to me to be a somewhat curious pursuit. In our country, we tend to make most of our celebrities into metaphorical cartoon figures, anyway. If you become famous enough, if you begin to be considered larger than life, then your humanity is almost inevitably supplanted by the garish image. Whether it is Madonna or Hulk Hogan, Roseanne or Ross Perot, whoever the person used to be is usually swallowed up by the object drawn in dense, broad strokes for consumption by the public. Usually the cartoonishness is merely symbolic. Did Jordan really want to make it literal?

"I've done it before," he said. "I did it in the commercial."

Indeed he had. In a wildly popular Nike television commercial, Jordan had acted alongside some of the Warner Brothers characters. Also, several years back, he had permitted a pen-and-ink cartoon version of him to be featured on Saturday-morning children's television.

"It's not that hard," he said. "You just pretend that the characters you're talking to are there. They draw them in later."

Certainly, if he chose to do it, Jordan had the acting skills to star in the feature film with the cartoon figures. He could undoubtedly pull it off. I tried to ask him whether this was really how he wanted to be presented.

"All I'm saying is that the movie contract is there for whenever I'm ready," he said. "I want to keep playing baseball if I can get good enough, but I know that I have the movie."

You just pretend that the characters you're talking to are there. Sort of like the life he was already leading.

. . . . .

He reported to Scottsdale and joined the Scorpions of the Arizona Fall League. But almost as soon as the league's short season began, he had to fly back to Chicago. His number was being retired at a lavish ceremony in the new United Center.

It was an evening conceived as a television show, broadcast nationally on TNT. A stage was set up where the basketball court was supposed to be; twenty thousand people bought tickets, some of them paying hundreds of dollars. Jordan, in a light blue suit and white shirt, appeared stiff and restless as he sat through speeches and comedy skits.

Woody Harrelson, Kelsey Grammer, Craig T. Nelson, Boyz II Men, Sinbad—all were a part of the program, which lasted two hours. At one point Jordan, live cameras trained on him, was escorted outside the new building, where Larry King unveiled a two-thousand-pound bronze statue of him, depicting him soaring toward an unseen basket. The statue had been commissioned by the Bulls organization for permanent display near the entrance to the arena. Jordan stood in the cold and looked at his metal image. Back inside, with his three children helping him, he tugged on a red rope and hoisted a banner featuring his number 23 to the ceiling of the new building.

The proceeds from the evening would benefit the soon-to-be-constructed James Jordan Boys and Girls Club of Chicago, named for his father. Jordan fidgeted during the tributes and the variety sketches. He was in a basketball arena again, and he was being requested to stay still.

Afterward, asked by reporters what he thought of the new building, he said, "Really nice. It looks like a mall."

"I have done some things in my life that I knew were stupid," he said when we talked later about that ceremony at the United Center. "I don't think I have ever taken part in anything as stupid as that."

As soon as he walked into the building, he said, he knew it was a mistake: "My instincts were not to take part in it all along, but it was for my dad's club, and it wouldn't have looked right if I had not showed up. Every time they explained to me what the night was going to be like, I thought to myself: Why am I doing this? But I told myself that they must know what they're doing."

As the songs and comedy routines went on, he said, he felt trapped: "I knew that everyone in the building was looking at me to see my reaction. That happens every night in sports, the people in the seats looking at you, but in sports your reaction isn't what counts—they're looking at you because they've come to watch you do something.

"That night, the stares were the same—but I wasn't supposed to do anything. They were just looking at me sitting there and standing there, and I knew it every second. I wanted to run out of there."

Was he thinking about how he should react during the two hours?

"Oh, yeah," he said. "I would laugh and smile at the stuff that was supposed to be comedy, and I would nod my head during the speeches. I knew it was on television and I knew the people in the seats were watching me. All I was thinking was: Get me out of here. And something else, too."

What was that?

"The guys in the Arizona Fall League—the baseball players. I was well aware that they knew this was being televised nationally. So those guys—who I want to treat me like what I am, which is someone who's trying his hardest to become an OK baseball player—those guys were in Arizona watching this thing, at least a lot of them were. They were watching this extravaganza, or whatever you want to call it. I can't imagine what they were saying about me as they were watching.

"I was standing there in the spotlight in Chicago smiling and nodding, but I was thinking about them. How in twenty-four hours I'd be back with them, back in the outfield. Playing. Even as I raised the banner with my kids—which was nice—I was thinking to myself: Get this done with and get out of here and go back to the guys who are supposed to be your teammates now. End this show."

CHAPTER 11

Peoria, Arizona, on a Friday night in mid-November was freezing and wind-battered; the heat of the desert day had disappeared, the sky was black and starless, and the Scottsdale Scorpions, in their vivid red jerseys and dark caps, prepared in relative quiet for their game against the Sun Cities Solar Sox.

Sports pages around the country were reporting that wherever Jordan played in the Arizona Fall League, he was attracting record crowds. That was technically true, as far as it went—but if people back East were imagining that baseball fans were lining up for standing-room-only tickets in Arizona, it was far from the truth. The six teams in the Fall League were accustomed to playing before virtually empty houses; the day before this game, for example, when the Mesa Saguaros had played the Chandler Diamondbacks, the official attendance had been 82.

Tonight, with Jordan playing, in a stadium that could hold 10,000 people the attendance would be announced at 1,523, and even that number would appear to be significantly inflated. Thousands upon thousands of seats would remain empty—the temperatures were too cold, the gusts off the desert too formidable, the baseball too routine. The noise and brightness and galvanic aura of the Chicago Stadium during the Pippen basketball game might as well have been some faint beeping picked up from another galaxy. Tonight Jordan, in the outfield, ran windsprints alone.

The Scorpions had arrived in full uniform on the team's bus; like a junior high school league, the Arizona Fall League did not provide locker rooms for the visiting teams—the men on the ballclubs dressed at their own parks, rode the bus to the away games, played, got back on the bus and, without showering, rode back home.

Out of the stadium's loudspeakers—the music echoing off the sea of empty seats—an Aerosmith song played: *Crazy, crazy, I go crazy.* . . .

A few fans walked in through the gates, wanting to be present for the first pitch of the contest. The coaches, bundled up and shivering under their team jackets—"If my apartment burns down tonight," one Scorpions coach said, "I won't lose anything. I'm wearing everything I have"—waited for the umpires to signal it was time to begin.

Full winter was on its way, even here in Arizona. Out there in center field, Jordan kept doing his warmup sprints, chasing something.

"Do I look like a statue to you?" he said.

If the basketball arena in Chicago seemed light-years away from Arizona, then that Civil War hero–style bronze sculpture of him in front of the United Center seemed even more removed from Jordan's present reality, like something from a hazy and half-recalled dream. Here in Arizona Jordan—fiddling with the laces on his spikes—was still struggling just to keep up with the other minor-leaguers. Back in Chicago, the statue had already become one of the town's top tourist destinations. Visitors from other cities, states, even other countries were making trips out to West Madison Street just to see it.

"I'm not a statue," he said. "I'm glad that people seem to like going to see the statue, but the whole thing makes me feel very strange. A statue just stands still forever while people stare at it. I'm a person. I'm alive."

"People are tossing coins at it," I said.

"Come on," he said.

"It's true," I said. "They do it as a good-luck thing. They try to make the coins land on the base of the statue and stick."

"If they were going to toss coins at me, I wish they would have done it while I was still playing," he said.

"Had you seen the statue before they drew the curtain back?" I said.

"Not the real thing," he said. "They'd shown me a model of it."

"Do you ever plan to drive by it, when no one else is around?" I said.

"No," he said. "It's not something I have a whole lot of interest in doing—driving out to see myself in front of a building."

"It might be an interesting feeling," I said.

"What am I going to do?" he said. "Get out of my car and toss coins at myself for luck?"

"So you have no desire to go out some night by yourself and look at it," I said.

"What do I want to look at a statue for?" he said. "It's a piece of metal. It's stuck in one place. It doesn't move. I'm a man."

He was hitting much better than he had during most of the Birmingham summer—crisply, with authority, his swing showing confidence. The tentative awkwardness of spring training was just a memory; he might still not be on the same level of skill as the other players on the Scorpions, but if you had walked into the ballpark, somehow not known who Michael Jordan was, and watched the athletes, he would not have stood out as not belonging. That was the difference here— after the long spring and summer, he was beginning to look like just another baseball player.

Which, for him, was progress. "I'm amazed by how far he's come," said Terry Francona, who had been the Birmingham manager and now was managing the Scottsdale team in the Fall League. "Some days I think I feel better about it than he does. He'll still get down on himself when he has a bad night, and I'll have to tell him that in this game you can't count on doing well every day. For all the times I've told him that this is going to come slowly, I think he tends to forget that. But the strides he's already made are really something."

Steve Gilbert got ready to approach Jordan in the dugout. Gilbert had been a substitute schoolteacher in Tempe when the Fall League had asked him to work in its front office. The league office didn't have a large staff—most years it didn't need one—and Gilbert had said yes, and then had come the announcement that Jordan was going to be in Arizona for the autumn. Now Gilbert—a wry, pleasant young man of twenty-five who had long been a Michael Jordan fan—found himself talking to Jordan every day. Jordan liked him—but in Gilbert there was still the inevitable hesitation to ask for certain things.

On this night, he had been ordered to do just that. "Michael," Gilbert said. "I have to get your permission for something."

"What's that?" Jordan said, looking up from the visitors' bench.

"The league wants to use your picture on the back of the scorecards," Gilbert said.

"Why?" Jordan said.

"We've run out of programs," Gilbert said. "So the scorecards are all we have. The league just wants to use that same little photo of you that's in the program, and print it on the back of the scorecards."

Jordan shook his head no. Gilbert seemed to think he was kidding.

"So can I say we can use it?" Gilbert said.

Jordan kept shaking his head. "This is your first hard job," Jordan said to Gilbert. "You've got to tell them no."

"Seriously?" Gilbert said.

"Seriously," Jordan said. He pointed down the length of the dugout toward Scottsdale third baseman Joe Randa, who was batting .350, third-best in the league. "Use him."

"They don't want to use him," Gilbert said. "They told me they wanted to use you."

"This league is supposed to be about top prospects," Jordan said.

"It's just that little picture," Gilbert said.

"I'm not a top prospect," Jordan said. "I'm not even a prospect."

. . . . .

"Now batting, with the Chicago White Sox, the designated hitter, Michael . . . Jordan. . . ."

The words from the stadium announcer rang through the sparsely populated ballpark. That was the P.A. style in the Arizona Fall League: Each batter was introduced not with the name of the Arizona team to which he was assigned, but with the name of the big-league club that had sent him here. Thus, Arizona was the only place in the world where Jordan was still considered a member of the White Sox.

I asked him if he had yet heard from any of the Sox. They hadn't kept in touch during the Birmingham season in the Southern League. Had they contacted him now that he was playing in Arizona?

"Actually, a couple of them have," he said. "I think Craig Grebeck is going to show up today or tomorrow, and if he does I'm looking forward to seeing him. And when I got out here, Ozzie Guillen sent a basket of fruit."

"Ozzie Guillen?" I said. "Did that?"

"Yeah, he did," Jordan said. "It really surprised me."

He paused.

"At least Ozzie's name was on the card," he said. "I assume it was really him."

There was a special Boy Scouts promotion at the park on this night; as small as the crowd was, it was larger than it would have been had the discounted tickets not been given out to local Scout troops. Many of the Scouts were with their fathers, or sitting with their troop leaders; they pulled their hoods over their heads in the cold—this was a long way from springtime, the place felt like a high school football stadium on an end-of-season Friday night. The Scouts let their teeth chatter in an exaggerated fashion, and looked toward the dugout at Jordan—the man from the commercials, the man from the television shows—with some perplexity. He might as well have been Thomas Jefferson, or some other distant figure from American history, sitting there in his red clothes.

"Now it's the basketball uniform that looks like it's wrong," I said.

"I know," Jordan said. "It looked strange to me at Scottie's game in Chicago when I put it on."

The uniform he had worn in the Pippen game—the sleeveless jersey and the famous baggy shorts—had seemed as out-of-place on him in November as the baseball uniform had looked when he first began to wear it back in the spring. What had once seemed like a second skin to him—the basketball clothes—had, at the game in the Chicago Stadium, seemed like a costume he was trying on. The baseball uniform had become his daily attire—it looked right. Yet all the changes—Bulls uniform to White Sox uniform, White Sox to Birmingham Barons, Barons to Scorpions, Scorpions to Pippen-game uniform and back to Scorpions again—seemed to epitomize this constant need of his to be moving around, not staying still, looking for something. Whatever the need was, he was still in the midst of trying to fill it.

"I saw myself in the basketball uniform, and it was like a whole different person," he said. "Like some guy I was watching."

"Like a guy you knew?" I said.

"Oh, I knew him," Jordan said. "I knew him very well."

The home field in Scottsdale was modern and clean, with a locker room built for the San Francisco Giants, who used it during each year's spring training. For the day games Jordan would arrive early, work on his batting, then wait by his locker for the contest to begin while his young teammates discussed bat weights and the women they had seen in the first rows of the seats the day before.

Jordan was escorted to and from the field by security guards. His presence in Arizona had taken on something of the feel of a rare animal that had been imported to a local zoo; at one game I saw two elegantly dressed Scottsdale women—they had been attending a party in one of the stadium's private press box–level suites—discussing him in the same kinds of terms they might, indeed, use for an exotic creature.

"Were you able to see him up close?"

"Yes, but you couldn't really see much. He had the bill of his cap pulled all the way down."

"But you could see his face?"

"A little of it, but he's awfully dark."

Jordan pretty much stayed away from this, and stuck to his baseball education. One afternoon I asked him what he had learned about baseball out here that he hadn't known when he arrived. He flashed an amused smile and said, "The lingo. I'm finally picking up the lingo. I'm starting to understand the language of baseball."

"Like what?" I said.

"Like they say 'steak' when they mean an RBI," he said.

"Steak?"

"Yeah. When you get an RBI, you say you got a steak."

"A steak is a run batted in?"

"Yeah," he said. "See, RBI. Ribeye. Like a ribeye steak. A steak."

"They told you that?" I said.

"Well, no, they didn't exactly say it to me," he said. "But I figured it out by listening. I wasn't going to ask them what they meant. I just try to figure it out on my own."

If he was the top-drawing exhibit in this particular zoo, he was also the explorer, picking up the customs of the natives. "They'd say, 'I got three steaks last night,' or 'I got four steaks,' " he said. "At first I thought they were talking about food, but then it dawned on me. Steaks. Ribeyes. RBIs. I don't think they know how closely I'm listening, even when I don't seem to be."

If Jordan's dream ending for all of this was to make it to the major leagues, the goal line had been moved back farther when the big-leaguers went on strike in August. It was the one factor he had failed to anticipate—that he would be working this hard in an effort to get to somewhere that did not exist. The country was angry and embittered toward baseball—toward the big-league players who chose not to play, and toward the owners who could not reach an agreement with those players. The Arizona Fall League was an entity out of time, a professional baseball league trying to get its players ready for major leagues that might or might not be in operation come the spring. There was a sense of futility every day.

On the highways between the Fall League ballparks at night, it was dark and often desolate, with occasional headlights appearing unexpectedly around the bends up ahead. One evening after a game Steve Gilbert was giving me a ride back to my hotel, and he told me a story about a ten-year-old boy—the son of a pitching coach for one of the teams.

"His dad lets him come into the clubhouse with him," Gilbert said. "The kid just loves being around the ballplayers—the uniforms, the equipment, the lockers.

"So one day, the ballplayers are talking about women, as usual. And the kid's sitting there, looking at the players, taking it all in, and he's got this real disappointed look on his face. He's not saying anything, but he finally gets up the nerve to speak.

"And he says to the players: 'Is that all you guys ever talk about—girls? I wish you'd talk about just baseball.' "

There were times in Arizona when the Jordan the world thought it knew—the multimillionaire celebrity, the man who could have anything he desired with a crook of his finger—appeared to have nothing at all in common with the fellow wearing number 45 on the red jersey. He seemed to understand this, and like it just fine.

One night when he was the starting right fielder, he would spend the Scorpions' at-bat time in the dugout all by himself, at the far end of the bench, just sitting back and watching the game. The cold snap was continuing; he had his hands jammed into his pockets. Except for the fact that he was in the dugout, he could have been anyone who had come to a small ballpark to watch the minor-leaguers and kill some hours. Sitting there alone at the distant edge of the bench, observing a ballgame in silence, he appeared to be giving himself a gift—the gift of silence and solitude.

And during a day game in which he was not scheduled to play—Terry Francona tried to give all of the Scorpions the innings they needed to prove themselves, so each man sat out once every few days—Jordan noticed that a pitcher named Joe Borowski was about to be sent in as a reliever. This was at the top of the seventh.

Without being asked, Jordan scrambled out of the dugout, borrowed a catcher's mitt from someone, and squatted to warm Borowski up. The two men took their positions in foul territory along the first-base line—Jordan near home plate, Borowski near first—and Jordan pounded his fist into the mitt and offered Borowski a target.

The crowd was minuscule at 3:30 on a Sunday afternoon closing in on Thanksgiving week. On days when Jordan was not playing, the box office personnel in Scottsdale were instructed to relate this fact to the customers before they bought their tickets; the league did not want to bring on the bad will that would accrue by taking fans' money and having the fans find out later that Jordan would not be in the lineup. Many people who had driven over to the stadium would get back in their cars and leave after they were told that they would not be seeing Jordan.

So on this day, with few watching, Jordan caught for Joe Borowski. He was unsure of himself as a catcher; he managed to hold on to Borowski's first two warmup pitches, but the third one popped out of his glove and onto the ground, and both Jordan and Borowski laughed, as did some of their teammates in the dugout. He seemed happy on that day.

One afternoon in the Scottsdale clubhouse, I was sitting talking with Jordan at his locker when, across the room, a television commercial came on, featuring him in a basketball uniform, floating in slow motion through the air, gliding toward an artfully lighted basket while stirring orchestra music played. One of the many products he endorsed was being promoted in the commercial; I saw his young teammates turn toward the screen and stare.

"Look at that," Jordan said quietly. "It happens all the time. They'll see something on TV where I'm playing basketball, and that's a person they never met. They'll watch that on the screen, and they won't turn their heads away from it.

"And meanwhile I'm over here. I guess it's like the statue. I'm not dead yet. I see them looking at the TV, and I think, here I am, guys, over here. That's not me. This is me."

We all define success in life in different ways. Midway through a night game on the freezing desert, Jordan had gone 0-for-2 at the plate.

This was one of those evenings on which he could be excused for wondering about the wisdom of some of his career decisions. The empty seats were only too evident, as were his failings at bat. As the game wore on, more and more of the customers, no longer willing to contend with the frigid wind coming off the sand and into the ballpark, were deciding to depart, and so they did not see the person who arrived even as they were leaving.

I did. I saw her come in and take her seat. Deloris Jordan, Michael's mother, settled in to watch her son play.

I walked up and said hello to her. She said that she had just arrived from North Carolina; she said she had not told Michael she was coming, that he had no idea she was here.

"You didn't call him first?" I said.

"No," she said. "You know, I called him last week, just to ask him how he was doing. He said, 'Mom, I'm tired.' I could hear something in his voice, the way he said it. I knew it was time for me to come."

So, she said, she had made her airline reservation, and here she was. "No one from the family has been out here lately," she said. "He's been at this for an awfully long time."

There were those who were still critical of Jordan's quest to become a baseball player, which had begun almost a full year before, and, except for a few days off, had not paused. There were those who laughed at it—many had—and others who looked at it with curiosity, or with fascination, or with admiration. But whatever anyone thought of what Jordan was doing, their thoughts had little to do with the one constant that had been a part of his life from the time he was a boy just learning how to play sports.

That constant was Deloris Jordan, who was there watching him on empty elementary school fields, and in junior high school gyms, and who ended up traveling to some of the world's most storied cities to see her son play basketball in the biggest and most prestigious of arenas. Her late husband was there much of the time; now he was gone, and now the crowds were no longer standing-room-only. Now her son did not always succeed.

Here she was.

Jordan's friend George Koehler, who had met Mrs. Jordan at the airport and had given her a ride out to the little ballpark where the Scorpions were playing a road game, was in on the secret—she had let him know that she was coming to Arizona. Koehler let himself onto the field through a swinging metal gate, and walked to the visitors' dugout. He said something to Jordan; whatever the words were, Jordan got off the bench and stood on the dugout steps and peered high up into the seats.

He was looking around, and then he found her. His face lit up. His mother waved down at him.

He returned to the dugout to rejoin his teammates, all of them much younger than he, and Mrs. Jordan sat back to watch the game. Some people might disapprove of what Jordan was attempting on his baseball journey, and others might think it was just fine, and the truth was that what anyone else might think didn't matter. None of them were there at the beginning, and they wouldn't be there at the end. Right now it had come just about full circle. A little field with few people present, and a son who doesn't know whether he will turn out to be good enough, and his mother in the seats, finding out with him.

Late in the game Jordan pulled a hard double down the third-base line, and what fans there were in the chilly ballpark applauded. He didn't seem to be hearing them. He was looking up to a certain place in the seats. "I could hear something in his voice," she had said. "I knew it was time for me to come." Over the course of a man's life, his successes are gauged in various ways, not all of them visible in a box score.

. . . . .

December was on its way, and with it the first interruption Jordan would have from baseball since starting this undertaking. His mother's observation had been accurate: He was beginning to sound weary.

"I'm looking forward to just taking a break," he said as we talked at the Scottsdale ballpark one afternoon. "Just not playing for a while, to see what my body remembers."

I asked him what that meant.

"I've taken in so much during the last year," he said. "I feel like I'm overloaded. Every day, I've tried to learn something, or to work on what I had already been taught. There were times when I thought I was taking too much in.

"I'm tired now. I'm ready to go home. If I've done this right, if I let my body rest for a while, when I start up again my body will have remembered the things I've learned this year."

There was that theme again—the theme of his body somehow acting as his brain. During the summer, when he had told me about trying to store all the information about baseball in his mind so that he could call it up without thinking about it, he had touched on this. Now it had become his body itself that he was depending on for the power of recall—as if his muscles and flesh had the ability to recollect certain things.

"That's really how it works?" I said. "You feel like your body has a memory?"

"It always has," he said. "But I've never tried to take in so much in such a concentrated period of time as I have for the past year. This will be a test—to see if my body could take it all in and process it."

When the Scorpions would play the other teams in the Arizona Fall League—the Peoria Javelinas, the Tempe Rafters, the various clubs that had their ballparks up and down the highway—he would often be asked to autograph balls and gloves by his opponents.

While this was nothing new for him—during the Olympic Games in Spain it had become almost a joke, the requests for autographs and snapshot sessions by men who were supposed to be trying to defeat him—there was a difference in Arizona. In Spain, the men from the other teams had known that he was better at basketball than they were. Here, the men asking him for his signature felt sure that he could not play baseball on their level.

Yet it never stopped. After a bad night on the road, he would walk in his uniform to the team bus, and trotting up beside him would be the opposing ballplayers who had just shown him up. "Michael, if you could just sign these two shirts." "Hey, M.J.—let me get a picture with you." "Mike—for my nephew and niece, OK?"

I asked him one night how many players were on the Scorpions.

"Thirty," he said.

"Where do you think you rank among those thirty?" I said.

"Last," he said.

"Dead last?" I said.

"Dead last," he said. "In no way am I even near the middle of the pack. I'm the worst player. But I'm not through yet."

I went from the field and into the clubhouse after one game. The young ballplayers were ragging each other about mistakes they had made during the contest just completed, postulating aloud how their performances in the last nine innings might have rated with Terry Francona and the rest of the coaching staff, arguing about when they thought the big-league strike would end, and about whether they would be called up to the majors when the strike was finally over. There was laughter and shouting, the sounds of young men with their baseball lives stretching out ahead of them.

Jordan wasn't among them. I looked over at the far end of the clubhouse. He was sitting on a folding chair, in front of a table. Deep in concentration, with no company, he worked intently at a hand of solitaire, paying no attention to the clamor around him, trying his hardest to defeat himself.

CHAPTER 12

"Yeah, I'm up about twenty pounds," Jordan said as the second spring training started. No one had any idea of how soon, for him, it would end.

Not that there weren't clear signs. A sportswriter, in the same White Sox locker room in Sarasota where Jordan had seemed so out-of-place a year before, asked him where the added pounds had come from. He wasn't fat; clearly this was intentional, he had decided to put some more muscle on.

"I've been working with weights all winter," Jordan said. "I'm trying to build up my arm strength—my right arm in particular."

"Well, you look good," the sports reporter said. "You look like a home-run hitter."

The writer walked away. Jordan, unloading his possessions from his gym bag and placing them in his locker, looked over at me with a small grin.

"The question is," he said, "can I still hit a jump shot?"

Spring training, on the surface, felt, as before, like the ideal place for any person to be. The eighty-degree temperatures in February, the dampness of the grass in the morning, the inviting sounds of baseballs pounding into the pockets of leather gloves, smacking off the barrels of wooden bats—for the first few moments, life at spring training seemed as if nothing had changed.

But everything had. The major-leaguers remained on strike as the training camps opened. The lockers where the world-famous stars had sat the spring before—the lockers that had borne the names of Frank Thomas and Robin Ventura and Tim Raines and Ozzie Guillen and the rest—were empty during the first days of camp, and no one seemed quite sure who would end up using them. What was being promised was some combination of minor-leaguers and the euphemistic "replacement players" being recruited by the owners. The physical accoutrements of spring training were up and running—the practice diamonds were ready, Ed Smith Stadium had a new coat of paint, the radio in the weight room blasted the words of a song that had become a hit in the months since this time last year—*All I want to do is have some fun* . . .—but only a relative few prospects were on hand, and the place felt forlorn. Jordan was present, having arrived early to try to get himself a head start on the other baseball players. He was clearly confused by the position in which he found himself because of the strike. And when he talked, basketball suddenly never seemed very far from his thoughts.

I had been thinking about this—Jordan's renewed attraction to basketball—ever since a call I had received from Steve Gilbert after the Arizona Fall League had ended its season.

Gilbert, having enjoyed his time in the Arizona league's front office, was trying to decide what to do with his life next. He told me a story about a night near the end of the fall season when he had done something he had never, in his most outlandish dreams, imagined: played in a basketball game with Michael Jordan.

"On Sunday nights, after the Scorpions' day games, the players had been going to an athletic club in Scottsdale and playing pickup basketball," Gilbert said. "Terry Francona told me about the games, and invited me to come by some Sunday night. So the next Sunday, I took him up on it.

"I got there, and the players were shooting around and Michael came out of the locker room dressed to play. It's funny—I had seen him so much around baseball that I had gotten used to him. I was very nervous when I first met him, but working with him every day, talking to him all the time—he was a good guy, and I was accustomed to him, and I stopped being so nervous.

"And then that night at the athletic club be walks onto the basketball court in those blue North Carolina shorts of his—and I look at him and I think: Oh, yeah. This is Michael Jordan. Different thing. Terry Francona tells me that I'm on their team—the way it was, it was Michael and Terry and the coaches against the baseball players. So I was put on Jordan's team.

"So the game started, and there I am on the same court with Jordan. I was assigned to guard Curtis Goodwin, and I knew I was totally overmatched—Goodwin stole forty bases in the minor leagues, and I'm supposed to keep up with him? But I did my best. One time, on offense, I got the ball and I thought I saw an opening in the lane. So I drove toward the basket and someone tripped me. I fell down and I lost the ball, and I felt pretty bad.

"I got up off the floor, and Michael was standing over me. He said, 'What were you doing?'

"I said, 'I saw an opening.'

"And Michael said, 'What were you going to do when you *got* there?'

"He was kidding with me but he wasn't kidding. He was so competitive. He said, 'When you get the ball, just throw it to me.'

"At one point Michael grabbed a rebound, and he saw me running downcourt, and he threw me a perfect pass—"

I interrupted Gilbert. "There's a sentence I bet you never thought you'd say in your life," I said.

Gilbert laughed. "I know," he said. "He threw me the pass, and I just froze. I stopped running as soon as I caught it. I put up a shot and I missed. He just threw that pass so perfectly—like he wasn't even thinking about it, right over the fingertips of the defenders, just high enough to clear their hands but not too high for me to catch. It was this little thing you never think about, that kind of move, and I must have seen it on TV when he was playing basketball a million times and not paid attention. Just this little part of the game, this perfection. . . ."

Competing against the baseball players who were on the other team, Gilbert said, Jordan was friendly but absolutely relentless. "Someone made a shot over him and said to him, 'Now I can tell my grandchildren that I kicked Michael Jordan's ass.' It was a joke, and the guy knew it and Jordan knew it and everyone else knew it.

"But on the next play Michael called for the ball and he took it downcourt and slammed a dunk right over the guy. And he said to the guy, 'Now you can tell your grandchildren that Michael Jordan kicked *your* ass. That's what you can tell your grandchildren.' "

During the game, some of the players on the sidelines pulled out video cameras to shoot Jordan, Gilbert said. "He didn't say anything about it, but he obviously noticed. Here he was playing this game for the fun of it, and it was being put on videotape forever. I tried to think about what it must be like for him to go through that kind of thing every day of his life, even in the moments that he's trying to spend away from the public eye."

After the game, Gilbert started having trouble breathing. "I knew I was in trouble," he said. "Playing in the game with Jordan—I don't remember breathing during the whole game. I could never catch my breath. And when the game ended it was pretty scary, because I still couldn't take a breath. I just couldn't breathe.

"They went to a telephone and called the team trainer, and he said he thought I was just hyperventilating, but that they ought to get me to a hospital just to make sure. So they drove me over to Scotts-dale Memorial Hospital. I was in the emergency room, lying on a table, and I guess the word got around about where I had been.

"Because all of a sudden all of these doctors and staff members were leaning over me. I'm being given oxygen, and I'm hooked up to an EKG, and I look up at all their faces looking down at me, and what do they say to me?

"They say, 'What's it like, playing basketball with Michael Jordan? What's it really like to play with him?' "

"I looked up at them, and I felt like saying, 'What's it like? What's it like to play basketball with Jordan? I'm in the fucking *hospital*, aren't I? What do you think it's like?' "

The next day—Gilbert was fine, he had, indeed, merely been winded from the game—he walked into the Scorpions' clubhouse while Jordan was putting on his baseball uniform.

"Jordan said, 'I ain't ever playing basketball with you again,' " Gilbert said.

"I asked him why. And he said, 'Because I can't have a good time out there if I've got to worry about you keeling over.' "

Now, in the opening days of his second spring training, Jordan was one of the few players on hand; enough were in camp for informal workouts, but the major-leaguers continued their strike and most of the fill-ins had yet to arrive in Florida. Willie Thompson, the fifty-six-year-old clubhouse man/equipment manager for the White Sox, who had worked for the team for sixteen years, looked around the quiet room and said, "I don't know what to do. I have no idea who the players on this team are going to be." He had plenty of blank uniforms in stock, but did not know who would be wearing them. He had ordered boxes of cloth letters and numbers, which had arrived. He would sew them onto the uniform shirts when someone eventually told him the identities of the Chicago White Sox.

Always a loud, jocular man, Thompson was subdued this spring. Every season he would wash the players' uniforms and underwear, cook chicken for them, consider them a part of his family. He had a wife and two children; he was not a wealthy person. Now the players' strike had shut down baseball. "I've worked all my life," he said. "I never thought I'd see this day."

I knew that Thompson genuinely had believed the players considered him to be a part of their family, too—their baseball family. I asked him how many of the White Sox had kept in touch with him after they'd walked out—how many had dropped him a line, called him to see how he was getting along, gave him some idea of what he might expect this season?

"Not a one of them," he said. "No one."

He thought for a few seconds. "Jack McDowell did write me a letter," he said. "To thank me for all the years. It really made me feel good."

McDowell, though, had been traded to the New York Yankees. He was no longer with the Sox. Neither were any of the men who had filled this room with noise and laughter a year ago. On the clubhouse table where their cold-cut lunch buffets had always been laid out was a copy of a publication called *Baseball America*. Usually it devoted itself to celebrating the game. On this issue the coverline had a somewhat different tone: "Lost Summer." Jordan, from the moment he arrived in camp, seemed like a man with one eye on the door.

He had become, by default, the biggest star in baseball. It wasn't much of an honor—there were no baseball stars this spring, the real stars were declining to play—but of all the ballplayers in all the spring training camps, Jordan was the most glamorous attraction. No one else was even close.

As the minor-leaguers and replacements arrived in Sarasota, Jordan was visibly more at ease in the clubhouse than he had been the year before. He knew the room; he didn't look like a man afraid a border guard was going to check his papers. He saw the young ballplayers and the replacements glancing around hesitantly—where were the showers, where were the toilets?—and he wasn't the new kid at summer camp anymore, he wasn't the one waiting to be told what to do. His posture at his locker—leaning back nonchalantly in his chair, flipping through magazines, exercising territorial imperative— was the same as in the old Chicago Stadium; a room in which he'd been a visitor was now his. The cigar wasn't literally in his mouth, but it might have been.

Television crews would come to Sarasota from other cities, other countries; the correspondents would stand in the sunlight and file reports about Jordan, and some of them, like the women in Scottsdale, would speak as if they were describing an animal they had observed behind the bars of a cage: "Tim Grover, Jordan's weight trainer, is ecstatic. He's got Jordan built up—much stronger in the arms, much more snap from the muscles in his wrists. . . ." Yet, while he was the biggest individual story, he wasn't the biggest story. The strike was the story.

So the reporters from the *New York Times*, the *Washington Post*, *Sports Illustrated* would visit camp, and while Jordan made a good sidebar, the main news account would be about the labor situation, and what it might mean for the season. On many days, Jordan sat alone in front of his cubicle, not faced with the wave after wave of questioners he had for so long been accustomed to. If what he had wanted was to be treated like just any other ballplayer, he was close to getting it. He had the peace and quiet he had asked for. The Chicago baseball beat writers were there, as they had to be, and they could sit with Jordan and shoot the breeze for long, casual intervals, no pressures, no deadline quotes, just a bunch of guys—Jordan one of them—talking. One day Jordan, out of nowhere—just for something to do—palmed the head of Paul Sullivan, the *Chicago Tribune*'s man in camp this spring, as if Sullivan's head were a basketball. "He palmed my head," Sullivan would mutter to himself later, simple declarative sentence. "Jordan palmed my head."

He had a baseball history now—in the media guide, all of his efforts of the last year were recorded in one line of agate type. The Birmingham summer, with all its texture and flavors and color, had been reduced to times at bat, hits, walks, errors, stolen bases, and that final batting average of .202. For better or for worse, he was a name in the record books, one name among thousands of ballplayers, from the majors down to the lowest Class A leagues, all of them trying to make a living.

Out on the back diamonds, only a handful of fans showed up each day to watch the workouts. They were the hard-core baseball enthusiasts, here to show their support for the young players and the trying-to-hang-on replacements who were defying the strike. Michelle Idzi, thirty, a clerk in a Sarasota clothing store, nodded toward Jordan as he waited for his turn in the batting cage and said, as if her presence here needed defending, "I'm here to watch baseball, not to watch him."

But others, to be sure, were. The Jordan Watch—that was its official name—had been a part of his world ever since he had reported to spring training the year before. Newspapers around the country would run daily boxes with that headline; the brief text inside the boxes would list how many times Jordan had come to bat, whether he had gotten a hit, what his batting average was, whether he had made any errors, the most quotable thing he had said that day—it had become a sports-page staple.

The Associated Press had included the Jordan Watch on its main sports wire all during the previous season; local reporters and stringers all over the Southern League had been assigned to get the information to the AP in time for deadline each night, as had freelancers in Arizona. I would see these reporters sitting in press boxes with pocket calculators, so they could swiftly compute his batting average as soon as each game ended. That average was usually just a little lower than it had been at the beginning of the game.

"I don't like it, but I know there's nothing I can do about it," Jordan said. In fact, he was courteous to the people in each town who had been assigned to the Jordan Watch—he understood that doing this little task was their job, that it was probably helping to pay their rent, and that it might well be just as bothersome a task for them as it was for him. He was always aware they were present, and that they would flash his baseball statistics around the world by midnight.

"If they did it for all the other players, I suppose I would think it was more fair," Jordan said. "No one else in the minors has to deal with their failures being reported to every paper every night. Or if I had done something to earn it, I would think it was OK. But the Jordan Watch isn't there because I've been good enough to earn it. It's there for the opposite reason."

With the new season about to begin, he was resigned to the idea that the Jordan Watch would be happening again—that wherever he might be sent in the minor leagues, the Jordan Watch would go with him.

"I would love it if they wouldn't do it," he said. "If I thought it would do any good for me to ask them not to do it, then I'd ask. But if I asked them not to do it, my asking would become a story in itself. And they'd do it anyway. So I just accept it. And feel embarrassed."

Dennis "Oil Can" Boyd, an eccentric, wild-eyed, past-his-better-days pitcher who was attempting to get back into the big leagues as a replacement player, had been brought into the White Sox camp by management. His locker was down the row from Jordan's; he would walk past Jordan's locker ten or twenty times a morning, usually wearing underwear and rubber shower clogs, just to have a word or two of conversation. Michael Jordan and Oil Can Boyd—two men no one would ever have bet would share the same space in the athletic universe—suddenly were seeing as much of each other as Jordan used to see of Scottie Pippen or Phil Jackson.

"M.J.!" Boyd would enthusiastically call out each time he passed Jordan.

"Oil Can," Jordan would say with a distinct lack of energy.

"M.J.!" Boyd would crow on his next time past.

"Oil Can," Jordan would say in a monotone.

"M.J.!" Boyd would trill brightly once again.

"Can," Jordan would say dully, trimming the first word to shorten the exchange.

"M.J.!"

"Can."

"M.J.!"

"Can."

"M.J.!"

"Can."

This second baseball spring of Jordan's, more and more, began to seem like something that could not last.

· · · · ·

"What are they being so greedy for?" Jordan said.

He was talking about the striking big-leaguers—the players who, on the average, had been making $1.2 million a year when they walked away from their teams. They were still on strike, and showing no indication that there was any chance they might come back during spring training. When Jordan spoke in front of microphones, he was always diplomatic as he talked about the strike. He was not a major-leaguer, he would say; thus, he did not want to be caught in the middle of this. It was something for the big-league players' union and the owners to work out.

Talking privately, though, he was critical of the players. It wasn't because he thought they were in the wrong; quite to the contrary, his sympathies lay with them. Where he thought they were misguided was in their assumption that they could ever beat the owners.

"They're being greedy without any hope of ever getting their money back," he said. "The kind of money they're giving up, they're never going to see again."

I asked him if he would do the same thing if he were in their position.

"But I'm not," he said. "You can't compare my situation to theirs. First of all, I'm basically not making anything playing baseball. And even when I was playing basketball, my salary with the Bulls wasn't where I was making my money. So what I would do in their situation has no bearing. We aren't in similar situations."

"Then why do you think the players are dumb for staying out on strike?" I said.

"The way I see it," he said, "the owners can always make their money back. All they'll do once the strike is over is raise ticket prices. The owners are going to be around for a long time. Believe me—no matter what, they'll figure out a way to get back every penny they lost. Time is on their side."

"And the players won't get it back?" I said.

"Not a chance," he said. "The money they've lost is gone forever. They've said goodbye to it. I'm not saying they're wrong for what they're doing—that's none of my business, it's their choice. But they ought to realize that the money they've walked out on is never coming back. They can play the rest of their careers and they'll never see it."

"Have you told any of them that?" I said.

"They don't need to hear it from me," he said. "I'm just a minor-leaguer to them. Which is fine. That's what I am. I'm staying out of their business."

I would think about his words the next summer—when Jordan himself became involved in a dispute with the National Basketball Association, as part of a group of players trying to decertify the basketball players' union. For now, though, as much as he said he supported the right of the striking baseball players to hold out for what they could get, he said he thought they were being foolhardy.

"You watch," Jordan said. "Their money's gone for good. And the owners will get back everything they lost."

At workouts, he hit balls over the fence on a routine basis. The balls that were thrown to him were only batting-practice pitches, true, but a year before he was clipping these same kinds of pitches into the dirt in front of home plate. Then, he had difficulty driving the ball out of the infield. This year the balls sprang off his bat. He was better.

Some days there were thirty people present to watch, some days less. "Come through on the fucking ball!" Walt Hriniak would shout at a young hitter. Here was Hriniak, under the sun, twelve months after he had met Jordan, his skin twelve months more leathery, like a drill instructor who is always aware that each season he must go through the purposeful tedium with a new class of recruits. "Come *through!*"

Jordan felt he was on his own now. "Walt was great for what I needed last year," he would say when Hriniak was not in earshot. "He showed me how he thought I should swing. But now it's up to me. No more of that hitting with one arm in practice, like he always wanted. I have to hit with both hands. I can't let myself think about all those mechanics anymore." It was as if now Jordan was trying to teach himself, with nothing to measure his success against except the sight of how far the ball went. The people who could tell him the truth—if only with a glance or a look away—were not here: Thomas, Grebeck, Raines, the ones who could do this well, time after time after time, without an apparent thought.

Rich King of WGN television in Chicago showed up one day with a camera crew, sent south to send back some spring training stories. Jordan was hitting on a sunbaked back diamond, and King said to his cameraman, "Get some footage. You can never get enough of Michael."

George Koehler, Jordan's driver and friend, was sitting on a wooden bench near the batting cage when he heard this. He said to King—whom he knew—"Want to bet? You can never get enough of Michael? I get up every morning and go to the bathroom carrying the newspaper, and there's M.J. in the paper. I turn on 'Good Morning America,' and there's highlights of M.J. when he scored twenty-five zillion points. I go out for a walk and every person I see asks me how M.J. is doing. I sit down to eat breakfast and he's looking back at me from the fucking cereal box. Try that for eleven years, three hundred sixty-five days a year, twenty-four hours a day. See if you get enough of him."

King laughed—he knew Koehler was trying to get a reaction from him. Koehler's life, perhaps more than the life of anyone else in the world, had been changed most dramatically by a chance meeting with Jordan. Jordan had arrived in Chicago from North Carolina in 1984 for his rookie season with the Bulls; the team had not sent anyone to pick him up at O'Hare International Airport. Koehler had been running a one-man limousine service, and the passenger he was supposed to pick up from a flight hadn't shown. Jordan emerged from the plane, looking around, young and confused. Koehler, thinking he recognized him from somewhere—sports? TV?—hesitated for a second and said: "Larry Jordan?"

Half right. He offered to drive Jordan downtown, the two men hit it off, and here was Koehler in the sun, eleven years later, having traveled the world at Jordan's side and seen things he'd never dreamed of. "Get the footage," Rich King said to his cameraman, and Jordan swung away, the deserted back diamond like the set of a silent movie.

After his jersey had been retired in the ceremony at the new United Center in November, Jordan had come to a Bulls game, sitting in a luxury suite provided by one of the team's owners. It had felt wrong for everyone in the arena—for the fans who saw him sitting in a chair in a coat and tie, for the basketball players who were aware he was present and watching them. I wondered about him—how had he liked being there, in that new building where he'd never shot a basket?

"I just wanted to find out for myself," he said. "I could have done without the people looking away from the court and up at where I was sitting, but I wanted to see what a basketball game felt like in there."

He was sweating in the Florida heat as we had this conversation—talking about a climate-controlled indoor basketball stadium as he sat near a diamond in the Sarasota sun.

"What about the court?" I said. "How did it look to you?"

"The court looked nice," he said. "It really did."

He paused, looking down toward the dirt.

"But from where I was sitting, it was very far away," he said.

At his locker one afternoon, Jordan, sitting with his back to the room, felt someone rubbing his head. Clearly annoyed—this was something he despised, few people were foolish enough to do it to him—he wheeled around.

The perpetrator, Oil Can Boyd, in underwear and clogs, beamed down at him. "M.J.!" Boyd called out loudly.

"Can," Jordan said, with more weariness than anything else.

It was one thing for Jordan to palm Paul Sullivan's head. In the natural order of things, such an action was allowed. But for Oil Can Boyd to rub Michael Jordan's head was yet another signal, if any more were needed, that in this particular spring the planets were miles and miles out of their customary alignment.

. . . . .

As the practice sessions neared an end, and scheduled games against other major-league teams—or at least teams bearing the names of major-league franchises—were about to begin, Jordan's tension over whether he would be asked to play by the White Sox increased. Unlike the year before, he fervently hoped not. In fact, he hoped it never came up; he hoped he would be allowed to merely practice.

He was aware that, if he played in games for which tickets were sold, he would be perceived as a strikebreaker. As long as he positioned himself as a minor-leaguer in camp, with no aspirations other than to be assigned for the summer to a minor-league team, then things would be all right. The minor-leaguers weren't in the players' union.

But if the Sox told him to play in revenue-producing games in which strikebreaking replacement players were on the rosters, then that would be a different story. He would be being used to bring paying fans into ballparks—and thus he would be working against the strikers. Not that he liked the major-leaguers so much—he felt considerably more fondness for the minor-league ballplayers with whom he had spent the previous summer, men with tiny paychecks and uncertain futures. But he knew that if the White Sox attempted to force him into being a strikebreaker, his standing with the public would be jeopardized, and he would be put in an untenable situation.

He had few voices available to offer him advice. He had been living with George Koehler and with his weight trainer, Tim Grover, in the same house he had rented the previous spring. Juanita had arrived in Sarasota with the Jordan children; Koehler and Grover moved into the Hyatt for a few days so the Jordan family could be together in the house. Gene Lamont, the manager of the White Sox, was asked by reporters what Jordan's baseball prospects were this year. "If I had to compare him last year at this time to this year at this time, there's no comparison," Lamont said. "This is going to be a big year for him, in terms of finding out what his future in the game is. The way he hits the ball this year—it sounds different. You can hear the difference in his game."

Lamont himself would be gone from the White Sox before the new season was even halfway over; he would be fired by general manager Ron Schueler and would leave the team upset and resentful. On this day, though, he said the season ahead was Jordan's in which to prove himself either a big-league prospect, or someone who would never be good enough.

"How are you going to end this thing?" I asked Jordan.

I wasn't talking about the near future; I was talking about eventually. He had conceded all along that he knew any baseball career he might have would not be a lengthy one; he had begun his quest as a thirty-one-year-old rookie, and the number of seasons available to him was clearly finite.

"How will I end it?" he said. "With a smile."

"You're sure?" I said.

"Yep. I'd like to get to the majors and play for a couple of years. That's how I'd like it to end—earning my way to the White Sox, and being a true major-league player for two or three years, and knowing that I've accomplished what I set out to do.

"But whether that works out, or I fall short, no matter how it ends, I'll walk away with a smile. It's the only thing I know about this for sure—that when it comes time to say this is over, I'll have a smile on my face as I say goodbye."

He didn't. Within days, he walked away from baseball full of anger and barely disguised bitterness. It happened so quickly it caught everyone in camp by surprise.

Ron Schueler had decided that any minor-leaguers who refused to dress in White Sox uniforms and play in White Sox exhibitions would be banished from the main clubhouse. There were to be no exceptions. One day Schueler was seen out on the practice field talking animatedly with Jordan. Jordan appeared furious. Word had been going around the Sox complex for days that Schueler was pressuring Jordan to play in the exhibitions, and to wear the uniform of the big-league White Sox; Jordan had said all spring that he had an agreement with Jerry Reinsdorf that he would not have to do this—that the day would never come when he would be forced to be not a minor-league prospect, but a major-league strikebreaker.

Jordan walked silently toward the clubhouse, his rage apparent. Within the hour he was gone from camp.

"I had told them from the beginning that I didn't want them to use me to make money in the spring training games," he said when we talked about it later. "We had an understanding. It was never supposed to even come up."

Most crises, with him, blew over rather quickly. He considered it a waste of energy to spend time fuming over past slights, harboring grudges. This was different. He felt he had been betrayed and lied to—put into a position in which he was being made to look callow and small. I asked him if Schueler had, indeed, made the direct request—if Schueler had told him the Sox needed him to break the strike in order to sell spring training tickets.

"I kept getting the hint, let's put it that way," he said.

Was he as angry as it had appeared?

"I was disgusted," he said. " 'Disgust' is a more accurate word than 'anger.' What had I done for the last year, other than to work as hard as I could, and to do everything I was asked to do? The one promise that was made to me was that they wouldn't put me in the position of being a strikebreaker—that if there were games in spring training that would be considered strikebreaker games, I wouldn't be asked to play in them."

And?

"I was disgusted that the promise wasn't going to be honored. I had my own reasons for not wanting to play in the games. But as disgusted as I was at what was being pushed on me, I felt even more disappointed for the guys from the minor-league teams. Look—I can walk away from baseball. I don't need it to make a living.

"But the rest of these guys—their jobs with the White Sox are the one chance they have. And they're being told that management wants them to break the strike and play in the spring games, and at the same time the major-leaguers are telling them that if they *do* play in those games, they'll be in trouble with the union members once the strike is over.

"How unfair can you be to these guys? Sox management is asking them to cross the line and play in these games—but where will the Sox management be once the strike is over, and the regulars come back? What assurance do these guys have that Sox management will look after them then? And if these guys listen to the major-leaguers, and refuse to play, what do they get out of that once the strike is over? If they refuse to play in the games because the major-leaguers have asked them not to, and they defy management, will the major-leaguers care about what happens to these guys once the major-leaguers have their own jobs back? Will the major-leaguers protect these guys, once the major-leaguers are back on the field and management doesn't need these guys any longer? You know that's not going to happen.

"So what you have is these young guys caught totally in the middle, with no one they can turn to. Yeah, I was mad—I was as mad as I've ever been. But my situation was nothing compared to theirs."

I asked him how he felt about Schueler.

"You don't want to know," he said.

I said that I did.

"You don't want to know," he repeated. Then:

"I no longer trusted him. And with me, once you feel you can't trust a person you once trusted, then it's over forever. I had to get out of there."

I said that some people were speculating that the thing that made him leave was the indignity of having to dress in the minor-league locker room. That's what was happening to the minor-leaguers who refused to break the strike—they were being sent to a different clubhouse. The theory that this bothered Jordan much hadn't made a lot of sense to me—the minor-league locker room at Sox camp was cramped and devoid of luxuries, but it was much better than most of the visiting clubhouses in minor-league ballparks where he'd spent the summer before.

"That's ridiculous, the locker-room thing," he said. "I knew Schueler was trying to make a point by sending me there, but I didn't care. The thing that did make me mad is something most people didn't even know about."

"What's that?" I said.

"I haven't said anything about it, because people wouldn't understand," he said.

He hesitated. "They made a rule that if you wouldn't play in Sox games, then you couldn't park your car in the lot," he said. "You had to park down the street.

"Schueler had to know that for me, that meant something completely different than for the other players."

The players' parking lot at the fenced Sox complex was patrolled by security guards, who stood sentry at the gates. One of their primary tasks was to keep people away from Jordan, and to clear a path when he drove his car out. If he was told he must park down the street, then he would have to fight his way through the crowds that would be waiting for him every day. Once the word got around Sarasota that Jordan was not allowed in the White Sox parking lot, he would face mobs every morning and every afternoon. While certainly not the stuff of war and peace, it was a situation that would without question needlessly complicate Jordan's days.

"I wasn't going to say anything to Schueler about it," Jordan said. "I tried my best not ever to ask him for special treatment. But after a year, if he didn't know my situation . . . if he really didn't know what would happen if he kept me out of the players' parking lot . . ."

Schueler obviously did know. He had to understand what would happen once people learned that Jordan would be walking to the ballpark from outside of the secured area every day, and that his car would be sitting unattended for anyone who might want to fool with it during the long mornings and afternoons.

"If he knew, then he was doing it on purpose, to put the pressure on me to play in those games," Jordan said. "If he didn't know, then that told me something, too. Either way, I knew I had to get out of there. I'm a person who keeps my word. I expect it from others, too."

· · · · ·

What followed, in the days after Jordan's departure from camp, was a public and press reaction so startling that even those who had witnessed the madness surrounding him for years could hardly believe it. He had not yet announced that he was through with baseball for good—in fact, Ron Schueler kept blithely announcing in Sarasota that he expected Jordan to return. He had not said that he was going to play basketball again—or even that he might.

Yet the simple act of his leaving spring training became the biggest sports story—one of the biggest news stories—in the country. National newspapers tracked the New York Stock Exchange, and reported how the speculation that Jordan might put on a basketball uniform again was causing certain stocks to soar. One published report said that the stock-market value of five companies whose products Jordan endorsed had jumped a cumulative $2.3 billion in three days.

Jordan showed up at a Bulls practice, worked out with the team, watched some game films with Phil Jackson, and broadcast stations cut into programming to offer that information as special reports. A microwave village was erected in the parking lot of the Bulls' practice facility in Deerfield, Illinois, sending live TV signals to the world— even though Jordan had said nothing. *Newsweek* magazine devoted its cover to Jordan—before he had said anything at all. After a Bulls game at the United Center during which the crowd—worked into a frenzy over the speculation that he might be returning to the struggling team—exploded with excited cheers the likes of which had not been heard in the arena all year (Jordan wasn't even in the building), Bulls guard Steve Kerr told the press, "The crowd obviously isn't cheering for us. They're cheering in anticipation of somebody else." Kerr, who had joined the team after Jordan left basketball, told a reporter that the Bulls themselves were talking about the same thing the fans were: "Sure, we talk among ourselves. A lot of us never got to play with Michael. When I played with Cleveland, I didn't play much. I sat [on the bench] in the best seat in the house and watched Michael Jordan play basketball."

The commentary focused on economics: What would a return to

the NBA by Jordan mean for the league's revenues—television ratings, sales of licensed merchandise, ticket demand? The commentary focused on inside-sports minutiae: What would happen to Scottie Pippen's contract were Jordan to return—would Jordan make sure that Pippen got a new, richer deal? The commentary focused on personalities: Would Jordan, if he decided to play, mesh well with the men who were currently the Bulls? Or would they resent his presence, turn against him for having left them and then having wandered back in?

I got a phone call during all of this from Elliott Kalb, the senior statistician for NBC's television broadcasts of the NBA. Kalb—referred to as "Mr. Stats" by Marv Albert at the end of each broadcast—made his living with numbers and dry figures. But he thought the essence of what was going on with Jordan could be found not necessarily in sports sections, but on the pages of works of literature. He sent me some passages from Samuel Beckett's play *Waiting for Godot*; he advised me to read the dialogue and to silently and randomly substitute for Estragon and Vladimir the names of coach Phil Jackson, general manager Jerry Krause, and the reporters staking out the practice gym in Deerfield:

> ESTRAGON: What exactly did we ask him for?
> VLADIMIR: Were you not there?
> ESTRAGON: I can't have been listening.
> VLADIMIR: Oh . . . Nothing very definite.
> ESTRAGON: A kind of prayer.
> VLADIMIR: Precisely.
> ESTRAGON: A vague supplication.
> VLADIMIR: Exactly.
> ESTRAGON: And what did he reply?
> VLADIMIR: That he'd see.
> ESTRAGON: That he couldn't promise anything.
> VLADIMIR: That he'd have to think it over.
> ESTRAGON: In the quiet of his home.
> VLADIMIR: Consult his family

ESTRAGON: His friends.
VLADIMIR: His agents.
ESTRAGON: His correspondents.
VLADIMIR: His books.
ESTRAGON: His bank account.
VLADIMIR: Before taking a decision.

. . . . .

ESTRAGON: And if he doesn't come?
VLADIMIR: We'll come back to-morrow.
ESTRAGON: And then the day after to-morrow . . .

When the announcement was made, it was not in the lyrical language of a transcendent playwright, but two unelaborated words on a statement distributed via fax machine by Jordan's agent: "I'm Back."

"I almost got scared away," Jordan would tell me, referring to his own reaction to the events during the period between when he left spring training and when the announcement of his return to the Bulls was made. "Some of the things that happened frightened me."

That conversation would come later, though, once he was on the NBA road again. Now it was time to start playing basketball.

CHAPTER 13

Steven Hill, an aspiring oil-on-canvas artist, had somehow managed to gain admission to the players' hallway in the basement of the Omni arena in downtown Atlanta. He had brought with him two impressionistic oil portraits of Jordan playing basketball. He had placed them on the floor, propped against the wall, in the hopes that when Jordan and the Bulls arrived at the building Jordan would see his artwork.

"He drives, he glides, he does what he wants to do," Hill said, explaining the theme of the paintings. He kept moving them; he wasn't certain which door the Bulls would enter when their bus pulled up, and he had a fifty-fifty chance of having his portraits displayed at the wrong end of the hallway. So he would prop them against one wall, then decide he had probably made the wrong choice; he would lug them down to the other end, set them up, then reconsider. Hauling his paintings up and down that corridor, he was putting on almost as much mileage as the basketball players would once the game began. I asked him if he was hoping that Jordan would like them enough to purchase them.

"I just want him to see them," he said. "That would be enough."

The Bulls had flown into Atlanta on their chartered jet after midnight and had slept at the Ritz-Carlton hotel, a few blocks from the arena. Now here, suddenly appearing through a doorway and walking down the windowless hallway, was Pippen, here was Phil Jackson, here was B.J. Armstrong, arriving at the gym just as they had arrived at every NBA gym all during this lackluster season. And here was the new man, Jordan.

He knew where he was going; he didn't need a guide. A traveling salesman whose territory is embedded in his mind, he had been here more times than he cared to count during all of his NBA years. He took a quick right into a smaller corridor leading to the visitors' locker room. He saw the two paintings on the floor, saw Steven Hill standing nervously next to them, nodded at Hill and said, "Nice." Hill beamed and pressed his palms together.

Sarasota and baseball seemed like a long time ago. "When you woke up in the hotel room this morning and looked up at the ceiling, did you know where you were?" I asked Jordan.

"Oh, yeah," he said. "I know exactly where I am."

The first games of his return had been covered as thoroughly as if they were Middle Eastern peace negotiations, not regular-season basketball contests. The day he first stepped onto the court again—a Sunday game on the road, against the Indiana Pacers—Larry Brown, the coach of the Pacers, made a comment that, on the surface, seemed overwhelmingly flattering to Jordan.

Brown said he was happy Jordan was coming back to basketball because Brown's own young son would now have a chance to see him play. "I'm like so many fathers whose sons never got to see Michael Jordan," Brown said. "Now they will."

It was an illusive comment. As laudatory as it was, it cost Brown nothing—it was like saying something nice about John Unitas or Arnold Palmer. The fact was, no one knew how much of a threat Jordan still was—no one knew if there was anything to fear. Why not say something gushing about him—and then go out and try to humiliate him? For all the hyperbolic public comments about the legend returning, the unspoken sentiment around the NBA was that Jordan was an entirely unknown quantity who would have to prove himself. Even on the Bulls, where it might have been assumed that he would pick up his old role as team leader, there was an uneasy sense that something important had changed.

He was like a husband coming home to a wife he had left. He was here, and it was a time of celebration, but the hurts that had preceded the return were being glossed over. The Bulls had become a .500 team without Jordan—this, within a year and a half of their third straight NBA championship. Human nature being human nature, his teammates could be excused for having genuinely mixed reactions to the public ardor over the news he had decided to come back.

In that first game, when his shots failed to fall, he kept shooting anyway, not so much out of the cockiness that used to be the emblem of his game, but in an effort to find out if he could still do this (that comment in the White Sox locker room: "The question is, can I still hit a jump shot?"). Was he the leader of this team? Was he really? On the court, not only among the Bulls but among the Pacers too, there seemed to be a sense of excessive politeness, a sense of "After you. *No*, after *you*." He had walked away from them—the Bulls, the NBA— and in his first game back he clearly was nowhere near as good as he'd been when he left. As he took the shots and they clanged out, his teammates appeared reluctant even to look at him askance. Before, his fellow Bulls would toss him the ball in key situations with the absolute knowledge that he would likely put it in the basket; in that first game back, the feeling was different, they were throwing the ball almost as a gesture of trying to help him: "Here, try again, you'll get it one of these times."

He had walked onto the court wearing number 45, his baseball number, a number he had never worn on a professional basketball uniform. Immediately the obvious market possibilities opened up by the number change were widely analyzed, as was the fact that Jordan was wearing a uniform in which his father had never seen him play. But there was something in addition to that: By wearing number 45, it was as if Jordan was accepting, and accentuating, the premise that he had inevitably become someone else.

All the comments in the press and on the air—"the greatest

basketball player who ever lived"—were utterly meaningless now. The world calling him a legend was no favor to him. You can't be legendary unless you prove it day after day, night after night, on the court and not in television commercials. You have to prove it all over again once you decide to leave your statue behind and put on your shorts. The Pacers won that first game 103–96 in overtime, with Jordan scoring 19 points; three nights later the Bulls defeated the Boston Celtics in Boston 124–107, with Jordan scoring 27. He was a good basketball player among other good basketball players. Which was not necessarily what the world was expecting from him.

Now, in Atlanta, the Bulls arrived at the Omni after losing to Orlando the night before in Jordan's first home appearance at the new United Center. Orlando 106, Chicago 99, and Jordan had at times looked close to awkward on his way to scoring 21 points. Shaquille O'Neal, interviewed on national television after his team's victory, standing on the Bulls' court, offered his own variation of Larry Brown's artful patronization. "Michael Jordan is the world's greatest player," O'Neal intoned soothingly. "It's an honor to be on the same court with him."

The easiest thing to say—after you've just run over him. There had been a Nike commercial running nationally when Jordan was still at spring training, designed to poke fun at his baseball failings. The key phrase, repeated at different times during the commercial, was: "But he's trying." The commercial was pulled off the air when Jordan announced he was returning to the NBA—yet the "But he's trying" tagline was, in a peculiar way, less insulting to him than were the "world's greatest player," "honor to be on the same court" lines tossed his way on nights when neither was necessarily true.

In Chicago, after the Orlando loss, Jordan uttered a rather unusual sentence at a post-game press conference: "I know I can play the game of basketball," he said, as if it somehow needed saying.

His arrival in Atlanta was Page One in the main news section of the *Journal-Constitution* (the fact that he and the Bulls had lost to Orlando the night before was relegated to an inside sports page, as if the results of the games themselves during Jordan's new tour were incidental, if not irrelevant). On the court of the Omni arena, as part of a radio-station promotion well before game time, a group of young local neighborhood hotshots were playing.

On the P.A. system, a high-energy announcer, apparently from the station, was making jokingly in-your-face comments to the teams as they played their game. "You foul him, we turn your car over in the lot after." "We fight you after." Across the way, a boy wore an Orlando Magic licensed jersey with Anfernee Hardaway's name and number on it. The basketball world had gone right along its way during Jordan's absence, with changes in stars, changes in tone. The assumption had been that he would never be back. Now, to these fellows playing on the Hawks' court—the "We-turn-your-car-over-in-the-lot-after" fellows—it wouldn't be enough for Jordan to stroll back in and presume to be the legend. It wouldn't be enough for him to be better than they were, or better than most NBA players, or even the best in the world. He'd better show them that he was the best who ever lived, still and again, or the jerseys they'd buy and wear would bear the name of someone else. Those were the rules. He had helped make the rules.

Not that the hotshots on the court even saw Jordan. Once the Bulls were inside the Omni and in their locker room, the floor was cleared and some of Jordan's teammates went out to warm up. He did not.

I asked him why he chose not to. He had been shooting poorly; in the Orlando game especially, he had looked worse than rusty. Why not shoot around before the game?

"I never warm up," he said. "You know that."

That wasn't quite true; in his first NBA career, there were some occasions when he would take practice shots with the team. Generally, though, he did one of two things. Either he would arrive at an arena hours before anyone else, and shoot all by himself, or he would wait until the team came out just before the game, and go through the perfunctory drills for a few minutes then. This, though the custom ary NBA players' routine of arriving at the gym, then going immediately onto the court for some serious work—was something he generally skipped.

"I know this arena," he said. "It's not like I have to find out what it feels like."

Even after not having been here for so long? Even after all the troubles he'd been having getting back his shooter's touch? If he wanted to show the world that he was as good as ever, would it make no sense at all to shoot for fifteen or twenty minutes before the opening tip?

"I don't want to magnify my shooting troubles," he said. "Maybe that's what would happen if I went out there before the game. I'd be thinking so much about the mistakes I've been making that I'd overdo it in trying to correct them. A lot of that can be in your head—it has nothing to do with your real shooting touch, it's just in your mind.

"So I don't want to put any more emphasis on it than I have to. Why go out and make it worse? You know what would happen—every other player warming up on the floor, every person coming into the arena, would be looking at me and passing judgment on every shot. Is he making them? Is he missing them? Is he getting better? Is he bad? I don't like going through that."

But doesn't that end up putting added pressure on him—playing a game, after all this time away, without doing any real warm-ups? Whatever judgments are being made about his game, aren't those judgments destined to be even more acute when the clock is turned on?

"Different thing," he said. "In games, I can concentrate. In games, I can really think about making the shots. Everything counts. It has meaning. That's how I do it. It'll come back. It will."

John Paxson, Jordan's backcourt partner during the championship years, had retired from the Bulls and was now in his first season as one of the team's radio broadcasters. He had been the perfect complement to Jordan—the selfless point guard always looking to get the ball to shooting guard Jordan. Bringing the ball up the court together night after night, season after season, in the packed NBA arenas spread across America, Paxson and Jordan had worked together more closely than had any other duo on the team. They had been like an old married couple, each aware of the other's strengths, weaknesses and idiosyncrasies.

I saw Paxson at the Omni, and asked him what his initial impressions of Jordan's return were.

"All I know is that he must really love to play this game," Paxson said, shaking his head. "Because these last two weeks . . ."

He didn't have to explain. For years he had seen the furor around Jordan from the closest vantage point; now that it had kicked into this overdrive, onto this almost religious level, with people camping out to catch a glimpse of him, people begging for tickets, people screaming at the mere promise that he might be on his way, Paxson was surprised that Jordan would willingly choose to put himself through this.

"I don't want to use the word 'grotesque,' " Paxson said. "But that's what it is, if you want to know the truth. There's something really grotesque about this whole thing."

"Have you told him that?" I said.

"He knows," Paxson said. "He says he's embarrassed by all of this, but that's what he's always said. I don't think even he had any idea it was going to get as out of hand as it has. That's what I mean about how much he must love playing basketball. Because, for him, this is what comes with it."

"Damn," Jordan said.

On his lap, in the Omni visitors' locker room, was a personal computer. The screen was up, and he was staring at it, his hands on the keyboard. He was not writing a story, he was not balancing a bank account, he was not going over his records.

"There," he said.

On the screen were images of playing cards. This was another card game in which he could play against himself—without the need for actual cards. He fooled with the controls on the keyboard, moving the electronic cards around, arranging them on the screen, trying to gain an advantage.

Jimmy Rodgers, an assistant coach who had come to the Bulls during the time Jordan had been gone, was in the locker room, as were Ron Harper and Toni Kukoc and Corie Blount and Larry Krystkowiak, all of them, too, having become Bulls since the Jordan championship years. They were sneaking looks at him. He looked only at the screen.

Ailene Voisin, basketball writer for the Atlanta *Constitution*, came into the room to chat with Jordan. He interrupted his computer game for a moment as she asked him something about Larry Bird.

"Bird was kidding my ass about my coming back to basketball when I played golf with him," Jordan said. "I said, 'Larry, you gained around forty pounds.' He said, 'I'm going to lose about five.' I said to him, 'Five? Five pounds? Somehow that doesn't sound right.' "

"He probably had a beer that day, right?" Voisin said.

"He had more than one," Jordan said.

He looked at his computer screen. "I'm about to lose my game," he said. "Quick, where's the plug? I thought they had a plug here."

His battery was dying. He found an electrical outlet and plugged the computer into it. Someone asked him whether he missed spring training.

"A little bit," he said. "I miss the sunshine. That's about it."

Someone who had just been in Florida said that some of the baseball writers were still checking out his White Sox locker every day, on the chance that he might change his mind and come back.

"Tell them to keep waiting," he said. "I may be back."

B.J. Armstrong, overhearing this from across the room, shot a quizzical look in Jordan's direction. This, at least, was the basketball Jordan of old—holding court at his locker before going out to do his night's work.

Someone asked him if he had been watching his alma mater, the University of North Carolina, in the NCAA tournament.

"I'm too nervous to watch 'em," he said, watching his computer screen.

Ailene Voisin turned to leave, to go to the Hawks' locker room, and she said so long to Jordan. He knew that her job was to analyze the NBA and its players; he knew, too, that she and her colleagues on the NBA beat had all been talking about the unsteadiness of his new beginning.

"Don't give up on me yet," he said to her.

Will Perdue, silent in the corner of the room, said that he wasn't unduly inconvenienced by the commotion around the team since Jordan's return. "It's not bad," he said. "Some of us have been through it."

Some of them had—but not many. There were only a few men remaining who had played with Jordan during the championship years. Perdue, Pippen, Armstrong—that was it now. All during this season, they had been able to check into hotels without facing excited crowds in the lobbies, had been able to get on the team bus and leave arenas without driving through hollering mobs. They might not have forgotten what that had been like—but they had become accustomed to doing without it.

"He came back and—boom! Just like that," Perdue said. "Everything changed, in one day. Boom!"

"Damn!" Jordan said, across the way, unhappy with the cards his computer had dealt him.

B.J. Armstrong came into the locker room again from the court, where he had been practicing his shooting before the game. He stopped to talk, and I asked him, "How much of the last two weeks has been fun?"

He smiled. "You want a percentage?" he said.

"Just an approximation," I said. "What percentage of the time since he's been back has been fun for you?"

"About half," he said.

"Is that right?" I said. "Fifty percent? I would have guessed lower."

"Not fifty percent," he said. "Half. Half of a percent." With him, it was always hard to read behind that smile.

. . . . .

Jimmy Rodgers stood by the locker-room chalkboard, where a screen roll play had been diagrammed for the Bulls to study.

"Fuck," Jordan said, perturbed by what the computer had told him about his card game.

Toni Kukoc asked him whether he used the computer for anything other than playing cards.

"Yes," Jordan said, overly solicitous, a kid caught reading a dirty magazine hidden inside his algebra textbook. "I do other work on it. But not right now."

On a television set near his locker, the local late-afternoon news was on. Tyrone Corbin, a player on the Atlanta Hawks, was telling a sportscaster that he and the team were looking forward to playing the Bulls tonight. The Hawks had been drawing disappointingly small crowds all season, and this would give them the chance to show their talents before a full house.

"I think we'll do well in front of a sellout crowd," Corbin said, not having to mention that the reason for the sellout would be a player on the opposing team. Jordan glanced at the television screen; not interested, he looked away again.

Someone asked him how he knew if he had won in this card game.

"The cards reshuffle," he said, staring at the computer.

The outlet he had plugged the machine into was a white metal bar that could be moved from place to place; the bar itself was plugged into a wall outlet via a long cord. Some of the other Bulls players and coaches were tripping over that cord.

"You want to put that thing down on the floor?" Jordan said to an Atlanta ballboy, who had been assigned to the Bulls' locker room.

The ballboy, hardly able to believe that Jordan was speaking to him, took the electrical bar from where it had been resting on a table, and placed it near Jordan's feet, where the cord would no longer be a nuisance.

"Good job, pardner," Jordan said to the ballboy, whose flushed and happy expression indicated he was processing those three words, storing them in his memory.

One of the Bulls' staff members put a cassette into the VCR hooked up to the television set. The tape was of a game earlier in the season when the Bulls had played against the Hawks—a game in which Jordan had not been on the team.

The voice of Johnny "Red" Kerr, the longtime Bulls television announcer, could be heard yelling: "Wennington goes up . . ." Bulls center Bill Wennington was fouled on the play; on the screen he went to the free-throw line. Wayne Larrivee, Kerr's announcing partner, could be heard: "He hits the first one . . . gets a second . . ."

Bill Wennington himself walked into the locker room, saw the Bill Wennington on the screen aiming a free throw. Wayne Larrivee's voice: "Luc Longley with the rebound . . ." Longley, in the locker room, turned toward the sound of his name, as if someone had called him.

They are used to this, the men who play professional sports at the highest levels—used to living both in the real world and on the television screens of strangers, living on highlights tapes that might pop back into their lives with no advance notice. "Armstrong on the drive, past Mookie Blaylock," Wayne Larrivee called out from a night now past, and on the screen the video B.J. Armstrong was taking the ball past Blaylock, in the locker room the living B.J. Armstrong was talking quietly with Scottie Pippen over in the far corner. Pippen, with his usual glum expression, wearing a black Bulls T-shirt and scholar's glasses, listened to Armstrong, who was already in his red game uniform; Pippen offered nothing back.

The two of them had reverted automatically to their wallflowers' roles in the locker room now that Jordan was among them again. During the almost two years he was gone, they had emerged as spokesmen for the team, finally, in Jordan's absence, learning what the full attention of the sportswriters and broadcasters felt like. Now, they understood, it was going to be the way it was before: a junior-high school dance at which all the boys wanted to dance with the same girl—and they weren't that girl. That's an analogy Phil Jackson had once used, and as out-of-place as it might have seemed in an NBA locker room, it was right on target. Everyone wants to dance with the prettiest girl, Jackson had said; it may not be fair, but it's the way of the world.

Jordan took a break from his digital card game. He asked me about some of the minor-leaguers and replacement players he had gotten to know at spring training; he wanted to hear how they had been doing after he left, which of them were making the best impressions on the White Sox coaching staff.

I told him that his friend Kerry Valrie appeared to be in special favor; everyone on the Sox staff seemed to think Valrie would make it to the majors one day. I asked Jordan if, before he left camp, he thought his own progress had been sufficient to be evaluated like that. The consensus among the baseball writers in Sarasota was that Jordan had improved remarkably from the year before; did Jordan, now that it was over, assess himself as being good?

"Good, yes," he said. "Good enough?"

He let it trail off.

"I don't know," he said. "I suppose I'll never know."

The facilities at the Omni were not particularly luxurious for the visiting teams; at most NBA arenas the players at least got to shower in the same suite of rooms in which they dressed, but at the Omni the Bulls had to walk out of their locker room and down a hallway to a separate shower room; it was not uncommon for sportswriters and arena workers to encounter the basketball players, soaking wet, walking among them, trying to find the right door back to their clothing.

"I bet you thought you'd done that for the last time," I said.

"I thought I'd done a lot of things for the last time," Jordan said.

Phil Jackson rewound the old Atlanta videotape. "Gentlemen?" he said to the room at large.

Jordan was back to his computer card game; Kukoc was looking over Jordan's left shoulder at the cards on the screen, Armstrong was looking over Jordan's right shoulder. The cards moved, shuffling themselves; Jordan had won a hand.

"If I'm not interrupting," Jackson said.

"That's OK, Phil," Jordan said. The two gave each other looks: wise-guy star student and the teacher who puts up with him.

Jackson hit the "play" button on the television monitor, and started to address his twelve players. "Scottie," Jackson said, speaking to the real Pippen in the room but motioning to the small video Pippen on the television screen. "*Penetrate* against this team. Up the lane." The Pippen in the room watched the show; from the blank expression on his face he might have been watching Al Gore or Mary Tyler Moore instead of himself. Armstrong was sitting on the floor of the locker room, like the youngest son watching TV after dinner with the family; on the screen he was dribbling, and Jackson said, "*Drive*," making a thrusting gesture over the head of the human Armstrong, pointing at the video Armstrong. Last night's loss to Orlando might as well have taken place in some previous century; within the hour it would be time for these men to make a new television show. They do this every working night.

I left the locker room and headed for the court. In the tunnel leading to the floor, I walked past several of the Hawks—Craig Ehlo, Greg Anderson, Andrew Lang—who stood in their white satin warmup pants and jackets, waiting to go to work, smiling and joking with each other, knowing: Here it comes again. A night with Jordan in town, the kind of night they thought they were through with, a night when their hometown fans would cheer wildly for the opposing team. Like the Washington Generals getting ready to go up against the Harlem Globetrotters, the Hawks knew that few eyes in the arena would be focused on them.

When the game started, the floor seemed so small—the ten starting players filled it up, crowded it, it could have been twice as big and it still wouldn't have felt too large. This was nothing new—just one essential difference between basketball and baseball, the one sport with its confined area and its huge athletes fighting for elbow room, the other with its expanses of grass, each fielder surrounded by empty spaces. If Jordan had left the tight and cloistered world of basketball floors to give himself the roaming room of baseball outfields, he was back for certain now, jostled by Hawks on either side of him, faced with the constant flashes of cameras from the close-in seats each time he turned, hearing the unremitting noise bouncing off the walls, bouncing off the ceiling.

And he seemed . . . home. He seemed like a man in his living room at the end of the day, utterly carefree, utterly at ease. The shots weren't all going in at first, but he was loose, his face was expressive, he jabbered at his opponents and smiled at their responses—he looked like a man who was exactly where he was supposed to be. All of the other stuff—the travel, the hotel rooms, the killing of time in the locker room—was incidental; this—these forty-eight minutes of scoreboard-clock play that stretched over two hours and more on a real-world clock—this was why he was here. Down press row I could see John Paxson, for the first year in so many years dressed in a light green business suit instead of the shorts and sleeveless jersey of the Bulls; Paxson had his radio-station headset clamped over his ears, he talked into his microphone to describe the action, and when Scottie Pippen stopped at the scorer's table to check back into the game he paused by Paxson's position, grinned at Paxson, said something to him.

But then Pippen was on the court, and Paxson, who used to trot out there with him, remained behind the table, and I watched Pippen join Jordan, saw them whisper something to each other before the ball was brought inbounds, and I looked over and Paxson was watching them, too, watching them so closely. In the locker room before the game, when Ailene Voisin had been joking with Jordan about Larry Bird, Jordan had said something about Bird, without being asked, seemingly out of nowhere. What Jordan had said about Bird was: "He'd play again in a minute if he could."

The ball was put in play, and Jordan, thirty-two now, his face tonight showing the eagerness of a child, moved into position to accept a pass. *He'd play again in a minute if he could.* The noise in the arena was one raucous and overwhelming voice, so when I looked again at Paxson, observing the game from a distance, talking into the microphone, I could not even begin to guess at his words, I heard only the noise.

For much of the game, Jordan's separateness on the court—the separateness that had always been there—was exaggerated by the response of the crowd to him. For years his skills, and his reputation, had caused the customers to look at him in a different way than they looked at the other nine men on the floor; now—with the circumstances of his leaving the NBA and then returning, with the troubles he was having getting back to the level he, and they, were accustomed to—there was separateness upon separateness, he was almost alien, at least two steps removed from every other person on the court. Midway through the third quarter he had nineteen points, but he had been shooting quite a lot to get those points, and the looks he was receiving from the fans said: What is he doing here? Why is he taking all those shots? If he's missing his own shots, what's he bawling out Will Perdue for?

With four-tenths of a second remaining in the third quarter, and the clock stopped, Steve Kerr, on the bench, glanced over at Phil Jackson. The two made eye contact; Kerr actually called to his coach—"Phil!" he screamed, to be heard above the noise—and Jackson sent him in. Kerr was an expert ball handler, ideal for situations like this, situations with little time on the clock; he stood up, ripped his red warmup pants off, stood by the side of the court with the ball in his hands.

He looked for Jordan. He saw him all the way at the other end of the floor, and heaved the ball. Jordan reached for it—the clock began as soon as Jordan's hand touched the ball—caught it, wheeled and shot, missing. But as the horn went off to end the quarter, Jordan signaled his congratulations to Kerr. Missing the shot didn't concern him—he knew the time would come when he wouldn't miss. The fact that Kerr, a man with whom he had never played as a teammate until two weeks ago, could find him and get him the ball with so little time remaining—that was important for Jordan to know, that was something new he could count on. That, for him, evidently had made the play a success.

The game remained close; with time running out in the fourth quarter both teams had a chance to win it. Jordan took the ball and tried to launch a shot to assure the Bulls the victory; Steve Smith of the Hawks blocked the shot, his teammate Mookie Blaylock took it to the other end for a layup, and by the time the clock had ticked down to 5.9 seconds Atlanta was ahead 98–97.

With the clock stopped at 5.9, the Bulls had the ball out of bounds. Jordan, with Smith assigned to guard him, stood all the way up the court from the basket the Bulls would have to get to, waiting for the ball to be thrown in from the sidelines. He and Smith were talking to each other, Smith still feeling triumphant about having blocked Jordan's earlier shot. Later, Jordan would say that as the two men waited for the ball to be tossed in, Smith "asked me who was going to take the shot. I told him, 'Pippen.' "

But the play had been called for Jordan. He caught the ball, the clock began to race down toward zero, and with Smith on top of him he dribbled the entire length of the court. Fourteen feet from the basket, with Smith running backwards and trying to stay between him and the basket, Jordan stopped, threw a move on Smith, went into the air and, slightly off-balance, with the clock all but emptied out, put the basketball into the net.

During those 5.9 seconds, it was as if time had frozen in the arena. It was that singular feeling Jordan had brought into so many buildings so many times—the feeling, even as it was taking place, of "Is this happening?" It was as if the world were moving at full speed and in slow motion all at once, as if this were unfolding present-tense, in front of your eyes, and yet was also some basketball film you've never seen before but you know you've seen somewhere. Down the row Red Kerr was shouting into his microphone, and I knew that up in Chicago, right at this instant, people were on their feet and screaming in the night, watching their television sets and howling right along with Red, and meanwhile Jordan was still down at the far end of the court, the ball had dropped through the net and onto the floor, 99–98 Bulls, game over, and Jordan began to run back toward the Bulls' bench, then realized there was no reason to do that; he stopped at mid-court, knelt toward the floor, made a little rolling-the-dice motion at the wood, talked to it, as if telling the floor something, and then turned in the other direction, toward the tunnel, and ran full-speed right through it.

Don't give up on me yet, he had said to Ailene Voisin tonight, before leaving the same locker room to which he was now returning. *I thought I'd done a lot of things for the last time*, he had said, talking about the lousy showers in the building and—99–98 on the scoreboard, game won at the buzzer by Jordan—about other aspects of the basketball life, too.

"It says something about us as a society," Phil Jackson mused. This was fifteen minutes after the game had ended, in a press-conference area of the Omni. Jackson was theorizing aloud about what the Jordan phenomenon signified; for most of the season, after the games were over, he had merely been called upon to analyze shots gone awry and free throws missed, but since Jordan's return he felt compelled to discuss what he found himself in the midst of. He wasn't talking about the national homicide rate, or the growth in homelessness—this thing that said something about American society wasn't a thing at all, but a human being currently putting his business suit back on over in the locker room.

Why did Jackson let Jordan play so many minutes tonight, after vowing to bring him back onto the team slowly? "He said, 'I'm finally having fun,'" Jackson said. "'Why don't you let me go a little longer?'"

Did Jordan seem to be in good shape? "I think his legs might have gone on him a little bit," Jackson said. "I didn't see him in that lather I like to see him in."

Did Jackson think Jordan was really back to what he had been? "He's on his way back. When he gets all the way back, we'll know it."

Jackson, addressing the gathered sportswriters, referred to Jordan's "original career," as if this tonight were a movie sequel, and off to the side of the curtain in the press-conference area Jordan appeared, watching, listening, as if the movie were about someone else. Jackson gave up his seat behind the table; Jordan sat in the chair his coach had just left.

This session was all for public consumption, he had learned to do it effortlessly years ago—little snippets for the late-evening newscasts. "I was able to finish the ballgame better than I have been finishing." . . . "It's always nice to be respected the way the fans respected me here." A sportswriter asked if he had known the final shot was good as soon as the ball left his hand: "I knew it had a chance," Jordan said, providing an audio track for sportscasts all over the nation to lay under the video of the winning shot going into the net.

This, the way it was going tonight, was the way he remembered it: winning the game, then coming out to be praised. No questions tonight about strikeouts or hitless streaks; no questions—not on this night—about why his basketball skills seemed diminished. By the time he and the Bulls were on the plane out of Atlanta, viewers not only here in town, but nationwide and worldwide, thanks to ESPN and CNN, would be watching what he did in those 5.9 seconds, hearing his voice talk about it. "I've been wanting to be successful, to be productive. . . . I was glad to do something tonight to help the team. . . ."

One thing he said at the post-game press conference, almost as a throwaway line, stuck in my mind because it seemed so odd.

"Never chase things," he said. "Let things happen."

I was thinking about it the next morning. I was at Atlanta's Hartsfield International Airport to get on my flight out of town, and as I walked down the long concourse the television sets hanging from the ceiling were all tuned to the same channel. Jordan's shot from the night before came on the screen—all up and down the airport, you could see him driving on Steve Smith, pulling up, aiming while at that unwieldy angle above the floor, then putting the ball in the hoop.

The marketing and distribution is so efficient, so routinized—yesterday at this time Jordan was still asleep at the Ritz-Carlton, twenty-four hours later he was back in Chicago—that now his calling card, the calling card he had fashioned in the time in between—the shot—was lighting up every airport boarding area.

Skip Ellison was walking with me. The director on WGN's telecast of the game, he had selected the camera angles that captured Jordan making the shot—it was Ellison's handiwork that was being used by all those stations around the world, it was his television picture of the shot that everyone in the Atlanta airport, Ellison included, was seeing on all the screens this morning.

"Does that make you feel weird?" I said to Ellison.

"It's Michael," he said with a shrug, meaning: Nothing is weird with Jordan. He affects everything around him.

"Never chase things," Jordan had said. That, from the man who could not, in fact, stop running, who could not even begin to give up the chase. "Let things happen." That, from the man who could never allow himself to leave well enough alone. Who had to be in charge of everything that happened, and then still had to see what else might be out there for him. On the airport monitor he hit the shot, Red Kerr's voice rejoicing in the background.

CHAPTER 14

"Check your mini-bar, sir?"

The hotel housekeeper was at the door of the room on the eighteenth floor of the Sheraton Meadowlands in East Rutherford, New Jersey. This was Jordan's room—actually a pair of rooms with connecting doors.

He was in the bedroom, where he'd slept. We had been talking in the room he was using as a living room, and the telephone had rung in the bedroom, and he'd gone in to answer. He had been lying on his bed, talking on the phone, when there had been a knock at the door of the living room.

I had walked from the living room into the bedroom and motioned out toward the door where someone was knocking. I had signaled to Jordan—did he want me to answer it or ignore it? The person kept knocking.

Jordan, still on the phone, still lying on the bed in a pair of gym shorts and a T-shirt, shrugged. The knocking continued. He nodded: Go ahead and open it if you want.

I had walked out of the bedroom, back to the other room, and opened the door. It was the housekeeper, in a hotel uniform: "Check your mini-bar, sir?"

She thought the room was mine. The mini-bar was right inside the doorway. "Sure," I said. "Go ahead."

She came into the room, opened the mini-bar with her key,

checked off what had been used since the day before and what needed to be restocked. Then she said: "Would you like me to check the one in your bedroom?"

I started to say no, then stopped myself. Why not? It would give her something she might want to talk about at the dinner table when she got home tonight.

"Of course," I said. "Go on in."

She walked into what she thought would be the empty bedroom. The next thing I heard was her voice—considerably more muted and constricted than it had been a minute before.

"Check . . . your mini-bar, sir?" I heard her say.

"Be my guest," I heard Jordan's voice say. "Go right ahead."

A minute or so later she came out. The numbness of her reaction—it wasn't that she was trembling, she simply was sort of sleep-walking, her face blank, as if she had just seen a ghost—was the stuff of another little Michael Jordan moment. She stood outside the door to the bedroom, looked back in, shook her head as if trying to wake up—then looked at me, shook her head again, and departed.

Coming into New Jersey to play the Nets, the Bulls had won five games and lost only two since Jordan's return. Any doubts anyone might have had about his potential to reclaim his standing as the best player in basketball had been effectively removed three days after he hit the winning shot in Atlanta, when the Bulls traveled to New York to play the Knicks in Madison Square Garden. Jordan's performance that night—55 points, 21-for-37 shooting from the field, 10-of-11 free throws, all of this in only 38 minutes on the court—could not have taken place in a better setting for him (the New York and national media were on hand in force), and could not have come at a better time (the game was nationally telecast, to an audience that had been reading the stories about Jordan's struggles, had been seeing the TV coverage of his missed shots and missteps). Since that night he had scored 23 points in a win over the Boston Celtics, then only 12 points on 5-for-19 shooting against the Philadelphia 76ers. But the evening in New York had defined the possibilities inherent in his comeback; now the world was clamoring to watch every shot he took, and tickets to Bulls games, always extremely difficult to get, were just about impossible to buy at any price. No one wanted to miss the next night when Jordan might explode.

"Isn't this where we came in?" Paul Sullivan said.

Before going to New Jersey for the game against the Nets, I had made a trip back down to Florida; Sullivan, who was still covering the minor-leaguers and replacement players at White Sox spring training camp for the *Chicago Tribune*, had told me that he and Dan Bickley of the *Chicago Sun-Times* were going to meet at a downtown Sarasota bar called the Sports Page. The Bulls were playing that evening in a game that was not on national TV, and the bar had a satellite dish that allegedly could pick up the local SportsChannel telecast from Chicago.

Sullivan and I used to sit next to each other at the press table in the old Chicago Stadium, watching Jordan during those three world-championship runs; we had watched him all during this spring training baseball season, and now, our elbows on the bar, we watched the proprietor reach up and try to find the right transponder number, the right coordinates, to pull the pictures of Jordan out of the night sky, lure them from the proper satellite circling the Earth and draw them down into this small tavern on the west coast of Florida.

The color pictures flickered onto the screen—the tavern proprietor was conversant in the newly mundane space technology, he had found the satellite, and there was Red Kerr doing his pre-game show, there were Jordan and Pippen and Armstrong on the court behind him, limbering up before the introductions of the starting lineups. More patrons began arriving through the front door. The word had gotten out that this was one of the few places in town to see Jordan tonight.

There were men in jerseys with the number 45 on them; women in T-shirts with the same number, Jordan's face, and the "I'm Back" slogan; other men with just-issued Jordan baseball-style caps, bearing basketball themes and his new number. It had been only a few weeks since Jordan had sat in that quiet White Sox clubhouse every day, with little agitation around him, nothing but time on his hands, time and the warm spring, talking about nothing and everything with Sullivan and Bickley and a few other beat reporters to while the hours away. If it was a calm center that Jordan had been looking for, he had seemed to find it, or something close to it, here. A baseball player among other baseball players, finally being permitted some peace.

Tonight his electronic image from the jammed arena up north was pulled into the Sarasota tavern from the satellite, and the customers in the mint-condition Jordan apparel continued to arrive, the live video pictures of him being delivered instantly from space, the clothing having taken a few days to go from marketing concept to manufacture to the backs and arms and heads of the people in the bar, but still, in the scheme of things, getting here remarkably quickly. Some people at a table whooped and barked approvingly at the sight of Jordan being introduced on the barroom screen, and there were times when all of this seemed as if it couldn't be real.

"Maybe he was lying to us," Sullivan said.

"About what?" Bickley said.

"All that stuff about how happy he was not to be bothered," Sullivan said. "About how much he liked being able to sit around without people swarming over him all the time. Maybe he never meant it."

The bartender adjusted the volume.

"He did palm your head," I said.

"He palmed my head," Sullivan said.

The basketball went into the air and B.J. Armstrong grabbed it and fired it over to Jordan, in an arena up north, in a tavern in Florida, in the blackness of the night sky above us all.

Now I was in New Jersey. Jordan, before I even saw him, seemed to be everywhere. In the airport before boarding my flight to Newark, I heard a customer at a newsstand begin a conversation with the woman working behind the counter. "I don't worship him," the man said. "But he does carry himself very well." He didn't identify the person he was talking about; I glanced over and saw that the man was looking at a stack of "Welcome Back, Michael" commemorative magazines that were stacked on the counter.

The cabdriver who took me from Newark Airport into Manhattan, where I was meeting someone for dinner, noted that traffic was heavy. "But it could be worse," he said. "The night last week that Michael Jordan was in town to play the Knicks, you should have seen the traffic jam around the Garden. It was like a World Series. Nothing was moving—people were paying six hundred dollars, seven hundred dollars, just for a ticket to see him." I asked him if he thought that was too much money for such a thing. "Not really," he said. "If I had it, I'd spend it to see Jordan play."

When I got to the restaurant, I went to the bar area to meet the person I was supposed to have dinner with. At the next stools two men in suits were talking; one of them said, "I heard he hit three from half-court. It was before the game started, but even so . . ." They were still talking about Jordan's night at Madison Square Garden the week before.

At the Sheraton Meadowlands, five or six security men were posted in the lobby when I arrived to check in. The Bulls' charter had been delayed into Newark and the team bus was running late; the lobby was filling with people who wanted to catch a glimpse. There was a bar that was part of the lobby, and from a conference room on the next level up the sounds of old rock hits—"Runaround Sue," "Hey, Jude"—mixed cacophonously with Frank Sinatra's "My Way" coming out of an unseen amplifier down below. Some bellmen had requested to stay on past their usual going-home time, to carry the Bulls' luggage to their rooms. By the time the bus bearing the team pulled up to the front of the hotel, the crowd just inside the doors looked like an endless reception line at the biggest wedding of the New Jersey spring.

Phil Jackson came in first, then trainer Chip Schaefer, then—few in the lobby seemed to have any idea who these players were—Pete Myers, Corie Blount, Dickey Simpkins. Jordan followed them, wearing a black leather beret, and as he always did in hotel lobbies he walked neither too quickly nor too slowly, having learned over the years that if he could surprise the strangers who were waiting—if he could come in like any other player on the team and be gone before it fully registered on them that he was here—then it could be done.

On a table to the right of the front door, the room keys for the Bulls had been laid out in envelopes so that no one would have to stop at the front desk. Jordan, behind Simpkins, walked three long strides from the door to the table, swooped his envelope into his hand and then into his pocket without stopping. By now—he was almost to the bank of elevators—the people who had been waiting had begun to buzz, it had struck them belatedly that this was it, and all their whispers sounded like an overworked vacuum cleaner. Jordan looked over at them and made his version of the same sound they were making—"Psssst," he said to them, playful—and in five more steps he was on the elevator and the door was closed.

Thirty minutes later the people in the lobby were still there. "Mr. Jordan has left the hotel to go out to dinner," a security guard told them. "There's nothing to see here."

"He can't have gone," a woman said. "We've been standing here the whole time."

"They took him out through the kitchen," the security man said. "Mr. Jordan is not here."

Brendan Byrne Arena, across the highway from the hotel, sat ready for Jordan to fill it. I met him on the morning of the game on the seventeenth floor of the hotel, where he had been attending a meeting. He was staying on the floor above—rooms 1826 and 1827—and he said he'd rather walk up through the fire stairs than deal with the elevator. Just another part of his life—the simple act of getting on a public elevator carrying hotel guests and business conventioneers in the middle of the day was something he knew he would be wise to avoid if he could.

So here was a man who could afford just about any luxury, walking up the grungy and dim cement staircase. We stepped out in front of his door, he opened it, walked in past the cart holding the remains of his room-service breakfast. The room wasn't as oppressively warm as he usually liked to keep his rooms—he had always thought that if a room was as hot as he could make it, he might be able to stave off the colds that he constantly caught during NBA seasons. "No winter cold yet," he said. "But I missed the real winter."

He sat on a couch with his back to the window. Behind him, across the Hudson River, was the skyline of Manhattan. It was breathtaking and looked somehow even more spread-out and expansive than usual on this bright April day; it was the kind of view of New York they used to open movies with in the 1940s, New York as a symbol for everything colossal and intimidating and beyond reach— New York as the top.

Because Jordan was close and New York was way across the river, the perspective was skewed—he, sitting in his room, was bigger than the skyscrapers in the distance. They stretched out to his right, to his left, but from here they appeared to be merely backdrop. There probably wasn't a person over there who didn't know who he was—not a person in any of those buildings who had never heard his name, never seen his face. He wasn't seeing any of this; he was looking the other way.

"Is that one the Empire State Building?" I asked.

Jordan turned around, looked out at New York.

"I don't know," he said. "Is it that one? Or is it the other one? I'm not really sure what it looks like."

"Is it the tallest one?" I said.

"Still?" he said, looking.

"That's selfish of them, not selfish of me," he said.

We were talking about a comment that had been made on an ESPN broadcast before he left baseball. The sports commentator had said that Jordan's insistence on trying out for the White Sox for the second year in a row was an act of selfishness—that to satisfy his own whims, Jordan was depriving all the people who loved to watch him play basketball.

In August 1993, James Jordan was murdered. Family members and close friends gathered to join Michael and his mother for the funeral.

Two months after his father's death, Jordan announced his retirement from the NBA. When next he came to a Bulls game, it was with his family, as a spectator. As the new United Center opened across the street from the old Chicago Stadium, he and his children, Marcus, Jeffrey, and Jasmine, raised his number 23 to the rafters.

OPPOSITE: August 1994; Michael Jordan, number 45, now playing for the Birmingham Barons.

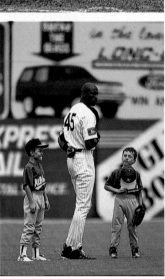

Jordan played 127 games for the Barons and was the biggest draw in the Southern League—while batting .202. As summer turned to autumn, he joined the Scottsdale Scorpions of the Arizona Fall League. The Chicago White Sox invited him to spring training for the second year in a row. This time, he left camp—and the game of baseball.

On March 18, 1995, Jordan announced that he was returning to the Chicago Bulls and the NBA.

In the last basketball game ever played at the old Chicago Stadium— a September 9, 1994, charity contest organized by Scottie Pippen— Jordan showed up and scored 52 points (LEFT).

Jordan arrived with his sons at the United Center, the Bulls' new arena.

When Jordan stepped onto the court again, he was wearing his baseball number—45. His first game, on the road against the Indiana Pacers, received worldwide television and press coverage. In the regular season he found himself facing Shaquille O'Neal and the Orlando Magic, and competing against his old adversaries the Detroit Pistons.

▲ BILL SMITH

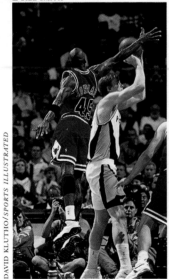

JONATHAN DANIEL/ALLSPORT

In the playoffs, Jordan and the Bulls met the Magic again—and he switched back to his old number as he faced a former teammate from the championship years, Horace Grant.

JOHN BIEVER/SPORTS ILLUSTRATED

NEXT PAGE:
A statue, a man; the many faces of Michael Jordan over the years.

MICHAEL JORDAN

CHICAGO BULLS

1984 – 1993

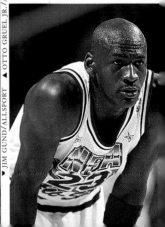

"I can't understand that kind of thinking," Jordan said. "That I can be called selfish because I want to do something with my life—but that the people who would have me do something else, because they think it provides them pleasure, aren't selfish. Is that what they're saying—that if they want me to do something to please them, and I don't do it, then I'm the one who's being selfish?"

"Well, it turned out you did what they wanted," I said.

"What, came back to basketball?" he said.

"That's what they asked for," I said.

"That's not the point," he said. "I just don't like being told I'm selfish because I do something that I think might be good for me. I didn't come back to basketball to make anyone else happy. I did it because I wanted to do it. And if I ever went back to baseball, or did something completely different with my life, I would do that because I thought it was good for me. How many people get called selfish for making decisions about their own lives? It's crazy."

"I suppose not many people are in that position," I said. "To have people they've never met resent it when they decide to do one thing instead of another."

"I think I've done a lot of things during my life to please other people," he said. "It just bothers me a little that when I make what I think is an important decision that seems right for me, some people get angry because I'm not pleasing them."

"Like I say—it's not something the rest of us have to spend much time worrying about," I said. "Whether we're pleasing strangers."

"You watch," Jordan said. "Someone will make a statement saying how selfish I am for playing basketball."

"I'm surprised you even think about comments like that," I said. "There are probably millions of people saying one thing or another about you every day."

"You can't shut out everything," he said.

When he had left Sarasota, he said, he hadn't made up his mind what he was going to do. The reaction during his first week away from baseball—when everyone was guessing whether he would return to the NBA—scared him, and almost made him decide that basketball was no longer an option for him.

"The following of my family and me was the thing that gave me a lot of concern," he said. "I was aware—I am aware—that people are interested in what I do. But I've never been followed around day after day like that, and the one thing I've always tried to do is to protect my family from that kind of thing. People began to follow my wife to the beauty parlor, and to follow her and my kids around, and I know that Juanita was becoming a nervous wreck over it. Not just her—me, too. I'm used to public attention, but there was something about that that made me feel it was dangerous."

It wasn't just the press, I said. There had seemed to be the same kind of tumult on the part of regular citizens.

"That's what I mean," Jordan said. "As public as I was before, this was different. People assume that I always have guards around me, but I don't—I'm not a guy who has the Secret Service with him, obviously. At the basketball arenas I have the guys who get me in and out of there, and at public appearances there's always security, but in my regular life it's usually just me. And that week when everyone was talking about whether I was coming back or not, it seemed that things were getting out of control. Going over the edge."

I told him I'd been down in Florida when I saw one particular piece of news coverage. Apparently he had gone into an office in downtown Chicago one day to take care of some business.

"Right off Michigan Avenue," he said. "Right."

I had seen the footage of him coming out of the building. It was nighttime, and he was descended upon by people, and for one of the few times I could remember he looked frightened. He was usually careful to wear the trademark smile any time he knew a camera was trained on him—it was as if he had made a decision to always appear confident and upbeat on camera no matter how he might really be feeling. That night, though, at least on tape, he looked close to panicked.

"I was just so surprised, it caught me off guard," he said. "I had gone into the building at around four o'clock in the afternoon. There was a big group of people on the sidewalk, but I got through them and went up to the office. I was there for a very long time—I came out around eleven-thirty at night. No announcement that I was coming, or anything like that.

"And they were still there. Some of the same people, and new people, and I just hadn't thought they'd be there. I had trouble getting to the car, and . . . yeah, I was scared.

"You know why? I just was getting a feeling that week like I was being put in the position of having to take care of all these people. Like I was somehow responsible for them—like whatever decisions I made, they thought it was going to affect their lives. And I kept thinking: I don't know if I want that kind of pressure, to have people feel they can count on me.

"I have three kids, and it's all I can do to be in that position for them. I can try to do it for them, but I can't do it for anyone else. I know the decisions I make will affect my own children's lives, but that's as far as I can take it. I don't want other people counting on me."

And yet . . .

"I know. I'm just telling you that there were times that week when I got this vision of what it would be like if I played basketball again, and it seemed like an impossible thing to do. Those special reports on TV—it had gotten out of hand. The last thing I want is to be treated like some cult item, or cult leader, or something. But there it was. It wasn't the happiest week of my life."

But he ended it by coming back to basketball.

"Yeah," he said.

His words were in sharp juxtaposition to his apparent mood. He was relaxed, conversational, seemingly with nothing worrisome on his mind. Yet the things he talked about kept veering toward the darker side of his life.

For instance: Over the years we had talked on more than one occasion about how he could physically feel the eyes of people upon him. He likened the feeling to a burning sensation—when he walked through crowds, he said, and every pair of eyes was on him, he could feel the eyes burning into his skin. At least that is what he had said during his first basketball career.

I asked him: Was that still the case? And if he still felt the eyes burning into him, then why would he willingly put himself through that again?

"It's still there," he said. "That feeling has never gone away. But in baseball it was worse."

It was? Even in those little ballparks, with only a small fraction of the people who used to watch him every night in basketball arenas?

"It was different and it was worse," he said. "Because in baseball the eyes were expecting to see something I could not guarantee that I could give them. I couldn't . . . I was not sure that I had the talent."

And that affected his perception of the eyes upon him?

"In basketball, for all those years, whenever all the eyes were on me, I knew I was capable of doing what they wanted me to do. It didn't matter how many eyes were looking, or where I was—if it was basketball, I knew that I could accomplish it."

But that's exactly the thing he had once said he welcomed about baseball—it was the thought behind those baseball dreams he'd said he had in the dead of night. The chance to have eyes on him that weren't expecting anything, that didn't know if he would be good or not.

"I know," he said. "That's how I hoped it would be. But I started to feel the inner pressure every time I came to bat, every time a ball was hit my way. I didn't know if I could be good enough to meet their expectations—and if I wasn't good enough, I couldn't figure out a way to get around those expectations."

The people in the baseball parks weren't looking on him with that in mind. He had to be aware of that—he had to be aware, now that he was back in the NBA, that those kinds of unyielding expectations might be facing him every night now, but in baseball he had indeed found precisely what he had been looking for: eyes that would judge him in a different way.

"That's what I thought it would be," he said. "But that's not how it felt. It felt like the eyes were burning worse than before. You asked me, and I'm telling you. I felt it every day."

And now, at least it seemed to me, he was in a place where he could conceivably find the worst of both those worlds. There were more eyes on him now than ever before, staring at him even more intently. And no one knew if, on a consistent basis, he would still be able to find the talent to satisfy those eyes.

"I never anticipated this to be the way it has been," he said. "I knew there would be a lot of publicity if I came back, and I was used to a lot of publicity. But publicity is one thing. This . . . it was like, am I supposed to be Santa Claus who saves the world or something?"

The adulation had been so extreme before—I could understand how this new plateau of hysteria had caught even him off guard. It would have been difficult to predict the escalation in the frenzy around him that had occurred in the last several weeks.

"I think I've figured out what it is," he said.

He paused.

"Some of this isn't going to sound right, and some of it may make me sound stupid," he said. "But I think it's close to right."

He hesitated again, as if he was reluctant to commit it to words.

"When something dies, you miss it, but you don't think in terms of having it again, because it's dead and gone," he said. "Having it again is something you don't even really consider.

"But if you could . . . Look, if I had a chance to get my father back, I would see him every day, spend every hour and every second of every day with him. I would value every second so much, I would never stop looking at him and never stop talking to him.

"That's what I mean about this maybe sounding stupid. I know that my coming back to basketball isn't like life and death—I may sound bad even trying to make the comparison. I'm not making the real comparison. I'm just trying to explain why I think people may be reacting so strongly.

"Because before I went away, everyone knew that I would be out there every night for the Bulls, playing, and that they could watch if they wanted. They might like it, but it wasn't something that had gone away.

"And then I did stop playing basketball, and in that sense the basketball player died. He wasn't going to be there anymore. So when I came back, it was like a person who you never thought you were going to see again, and there he is. He was dead, in your mind, and then all of a sudden one day he's not dead anymore. It doesn't happen in real life—when your father is gone, he's gone forever, he's never coming back.

"But maybe, in my situation . . ."

He sat there for a moment.

"That's all I can figure out about it," he said. "That it's not really death becoming life, but it feels like it. And the question is, how long does that last? The feelings that people are having now—when does that go away? Because when it goes away this time, I think it probably goes away for good. So the people who say that they're happy you're in their lives again—how long do they stay that way? When does it stop?"

And still, that didn't answer the question. As complicated as his life had become, as many directions as he had looked in the weeks and months after his father's death to change it, redirect it—why was he here, in this place? Why, of all the things he could have decided to do with his life, was he in this hotel room, a few hours away from crossing the street and, once again, on one more night, at the age of thirty-two, playing in a basketball game?

"I was lost," Jordan said. "I was lost within myself, and I didn't even know it.

"That was the worst part. I knew something was going wrong with my life, and everything was starting to feel wrong—and I didn't even understand that I was lost."

I asked him what he meant.

"For so long everyone was seeing me as—I don't know what word you want to use," he said. "Object? Product? Whatever it was they were seeing me as, I was starting to see myself the same way. I was becoming an object to myself. In my own eyes.

"The object was an object that was being shot at and misunderstood, and I misunderstood it right along with everyone else. People thought that I was this great businessman, that I knew all the answers in business. But I'm a guy who has never had a job, a real job—never wanted a job. And I was supposed to be this businessman, and this logo, this idol. All these things to all these people, and I was believing it myself.

"And then I realized—all I've ever wanted to do was to love every minute of my life, playing games that I love. I don't think I had ever sat down and thought about it before, because things were going so fast. But I finally realized it: All I am is a basketball player. That's who I am and what I am, and that's all I am. And when I realized that, it made me feel relieved and happy. Because none of the other things matter, and I didn't want to think about any of them anymore. . . ."

He was silent for a minute, New York City behind him across the river.

"So this is it," he said. "Here I am."

Before going over to the arena, I went down to the hotel coffee shop for a late lunch. The restaurant was mostly empty. Two tables down from me, eating a sandwich and reading the sports page of *USA Today*, was Steve Kerr.

It was a staple of life in the NBA, something you could observe in every team hotel in every city. Not the most dramatic anomaly in the world, and easily explained, but still something to occasionally give brief pause. These men, who each night entered arenas packed with thousands upon thousands of screaming fans who waited breathlessly for the first sight of them, fans who had paid top prices and stood in long lines just for the chance to look at them from a distance; these men, for whom jostling crowds would wait for hours to gaze at for a second or two during personal appearances at sporting-goods stores, for whom fathers would take their sons miles out of their way in the hopes of catching a quick peek; these men, to whom people from around the world sent letters in care of their teams and their arenas, hoping that by chance their letters, out of all the sacks of letters pouring in perpetually to the offices of the NBA teams, might somehow actually be seen by these men, these distant and unreachable men . . .

These men, sought out and chased after by the multitudes—these men who, as a part of their daily life on the road in the hours before the games, so often found themselves saying the solitary words:

"Table for one."

"The statistic everyone was looking up on their way to the arena tonight was most points in a game in NBA history," the radio man sitting next to me called out in crisp, staccato tones to his unseen listening audience. This was during the first quarter; he was broadcasting live for a New York City station—not the play-by-play of the game, but periodic on-scene updates for his station's newscasts.

"It was Wilt Chamberlain, 100 points in a single game," he called into his microphone. "Everyone remembers what Michael Jordan did when he came to New York and scored 55 against the Knicks, so everyone's looking for him to top that tonight. . . ."

The radio man finished his report and returned to watching the game—a game in which Jordan, once again not having warmed up, was having his early troubles putting the ball in the basket. "Do you remember exactly when that Knick game was?" the radio man asked me.

"Eight days ago," I said.

"It was only eight days?" he said.

An eternity. If, at the tavern in Sarasota, the Jordan merchandise had been making itself evident, here at Brendan Byrne Arena the sight of the people adorned in the boundless array of products bearing his number—new number, old number—and his name and his image was not so much amusing as vaguely troubling.

In the bright lights of the indoor stadium, all the way up to the ceiling, all the Jordan garments on all the people who were wearing them bled together—red garments, white garments, black garments, in dozens upon dozens of designs, all of them bearing devotion and allegiance to that man down there on the court. There was a certain dull-eyed mindlessness to the process—the process that had become so accepted in American life by now that it was seldom called into challenge. A person becomes adept at a sport, and soon enough millions upon millions of men, women and children are draping themselves in public tribute to him, are making sure to be wearing their ceremonial robes before walking out their door. The Jersey Girls—the Nets' cheerleaders—gyrated on the court below, and the man whose name and number were imprinted on the garments of many colors held on to the bottom of his shorts as he leaned over to catch his breath, and all through the stands the people who should have been urging their own team on stood and screamed for him, pointed their arms toward the floor where he stood, chanted his name. If he were a political leader in a country with policies adverse to the United States, this scene would be a chilling one—all that unquestioning and bellicose ardency, all that zeal.

But he wasn't a political man, he was something beyond that. The people dressed in his clothing stood to honor him, and at chest level down on the court he accepted the orange ball thrown toward him by Scottie Pippen.

"Back in the game for Chicago," the Nets' P.A. announcer informed the crowd, "Dickey Simpkins and Michael Jordan, replacing Steve Kerr and Toni Kukoc."

That sentence is one that Simpkins—a Bulls rookie from Providence College—may never have imagined he would hear spoken. Simpkins was all of twelve years old when Jordan was already a star in the NBA. Now here they were, stepping side by side onto the court in New Jersey, Simpkins, for this one announcement at least, getting billing over Jordan.

But if the sentence rang off-key in Simpkins' ears, it must have sounded just as dissonant to Jordan. The three other men involved in the substitution—Kerr and Kukoc coming out of the game, Simpkins going in—were men Jordan had never played with before this spring's return. It was commonly stated that Jordan had come "back" to the Bulls—but the majority of the team was new to him, as was the arena where they played their home games. There were nights when he looked around the court like a fan, trying to place the faces with the names.

Wilt Chamberlain's scoring record was under no threat in New Jersey. Jordan was 1-for-11 in the first quarter, 2-for-13 in the first half, and at halftime his goal for the evening seemed to be to elevate his game to the level of ordinary, never mind magnificent. But then— perhaps he had needed the first two quarters as a warmup—he was all over the floor in the second half, leaping between Nets players to grab away passes, twisting past their outstretched arms to lay the ball into the hoop, battling much taller players to pull rebounds off the backboards and then fire the basketball out to his own teammates. There were sixteen ties in the game, but once Jordan started hitting his shots the Bulls were never behind; he finished with 37 points, and the Bulls walked off the court with a 100-101 victory, their fifth straight, their longest winning streak of the season.

Jordan had decided the separate post-game press conferences that had been arranged for him since his return—held in a room apart from the team, like the one in Atlanta—were sending a message he didn't like. He thought the rest of the Bulls might be displeased at the symbolism of him walking away from them to talk to the local media in each city.

So he had let it be known to the Bulls' staff that if sports reporters wanted to talk to him after the games, he would talk in front of his locker, just like all the other players. Of course, this only further em- phasized the dilemma—with scores of reporters and camera crews crammed into the post-game visitors' locker rooms, there was always a scramble among the journalists in the limited space to get close enough to Jordan so they could hear, and meanwhile the other Bulls had to get dressed in the middle of all this. At least when Jordan was giving post-game briefings in other rooms, his teammates weren't re- quired to witness this kind of scene.

Tonight with the press he was on automatic pilot—"I guess I haven't given myself a reasonable grace period to get my skills back.

But being the competitor that I am, I expect a better performance every night"—and the other Bulls, not that they needed reminding, had only to look across their locker room at actor Bill Murray, who had come in to watch Jordan talk, to understand the new realities of life with the team.

Darryl Dawkins, a former NBA player who had been known as "Chocolate Thunder" during his career in the league (professional basketball had placed a little less emphasis on understated elegance in those years), had somehow materialized in the Bulls' locker room, too, proclaiming loudly that if Jordan could come back, then so could he: "Just give me two hundred thousand dollars, we'll talk!" B.J. Armstrong, in boxer shorts and ready to get dressed and leave the arena, walked past Dawkins, who grabbed him and bellowed, as if to a young autograph-seeker, "How you doin', little guy!"

The atmosphere around the Bulls had been surreal ever since Jordan's return, but on this night in New Jersey it seemed especially exaggerated. Armstrong, always a quietly thoughtful man, extricated himself from Dawkins' arms, moved as far away from the commotion as he could without leaving the room, and looked at the hordes of people pressing in toward Jordan.

"When did you start to believe that he was coming back to the Bulls?" I asked him.

"I always believed," he said.

"Always?" I said. "Even when he said he wasn't coming back?"

"Always," Armstrong said.

"Why?" I said.

He nodded toward Jordan, lighted by klieg lamps, the center of attention in the middle of the throng.

"You are who you are," Armstrong said.

CHAPTER 15

"Scottie knows how I feel," Jordan said. "I told him from the first day I came back to practice—I told him, 'I'm trying to catch up to you. I'm not on your level yet.' And I've constantly reiterated it to him, all the time."

"You think Pippen's better than you are?" I said.

"Yes," Jordan said. "Right now, he is. He's a consummate basketball player. I'm trying to reach his level."

It was quite a thing for Jordan to be saying. Every day, in newspapers and on television and radio, he was being called the best basketball player in the world—and here he was, saying that he wasn't even the best on the Bulls.

"Pippen reads the same things everyone else reads, and watches the same TV shows," I said. "He hears everyone going crazy over you and saying that the best basketball player is back on the court."

"It doesn't matter what anyone else says," Jordan said. "He and I know. He knows how I feel about it, and he and I have had the conversations, so anything anyone else might say doesn't have anything to do with it."

We were talking about what it had been like when he came up from Florida and walked into the Bulls' practice facility. Here was this team, nearing the end of a dreary and disappointing season—and then Jordan's in the doorway. It must have been more than a little awkward.

"It was," Jordan said. "It was awkward. I was putting them in a difficult position. But whatever they might have been feeling inside, they made me feel like they needed me. From the very first day I came to see them, they were saying, 'If you were here, blah, blah, blah.' 'If you come back, we can do this and that and the other thing.' So it might have been awkward, but I also had the feeling that if I came back, I could bring a new attitude to them that might help."

And there weren't people on the team who resented him coming back in at the very end of the season?

"Some," he said. "But I was only worried about the guys I most respect, and they encouraged me, they said they'd like to have me back. I think Phil is happy I came back—I know he's happy, he told me. And I told him that I didn't have to be a team captain."

"You turned him down?" I said.

"I didn't turn him down—I just made sure that he knew, and everyone else knew, that if they thought it was better if I came back to the team but didn't take over my old role as one of the captains, that was all right with me. I told Phil that it was OK with me if everyone just let things go the way they'd been going, and that I would try to fit in. I told the players to let me work my way back in—I told them, 'Don't give it to me—don't give me the bull all the time.'"

I smiled at the thought of that—Jordan asking not to be given the basketball—but he insisted it was true. "I thought that was the best way to do it." he said. "For me to try to fit in with the others, rather than to make all of them try to fit in with me."

"That's a nice thing to say, but it sounds like you were just trying to be diplomatic," I said.

"Nope," Jordan said. "Up to the point when I made that shot at the buzzer in Atlanta, I hadn't really done anything to earn the guys' respect. I had a reputation, yes, but it was a reputation from two years ago. I'm the one who has to prove myself as a teammate—they have nothing to prove to me. Even if they don't say it out loud, I know there are times when they look at me on the court and think: *Who's he?* Like, what am I doing there, and what do I want? They have every right to think that. I'm the one who left and then came back."

. . . . .

At the highest level of the United Center, late on a Tuesday afternoon, I passed a door marked with a sign: "Microwave Room," behind which electronic communications equipment was contained.
The new home of the Bulls, a place meant for noise and marketed
bedlam, was, at these upper reaches, in these hours before the doors
would open to the evening's customers, as silent and cool as a cave
within a cave. Expensively framed color photographs of past Bulls
teams hung on newly painted walls; uniformed waiters and waitresses
prepared to serve dinner and drinks to the owners of the luxury suites,
soon to be arriving for tonight's game against the Indiana Pacers.

The hallways were richly carpeted, the colors muted; while the
ambience of the new arena had frequently been compared to that of
an airport, the more precise analogy up here was to one of those private preferred-travelers' clubs inside airports, where the airlines'
most valued passengers could wait behind solid oak doors until just
before boarding time, sipping cocktails and reading the business
pages, pretending that they weren't in a public air terminal at all.
That's what the luxury levels of the United Center seemed designed
to strive for: to reassure the patrons that they were not in a mere
gymnasium.

I had been walking around, just looking at things. I stepped into
one of the suites—it was unlocked—and peered down toward the
basketball court. The suite was higher in the building than the scoreboard—the court itself was like an elongated postage stamp down
below. If the airport analogies applied, then this vantage point was
more like flying over a basketball court in an airplane than actually
being inside an arena. Down on the court, in front of the tens of thousands of empty seats, so small I couldn't be sure who he was, was a
single figure dressed in white. Shooting baskets.

I headed downstairs. When I got to the escalator a uniformed
attendant (the old Chicago Stadium never had uniformed attendants,
but, then, it never had escalators, either) said the moving stairways
only carried people up, not down. I saw no staircase in the public
areas, so I walked through a fire door and made my way to the main

level, through the gleaming, pristine lobby, and onto the court. There was Jordan, in sweatpants and a white sweatshirt with the sleeves cut off, working. He and one ballboy, alone on the floor.

"Terrible lights," he said. He motioned up toward the ceiling. Up there, where he was pointing, were the three world-championship banners, and the banner bearing his own number 23, the one he and his children had raised to the rafters back in November. It was as if he chose not to see those items. Rather, he was gesturing to a row of extremely bright lights that glared in his eyes when he shot.

He tried a jump shot, saw the ball bounce off the hoop. Some ushers, reporting for work, were standing and watching him.

"New building," Jordan said to them, as if he owed them an apology for missing.

Since coming back to the Bulls, Jordan had been shooting woefully at the United Center—33 percent at home in the Bulls' arena compared with 44 percent on the road. Here he was this afternoon, the only player in the building this early, practicing.

Kent McDill, who covered the Bulls for the suburb-based *Daily Herald*, was walking in, on his way to work. He said to Jordan, "That's the rim that's tight."

This was the word around the new arena—that the rim at the west end of the building, on the basket beneath the banners, was tight and unyielding. It seemed improbable—with all the details that had been checked and rechecked before opening up the new place, would one of the two rims be unsuitable for play, tighter than the rim at the other end?—but that's what people kept saying.

"I'll loosen it up," Jordan said to McDill.

From the free-throw line, Jordan raced toward the basket, leaped into the air, grabbed the rim with both hands and hung from it. It bent underneath his weight, and he kept hanging. Then he dropped to the floor.

"Watch," Jordan said.

He picked up a basketball, stepped behind the free-throw circle, and lofted a shot in the direction of the hoop, but way too high, the ball towering more than twice as high as any shot should go. It was a lob—more like a pop fly—twenty, maybe thirty feet up in the air. It hit the front of the rim, which is what Jordan had intended.

"This is the way to do it," Jordan said. "This is how you loosen it."

And so—no other players around—Jordan kept at this do-it-yourself chore. Who knew if this really worked—if bouncing high, looping shots off the rim really was the way to make the metal more forgiving? Or even if the metal on this particular basket truly was too tight? But Jordan continued to heave the ball toward the ceiling in steep, exaggerated parabolas, continued to aim not for a through-the-net shot but for that front rim.

"You have to do it a hundred thousand times to get it loose," McDill said to him.

"That's OK," Jordan said. "I'll do it."

His next two lobbed shots went in—trying to miss, he scored.

"You ought to do it that way during the game," McDill said.

Jordan motioned for the ballboy to stand next to him. "Look at this," Jordan said. He took a jump shot from the left side of the basket. As the ball was in the air, he directed the ballboy's vision to the path of the ball.

"Look at that arc," Jordan said. The ballboy watched the ball's flight.

"You can't follow the arc," Jordan said to the ballboy. "See? When it gets near the top of the arc, the lights screw up your eyes."

Indeed, the harsh glare from the close-together line of lights up by the ceiling was temporarily blinding when you looked up there. The effect was like glancing directly into the sun in summer daylight: For a few seconds afterward, everything else was indistinct and fuzzy. Jordan said this was what he was seeing every time he took a shot.

If that was correct, it would seem logical that someone in charge of the building would have taken it into account when constructing the place. After all, the basketball players would be looking up there all game, every game.

"I hate this place," Jordan said, going into the air with the ball in his hands.

. . . . .

As Jordan worked at his shots, a United Center security official no-ticed that there was a scuff on the court—an abrasion on the wood to the right of the foul line.

The security man said to a building worker who was standing nearby, "You ought to try to get that up."

The worker came onto the court to look at the scuff, attempting not to disturb Jordan. Jordan said to him:

"While you're at it, blow the whole fucking building up."

The security man, hearing him, said, "They'd just build a new one for you."

"Maybe then I'd stay," Jordan said.

A joke, but for a few seconds everything stopped. The security man, the arena worker, the ballboy—everyone stared at Jordan. He had, after all, been back for only a few weeks; there was no guarantee how long this return to basketball would last.

He held the ball to his hip, trotted back behind the foul circle, and once again started to lob the ball, higher still this time, as if he were the one who had to take the responsibility for making sure the rim was finally loose and friendly, the way it ought to be on his home court.

The old Chicago Stadium, directly across West Madison Street from the United Center, was still there—at least its shell. The wreckers had been working for months to take it down, but the task was evi-dently going slowly. Knowing that the Stadium was going to eventu-ally and unavoidably be leveled, it seemed somehow worse that it continued to stand, in full view of everyone who arrived for each game at the United Center—you could walk past the Stadium and know that, had the new place not been constructed, there was no rea-son they couldn't still be playing basketball games in there, right now.

The new place was objectively beautiful—very big, very clean, every convenience provided for the customers. The new place, with, on its street level, doors that looked like handleless panels and panels that looked like unwelcoming doors meant to be opened only from the inside, had the exterior feel of an urban shopping mall afraid of the city it's in. These were the buildings of the American future, buildings with interiors designed to appear free and open and airy once the people who are supposed to be inside get inside—and designed to make sure no one else even thinks about it.

Across the street, the old Stadium waited for the end. Most people had expected it would be gone by now; the regular season, the Bulls' first in the United Center, was nearing its finish, the playoffs would begin soon enough, yet large portions of the gray old Stadium, with all its memories, were managing to resist the wrecker's ball in full sight of the customers who used to fill it, the same customers who were arriving for the games across Madison Street.

"It almost seems like it's fighting," Jordan said. "Like it doesn't want to die, and it's standing up for itself and fighting back. Like it doesn't want to go down."

If Jordan had been a key factor in the building of the United Center—if the success of the Bulls during his years on the team was the driving economic force behind its construction—then it had plainly been designed for the years after he was gone. Whichever team, the Bulls or the Pacers, won tonight's contest, the outcome of the game—of any game—was irrelevant in the master plan of the new arena.

It was a place of commerce, boldly and unapologetically. Devised as an entertainment center that did not depend on the ebbs and flows of the teams that played in it, every square inch appeared devoted to merchandising and advertising and profitable promotion. The concession stands were plentiful and expensive, the gift shops had the glitz of upscale department stores; there was a blowup of a team picture beside which fans could stand and pose (the team was missing one man—Jordan—because the photo had been taken at the beginning of the season), there were stopping-off places where customers could match the size of their hands against handprints of NBA stars, compare the size of their feet to the shoes of prominent NBA players. Like all new U.S. sports complexes, this one was designed to be bad-team-proof, to prosper regardless of the skills of the athletes during a particular season or string of seasons; the wholly understandable goal was to extricate the dollars from the customers' wallets as gently and lovingly as possible—to take the money and make the customer say "Thank you" for the taking, and be eager to be allowed to come back another night.

The off-duty police officers from the old Stadium—the men in the utilitarian yellow cop windbreakers who had guarded Jordan and the team in the building across the street—were on duty here, but in blazers and dress pants. They seemed less than at ease in the new clothes, like boys who have been taken off the ball diamond and made to get dressed up for dancing school—or, more to the point, like policemen who have been promoted to desk jobs they never wanted, and would like nothing better than to give the promotion back and return to the beat. I saw a fellow I knew from the old place, walking on the second-level concourse of the United Center; in the sport coat and slacks I didn't recognize him for a second.

"Do they wash that stuff for you?" I said.

He put his fingers on the lapel of his blazer. "They're *supposed* to," he said. "Give me my old yellow jacket back."

In the first-floor lobby, one of the musical combos hired for the evening was setting up and testing its instruments. This was part of the new formula: music in the lobbies, to give the fans a total entertainment experience (when they left after each game, they were handed mints on their way out the doors). The combo ran through a practice rendition of "Brown-Eyed Girl": . . . *behind the stadium with you* . . .

In the basement—even the basement was sparkling and brilliantly lighted and scrubbed, like the underground control center of a nuclear power plant—I saw B.J. Armstrong, on his way to the locker room to get ready for the night's game. I told him that I'd been walking around the place, and asked him what he thought of it.

"It's for business, not for the players," he said.

But, of course, the players were the business—and the businessmen who owned the team and the building had to run it this way in order to write the checks that paid the players' salaries.

"All right," he said. "But upstairs is for the revenue. It's not for us."

I asked him what his impressions were of all the features built into the building—the luxury suites, the stores, the elegant concourses.

"I never have gone up there," he said.

From the bronze statue outside the entrance, to the multiplicity of displays and products designed to commemorate his years on the Bulls, parts of the United Center felt more like a Michael Jordan theme park than a place to play basketball. Knowing that he would not be on the team as the building opened, the owners had given the place the feel of a Jordan museum—he would not be present on game nights, the executives had figured, so the memory of his years as a basketball player might as well be used as an enticement to bring people to the premises.

The one thing no one had counted on was that, in the Jordan theme park, the real Jordan would be out on the court early on a day like this one, not a photo montage or a licensed cap or a souvenir program, but a man in shorts and basketball shoes. Watching him working on his game beneath the luxury suites and their catering staffs, beneath the computerized heating and cooling and lighting equipment, beneath his banners, the thought occurred that if this place had been declared a shrine to him, it was a perfectly cold shrine—and that maybe what he was doing down there on the court by himself was trying to make it a gym.

That's what it seemed like—after all that had happened, he seemed like a man in a palace, trying his best to turn that palace back into a gym.

"It's not the Stadium," he said. "You don't want to hold that against this place, but I played in a place that I loved, and this isn't the place."

When he talked about the United Center—in those moments he wasn't wishing facetiously that it would explode—he conceded that his lack of luck with his shots in the new building, his troubles with the baskets, weren't the real reason he felt out of place. Had every shot he tried gone in, his feeling of disconnectedness would still be there.

"It just feels a little distant," he said. "In the Stadium, I could see everyone's face. It wasn't just that the people were physically closer, although they were. But it was like I could look off the court, and the people were *people*—I could make out every face, every personality. It even seemed I could do it in the farthest seats.

"It's not that I was looking for people who I knew—that's not what I mean. But the people in the Stadium just seemed like people to me—like individuals. I don't know what it is about the new place. It holds more people, and it's bigger than the old place, but when I look off the court nothing feels as real."

I asked him if that affected his game.

"I don't know," he said. "When I leave the floor after the game, it doesn't feel like I'm leaving a big room full of people I know. That's what it felt like in the other place. This place, it feels like I'm leaving a show. Like I've been to the movies or something, and it's time to go home."

When the Bulls had last played the Pacers, it was on the road, that first game back for Jordan. That game had been promoted into a national event—by the time it began on television sets all over the United States, it had taken on the aura of Academy Awards night. Now, though, with Indiana visiting Chicago, the NBA season had reverted to its regular routine. What had seemed unlikely just a few weeks before—Jordan playing in a game and having it treated merely as a game—was here. Everyone knew this would change when the regular season ended, and the playoffs began. But for now, the national press was absent, the contest was televised only locally and not on any network, and this was as close to the feeling of just being a ballgame as anyone had the right to hope.

Neither Jordan nor Reggie Miller of the Pacers was shooting especially well, and Pippen had the stomach flu. The Bulls took a big lead early, and the fans—finally able to sit back and enjoy Jordan and the Bulls as a pleasant weeknight diversion rather than as a spectacle the press and TV had told them in advance they would remember forever—were appreciative and vocal but hardly boisterous.

Jordan was beginning to look like his dad. If the arena was new, he wasn't—he was entering into full maturity, and it was hard to look at him and not see the face of James Jordan. For the last several years of Jordan's original time in the NBA, fans who were watching him in person for the first time would depart stadiums marveling aloud about how high he had soared in the air, how he had flown toward the basket and hovered above the court longer than any mortal, under the laws of physics, should be able to do. It was nice they thought they were seeing that—but in fact, they were not. They had desired to witness the flying, airborne Jordan of legend, and because that's what they had arrived wanting to see, that's what they walked away believing they had seen.

But in those last years in the league before he left and went to baseball, Jordan had changed his game almost completely. He still dunked, he still could make people gasp when he got into the open court and created some impromptu move as he stuffed the ball into the basket. More and more, though, he had kept his game closer to the ground—hitting long jumpers, working his way free for bank shots from the sides, implicitly acknowledging that he wasn't a twenty-three-year-old anymore.

That's not what the first-time fans wanted to see, so that's not what they left the arenas telling themselves they had seen. Jordan, had they been able to ask him, would have verified that he was a vastly changed basketball player from the man in the vintage highlight reels and the early Nike commercials—"I see that guy, and I know it's me, but he's so young, he's so cocky and full of energy, it's like he's someone else"—but that's not necessarily what they would have wanted to hear. They saw what they chose to see.

Now Jordan, back in the league, was thirty-two, and the changes in him as a player were even more pronounced. His game was smarter and more precise, to make up for the fact he was no longer a young whiz in his twenties; many basketball experts said that it was even more fascinating to watch him now, to observe his mind and body working together. And the same way first-time fans wanted to see the gravity-daring Jordan of old, they also wanted to see the laughing, tongue-wagging eternal kid from the posters and the videos.

The man on the court was not that man. There were nights when I looked at him taking the ball up the court, and at certain angles his resemblance to his father was so pronounced it was almost chilling. So recently, his dad had been coming to these basketball games, standing around the court before the tipoff and at halftime, watching his son from the seats. Now Jordan, past thirty, took aim at the basket, and when the light was right his face was the face of a man now gone.

Before the Pacers game, as I had walked around the United Center, I had passed the glass windows of Fandemonium, a large gift shop in one of the main concourses, devoted to selling Bulls items. It was locked—it would not open until the public was allowed into the building—but its staff was already inside, stacking the merchandise onto the shelves. I saw two men hefting piles of jerseys with the number 45 and Jordan's name on them. Obviously the shirts had become a staple of the store's inventory, a product that had not existed a month ago but that now was hard to keep in stock before the daily supplies were depleted. The men in the window lifted the shirts onto a shelf, arranged them so even more could be loaded on top of them for the customers who would soon arrive and begin carting them away.

Now, down on the court, with forty-one seconds left in the first half, Jordan drove, stopped, whirled to take a shot. For that moment, his face was his father's; for that moment the white jersey with the unfamiliar number on the front seemed not so much something he was wearing for the game, but something he, like all the men and women and children dressed in duplicates of it up in the stands, had bought at a gift store, had purchased to try to be like the person they thought was Michael Jordan. He as much as they. The ball went into the net, and he turned to run back down on defense, and the face of the person in the shirt was the face of a man growing ever older.

. . . . .

He had said something a few days back—after a Bulls loss to the Cavaliers in Cleveland—that was more than a little intriguing, but that had barely been noted because it came during his regular post-game comments, along with his usual boilerplate statements about how his shooting was progressing, and how the fans on the road were treating him, and whether he thought the Bulls had a chance once the playoffs began.

In the loss to Cleveland, Jordan had taken a shot as the clock ran out that would have given the Bulls the win. Had he succeeded—had his three-point attempt gone in—it would have been one more in a famous line of Jordan shots that, over the years, had sunk the Cavaliers. But the ball banged off the back of the rim, Cleveland won, and Jordan, not seeming particularly upset, said it had been an enjoyable moment for him.

"I knew everybody was watching," he said. "And I guess that's the thrill of it all—that you have the opportunity to make people sad or make people happy. That's a fun position to be in."

As if even he had accepted that this was now his station in life—as if the Michael Jordan theme park were literal, as if he were not only the amusement park ride, but also the proprietor of the park, a calculated human catalyst for other people's joys, and not his own. Anyone else would have walked off the floor furious and disappointed—the Bulls' six-game winning streak was over, they remained in fifth place in the Eastern Conference, hardly the status they had been accustomed to occupying during Jordan's first term in the NBA. Yet—or so he announced—it was all right, "a fun position to be in," because he knew that the happiness or sorrows of strangers were his to determine.

He may very well have believed it. I was seeing Carmen Villafane again every night. The year and a half that Jordan was gone from basketball had left something of a void in her evenings; from the day she had first worked up the courage to give him that Valentine at the old Stadium, he had been one of the most important people in her life. With the seat he had given her behind the Bulls' bench, and her constant conversations with him on game nights, he had brightened her world in a way so profound that dry words are insufficient to summarize it. She was out making a living on her own now, having found a job in a medical facility, coming to work in her wheelchair and making full use of her intelligence and her diligence, regarded at her office as a full and independent person despite her severe physical disabilities. And Jordan, even when he was no longer a Bull, had made sure that she still was sent her tickets.

Yet it hadn't been the same for her, going to the games and knowing he was gone and wasn't returning. "I still like it, but sometimes it feels kind of empty," she had told me during that first full year he was absent. Now, with him back and the Bulls playing in the new building, she was at the arena again early every night, her game days built around him.

The security men at the new arena knew to allow her to steer her motorized chair past the various checkpoints, and to wait for him directly across the hallway from the Bulls' locker room door. Which she did, each evening, and Jordan would stop to say hello and exchange some words with her, on his way in and on his way out.

Everything was back to the way it had been. Which for him, or so he seemed to tell himself, meant having the "thrill"—and the obligation—of altering the emotions of other people, to "make people sad or make people happy." As if he were trying to persuade himself that the things he might feel were not what was essential in his life—that he had really become that public catalyst, full-time, a calling he was no longer in any position to change.

Now, as the Pacers mounted a second-half comeback against the Bulls in the United Center, I looked around the place. There were no real memories here yet—most of the Bulls players, at one time or another during the season, had pointed out that, in addition to the newness of the physical plant, the building felt barren because nothing of importance had ever happened here: It lacked emotional weight.

The idea of a building as a community—a place of shared experiences and fond recollections—is something some people might question. After all, a sports arena is only a floor and seats; no one lives there. How much resonance can those shared recollections really have?

During the game, a man at the press table—a sportswriter from Bloomington, Illinois—had been gracious enough to come over and tell me that he had just read *All Summer Long*, a novel I wrote after *Hang Time* was published. It was my first venture into fiction, and like anything you do for the first time, it had special meaning for me; I was flattered that he wanted to talk about the book. It was the story of three old friends, now in middle age, who meet at their twenty-fifth high school reunion in the small town where they grew up, and decide to take a leave from their jobs and families, and to give themselves the freedom and friendship of one more summer in the sun, like when they were seventeen. The fictional town in the novel was modeled after Bexley, Ohio, the town where I grew up.

The sportswriter from Bloomington wanted to know how close the parallels were between the fictional Bristol, Ohio, in the novel, and the real-life Bexley. We talked about it for a while—Bexley, and the sense of home and community it has always represented to me, has echoed so deeply for me for so long; my memories of what went on there are as clear, vivid and complicated as anything that has happened in the bigger world since I left to go out on my own. Bexley was, and is, a universe—Bexley for me, as hometowns are for so many people, has its own time span and history and cast of characters, there is a story in that town that goes on forever.

The man I was talking with asked me how big Bexley was. I told him: fifteen thousand, maybe fewer. We sat there, and I looked around the United Center, filled to capacity for this game, and I realized something. There were more people here tonight—more than twenty thousand—than lived in the town where I grew up. If all the people who live in Bexley came to the United Center, and were assigned seats, there would be thousands and thousands of empty seats left over. The Ohio community that meant so much to me, with all the emotion it carried, had a population much smaller than this basketball arena on game night.

On the court, Steve Kerr and Toni Kukoc were having a good run for the Bulls, and Jordan was on his way to scoring 25 points en route to a Chicago victory. The crowd, toward the end, was on its feet and yelling; the building might not be broken in yet, and the musical interludes in the lobby, the free mints on the way out, might seem like an artificial method for a basketball team to build a sense of home. But can it happen? In the midst of a vast and often indifferent outside world, can a place this confined and relatively small become a community that means anything, that can provide warm remembrances and shared experiences that will last over the years?

It can. It just takes time. Some of us grew up in places with fewer people than were in this building right now. The memories can come. And will.

"I still have to find out where he hides," Jordan was saying after the game.

The Bulls would be taking a bus to the airport, then flying directly to Detroit for a game the next night. Now, sitting at his locker, Jordan was talking to a group of sportswriters who were on deadline. Someone had asked him whether he was having trouble getting rid of the ball when he didn't want to shoot it himself. He had been just 8-for-27 tonight; he needed to be finding an outlet man instead of taking the shot every time the clock ran down.

John Paxson had been his consistent and steady outlet man during the championship years; Paxson had always seemed able to be free so that Jordan could get the ball to him if he didn't have the shot himself. What about Steve Kerr, Jordan had been asked—was he having trouble finding Kerr?

"He likes to hide out," Jordan said. "I always knew where Pax was. Pax was foul-line extended, right behind the three, and it was easy to find him."

It was easy to find Paxson tonight, also, as a matter of fact—he was directly across the locker room, having broadcast the game on radio. He was hanging out here prior to going to the team bus before the flight to Detroit, where he would broadcast again. It was a quietly melancholy moment: Jordan sitting there talking about Paxson in the past tense—glowingly, but in the past tense—and Paxson, twenty feet away, with all the reporters' backs to him.

Jordan, surrounded by the reporters, didn't see him. And he kept talking about finding Paxson for the pass:

"I could do it with my eyes closed. But with Steve, he moves around a little bit."

Paxson decided to leave the room. He walked out by himself, past the sportswriters. Jordan was always the last man on the bus, then and now; this would not be the first time Paxson had waited for him.

"Top of the key, foul-line extended," Jordan said of Kerr and where he most often had stood on the court during the game just completed. "In the corners. I know where he was. So it's just a matter of finding Steve."

Paxson wasn't the only person to have left the room early; B.J. Armstrong had departed, too. Armstrong, the guard who had replaced Paxson as a starter, was now losing minutes to Kerr—Phil Jackson suddenly seemed to like Kerr's play better. Tonight Kerr had played thirty minutes, Armstrong only twenty. Jackson, asked to explain Kerr's sudden prominence in the lineup, said, "Steve just happens to be playing hot. He had a good first half and we just felt we had to come back to him in the second half."

As Jordan answered the questions, both Paxson and Armstrong, either inadvertently or by implication or some combination of the two, had been subtly relegated to the basketball past. Armstrong once told me, when a teammate had suddenly been traded away by the Bulls: "Whenever you start thinking about how good life in the NBA is, you should always remember something else: This is a very cold business." By the time the next season would be ready to begin, Armstrong, one of the Chicago fans' favorite players, would himself be optioned away by the Bulls. Tonight he was gone early, and Paxson, beloved in Chicago as a hero in the Bulls' three championships, but not a member of this team, waited on the bus.

· · · · ·

Jordan, when we talked about his chances for success in his second NBA career, said everyone who was predicting whether he would be a winner again was missing the point.

"If they think the main thing of this is about winning, then they don't understand," he said. "It's about riding the elevator as opposed to taking the stairs."

He said that before he had gone off to baseball, he was so used to riding the elevator—symbolically—in his life that he had forgotten what the stairs were like.

"Everything had gone so well for me in basketball for so long," he said. "I was winning the scoring title every year, being named most valuable player in the league, winning the championships—it was like everything was due me.

"I had gotten so used to riding the elevator that I had forgotten how to take the stairs. Then I went down to the minor leagues, and whatever I might have been expecting from baseball, my days on the elevator were gone. I had to deal with my lack of success every minute.

"And I had to work so hard, and even the work didn't make me good enough. But the work got me reacquainted with the stairs. I liked the work—I liked going out there and taking all that batting practice, I liked taking nothing about my game for granted. I liked the feeling that I could never assume that I could succeed.

"That's what I've brought back here with me. I was taking the elevator in basketball before, but now that I'm back I'm going to stick with the stairs. The stairs are for me."

His reluctance to warm up in arenas before the games had nothing to do with the point he was trying to make, he said: "My real practice comes with the team, when no one but us is around. The other thing, before games, with people I don't know watching me, is a different thing."

I asked him if the elevator-versus-stairs analogy meant that he was making himself climb all the way back to a fourth world championship before he could feel he had reached the top.

"I don't feel that I have to win the championship again," he said. "That doesn't mean I don't want to—I wouldn't be here if I didn't want to. But before I left, it was expected by everyone that we were supposed to win a fourth championship, and that if we didn't we had somehow failed.

"Now, I have to prove that I can win again. It's not expected of me—no one knows. Now some people are saying, 'Chicago can never win another championship.' Whether we can or we can't, this year or next year or the year after that, will have to be determined.

"But the one thing I know is that I like the stairs. That's where I'm at my best—climbing the stairs. I'd forgotten that, and baseball gave it back to me. It let me find out what the stairs felt like again. The stairs feel good. They're where I belong."

CHAPTER 16

"It's Easter," Jordan said. "You've got to give. Start giving."

Standing all the way back by the half-court line, surrounded by four security men, Jordan launched a shot using his left hand. *Start giving.* It was a joking challenge, an invitation to a mock wager—*start giving*, the ball's going in.

The ball sailed left of the basket, banged off the glass, bounced to the floor.

"Go back to your right hand," said one of the security men—all of them were off-duty police officers, the former yellow jackets, now in their constricting United Center blazers.

"What's the difference?" Jordan said, laughing, lofting another long shot, missing again.

It was 3:03 p.m., Easter Sunday. The New York Knicks were in town. Jordan had arrived early, to get this work in before he had an audience. The police officers—they had become his friends over the years, they sometimes went out to dinner with him after games, played cards with him, he could relax around them—had come onto the court with him to keep away anyone who might have sneaked in before the doors opened.

No one had sneaked in. Joe McConnell, the "voice of NBA Radio," was there; he and his engineers were set up at courtside, testing their equipment and conducting game-day soundchecks.

McConnell, fifteen feet away from Jordan, read from a card and spoke into his microphone: "This is Joe McConnell of NBA Radio. If you're listening to the NBA Finals in middle Tennessee, you're listening to . . ."

These were not the NBA Finals. This was still the regular season—the tail-dragging end of the regular season. He wasn't on the radio live, merely recording a taped promotional announcement.

"Why are we doing a promo for this station?" McConnell said to his engineer. The engineer shrugged.

McConnell, lowering his voice an octave, read his next promo: "This is *Joe McConnell*, the voice of NBA Radio, along with my partner, Wes Unseld. And you're listening to the voice of sports in northern Arizona. . . ."

"Are *you guys* back again?" Jordan said.

Turning to a sound he had heard behind his back, he had found a cameraman and sound technician from NBC television. NBC would be broadcasting the Bulls–Knicks game live on national TV; its crews had a contractual right to be in the arena this early. Jordan knew this crew, and was saying it good-naturedly, but making a point.

"I was trying to beat you guys out here," he said.

Meaning: I was trying to get here early enough on Easter Sunday to practice without my mistakes being shown in every city in the country. Meaning: As early as I wake up, as early as I try to be alone, I ought to know that I can't be alone.

"Jordan's 55-point barrage in Madison Square Garden set an all-time record for a Knicks opponent," Joe McConnell boomed into his courtside mike. "More importantly, Jordan's performance sent a message to the Knicks, and to other opponents in the East. . . ."

His words weren't going anywhere. Still a rehearsal—just like Jordan's.

By now there were six security guards around Jordan. Six security guards, one ballboy, one NBC camera crew.

"Happy Easter," Jordan called to the security men, celebrating in advance as his shot from half-court rose in the direction of the basket.

It missed.

"Yeah, right, Happy Easter, Michael," one of the security men scoffed.

"You're listening to the NBA Finals . . ." Joe McConnell read from a script.

"Happy Easter," Jordan called, shooting, not giving up.

"We smell the blood," Anthony Mason said. He was playing his part.

Mason, the glowering power forward for the Knicks, was sitting in front of his cubicle in the visitors' locker room of the United Center. During the final years of Jordan's first domination of the NBA, the Knicks had become something close to the designated villains of the league. Their own fans in New York loved them; that was to be expected. But around the rest of the NBA, and especially in Chicago, Mason and his teammates had been cast in the necessary role of the thuggish bad guys. Someone had to do it.

In that respect, the theatrics of the NBA were not all that different from professional wrestling. If the Jordan-era Bulls stood for grace and beauty, the law of supply and demand called for someone to assume the converse role. So here was Mason, here was Greg Anthony, here was Charles Smith, here was John Starks. Their blue jerseys with orange numerals hung above their heads in their cubicles, and in a way it seemed that the men themselves were not needed, or at least interchangeable—the jerseys would do for the villains' role, regardless of who was selected to fill them.

"Excuse me," Patrick Ewing said courteously. The Knicks' seven-foot center was asking some people standing in front of him if they could move out of the way of the television set. His pleasant voice belied the ferocious on-court image of him the NBA liked to market; on the television set—this was a show Ewing might well have chosen to skip—was a videotape of Jordan's 55-point game in Madison Square Garden. Someone on the United Center building staff had stuck the VCR securely to the top of the TV set with white athletic tape, the kind used to prepare the players' ankles for the games—this precaution against VCR theft would not have seemed to be necessary in a league where the average salary was in excess of a million dollars.

Pat Riley came into the main locker room. Weary and pale, the Knicks' coach glanced around at his players. "If I hadn't been suspended . . ." Anthony Mason complained to someone. Riley, not needing to hear this, turned around and returned to his office.

"Will you get me some pre-wrap, please?" Ewing said to a locker attendant. Trapped in his enormity, he was as courtly as a waltz instructor.

John Starks listened to music through headsets. In this NBA movie, he was cast long ago as the icy-eyed punk who challenges Jordan's James Dean to a game of chicken—Starks had been given the role of the anti-Jordan. The television cameras loved to inhale his every scowl, pout, grimace; if Jordan could light up the screen with a smile, Starks could darken it with a twitch of his mouth. If he hadn't existed to be night to Jordan's day, the NBA would have had to recruit an actor for the role.

Except this wasn't acting; it was great television, but these men were only basketball players. Starks laced up his shoes, aware that whatever the nation might think of the histrionics of his encounter with Jordan today, he was the one who was going to have to walk down the hallway and onto the floor and defend his celebrated rival. For him it wasn't a TV show; he was shorter than Jordan, less limber, less acrobatic. He may have been the anti-Jordan because of factors beyond his control, but for forty-eight minutes of regulation today he was going to have to go into the big room of the United Center and play basketball against him as if they were athletic equals. No one could do it for him. He wasn't going to be in the audience.

"Thank you very much," Patrick Ewing said to the locker-room attendant, who had handed him the roll of tape he had requested. He took off his ring and his wristwatch and, to keep them safe during the game, put them carefully into a little sack that looked like a ladies' black leather purse.

. . . . .

If there was a person who most assuredly had not been cast as the anti-Jordan—if there was a person the NBA was counting on to carry it into the twenty-first century—that person was Grant Hill, the rookie star of the Detroit Pistons.

Quiet, polite, deferential—and an absolutely wonderful basketball player—Hill was the NBA's antidote to the surly crop of athletes who had dominated the younger echelons of the league in recent seasons: Starks, Derrick Coleman, Chris Webber, Alonzo Mourning, Larry Johnson and numerous others the league's imagemakers would just as soon forget they had ever heard of.

Hill, on the other hand, was being called "the new Jordan." This did not sit particularly well with the old Jordan.

"They did the same thing with me," Jordan said. "When I came into the league, Dr. J"—Julius Erving—"was the one they compared me to. It didn't help him to have them say that, and it didn't help me. You can't stop them from saying things like that, but it's kind of stupid, if you ask me."

"So you're annoyed when they say Hill is the new you?" I said.

"It's flattering, I suppose," Jordan said. "It's not supposed to be annoying—if you want to think about it that way, it's flattering to both of us. It's flattering to him because he's being compared to someone who has already achieved some success. It's flattering to me because I'm being held up as someone to be compared to. But it's also dumb."

"Why?" I said.

"Because no one's the next anything," he said. "With all the things that have happened to me since I was a rookie, do you think there's anyone still going around saying that I have become 'the next Dr. J'? Of course not. If you succeed, the comparisons stop. If the people are right—if you turn out to do well—then they stop saying that you're the next whoever. The only people they keep saying that about are the people who were supposed to be really good, and didn't do it. Then they keep saying that the person 'was supposed to be the next so-and-so,' and never lived up to his potential."

"So the next you isn't out there?" I said.

"There's a person out there who's going to be great," Jordan said. "We don't know who he is yet. But whoever he is—whether it's Grant Hill or someone else—no one's doing him any favor by comparing him to me. When the person comes along, and he's the real thing, you'll know it, because he'll be so good that no one compares him to anyone else."

Before tipoff I rode an elevator up to the seventh level of the arena. Inside the elevator car there was music—the rendition of George Gershwin's *Rhapsody in Blue* that United Airlines had made its corporate theme song. The version in the elevator was the same arrangement heard in United's television and radio commercials, and played regularly in the main United concourse at O'Hare International Airport. The airline, having entered into an agreement with the owners of the new building, possessed the right to permeate the premises in large ways—the United Center name—and small.

In the carpeted hallway of that top level, I walked to the big windows facing north. Across the street and down below was the old Stadium, now much closer to being gone forever. In the afternoon light, you could see the bulldozers parked inside, see jagged portions of its famous balcony, see hanging and jutting bits of pipe and wire. From this angle in the new building the Stadium looked like an egg diorama rudely cracked open. Everything was visible and everything was asunder. The door where Jordan and the Bulls had come into the building each winter night, the door inside of which Carmen Villafane had always waited—that door, and the wall it had been a part of, were vanished. The Stadium seemed to have only a few days left, a tired and beaten warehouse that had stored . . . what?

In the first half against the Knicks, the Bulls looked as thrillingly skilled as they had during the most exhilarating nights of the three championship seasons. Jordan, Pippen and Kukoc sprinted up and down the court together like three friends trying out for a team and trying to impress a coach who had never seen them before; they played with joy and energy and something that looked like love, and the Knicks played like men who wanted to get this over with so they could keep a dinner reservation. Pippen, by the end of the half, had 25 points, four rebounds, four assists and four steals. Jordan would say later: "Teams can think about me, and I'm thinking: Yeah, but that guy over there is the one who is beating you."

The United Center's advanced technology did not at all decrease the players' inexplicably hypnotic reaction to the dot race. In the old building, once each game, the Stone Age scoreboard would be used during a time-out for that pre-programmed "race" between globs of light. It was an advertising promotion—one year the dots were supposed to represent a certain brand of potato chip, one year a certain brand of candy. In the midst of the closest games, at the most tension-filled junctures, while Phil Jackson was talking to his team and dia-gramming plays on his clipboard, at least some of the Bulls would apparently find themselves physically unable to look at him and pay attention; instead, like men whose heads were being drawn skyward by a giant magnet, they would stare open-jawed up toward the dot race, as if the outcome were the most important thing in their day.

Here in the new building, with a computer-driven, multi-hued, video-enlivened scoreboard that seemed as if it could fly to Europe if someone punched the right buttons, the dots in the race were no lon-ger amorphous globs. Here they had faces and legs and personalities all their own: The prehistoric dots had evolved into perky modernity over the long continuum of dot life. The Bulls had led by 20 points at the half, but in the second half the Knicks began to mount a come-back. Phil Jackson addressed his athletes. At least the majority of his athletes: Will Perdue, Pete Myers and Corie Blount stared blankly skyward at the dots, evidently unable to stop themselves.

The Bulls held on to win the day's main event 111–90. The most electric moment came with less than five minutes remaining, and the Knicks showing a burst of energy. Jordan, near the baseline with the ball in his hands and the shot clock about to expire, launched a shot. Charles Smith of the Knicks swatted his hand at the ball, knocking it off course. Jordan snatched the ball back, jumped into the air, and threw a ludicrously high lob—"a rainmaker," Phil Jackson would call it later—up toward the ceiling. It looked like nothing if not one of those fly balls he had played around with before the Pacers game, when he was trying to loosen the tight basket.

And it went in.

Asked by reporters after the game what he'd had in mind when he had sent the ball towering into the air like a looping rocket, Jordan said, "I was only trying to hit the rim." The reporters logically took that to mean that he was trying to save the possession—that if he had hit any part of the rim, the Bulls could have had a new twenty-four seconds on the shot clock.

But who could be sure? Perhaps he meant it literally—perhaps he was "only trying to hit the rim" so that he could keep loosening it.

"Maybe that's how I should shoot every one," Jordan said to the reporters.

Precisely what Kent McDill had advised him when there was no one in the arena.

"Michael is with Ahmad," Marv Albert's voice proclaimed from a television monitor in the basement of the United Center, and onto the screen came picture and sound, Ahmad Rashad of NBC Sports interviewing Jordan on the court.

But Michael, at this moment, was not in fact with Ahmad—at least in real life, which often didn't count. A minute or so before, I had run into Rashad on his way out of the building, where a car was waiting to take him to the airport. He had spoken with Jordan in the seconds following the Bulls' victory, while the network had been in a commercial break; the conversation had been stored on tape, the scheduled commercials had run, and now the Jordan–Rashad conversation was being seen in millions of homes all across the United States.

So at this moment the millions were seeing the two men talk on the Bulls' court, listening to the electronic Jordan even as the real Jordan took a shower. Since the entire purpose of the brief conversation was to provide a sending-off for the day's broadcast, since the conversation would have no reason for being unless it was aired to those millions, it could be argued that Marv Albert was only being accurate when he said "Michael is with Ahmad." Rashad might be on the expressway heading for O'Hare, Jordan might be adjusting the temperature in the shower, but in the only places that mattered—on all those millions of television screens—they were, indeed, together, in real time, the realest time of all.

Because what, of all this, was real? The writers prepared their stories for the morning papers, as if the result of this game, this season, was the thing of consequence, and the NBC staff took the conversation that had occurred on the floor upon which right now no conversation was occurring, and sent that conversation into the sky and bounced it off a satellite, and Jordan prepared for the bus ride to the Bulls' own flight, which would transport him and them to Miami for yet another game. "Michael is with Ahmad," the voice had said, as if anyone is with anyone, as if any man is ever really anywhere.

"When you want to go one-on-one?" Jordan said to Bill Wennington.

Wennington, a seven-foot center for the Bulls in his eighth year in the NBA, looked at Jordan as if to ask: Who, me?

This was on the last Saturday of the regular season, hours before the Bulls' final home game in advance of the playoffs—a game against the Charlotte Hornets. Jordan had been shooting around by himself, and Wennington had walked onto the court in his warmup clothes. He had not played with Jordan during the championship years—in fact, Wennington had left the NBA entirely for a couple of years to play in Italy. Now here they were—Jordan, the ultimate shooting guard in the history of basketball, and Wennington, a journeyman center—and Jordan seemed to be challenging Wennington to a game.

"Any time," Wennington said. He smiled at Jordan and joshingly said: "You just need the confidence."

Jordan grabbed the ball, dribbled hard at Wennington, pulled back, went into the air and sank one.

"Oh, who said I don't like this building?" Jordan called out.

Wennington dribbled; Jordan stole the ball from him, turned, went into the air in the same motion, double-pumped to get Wennington's arms out of the way, then hit another long jump shot.

"*Confidence,*" Jordan said, wagging his finger at Wennington.

Wennington put in a layup. Jordan retrieved the ball and slammed a dunk over Wennington's extended arms.

"I *like* this building," Jordan said. "I *like* it."

Wennington, using his bigger size, backed Jordan into the key, moving Jordan out of his way with his body. "That's not fair!" Jordan yelled out in feigned indignation, a kid on a playground. "You shouldn't back me in!"

Wennington dunked the ball. Jordan grabbed it from the floor, dribbled behind the key, let Wennington get within a foot or two of him, and then let sail a shot toward the basket. It went in.

"*Confidence,*" he called.

Jordan was jokingly taunting Wennington, the two of them being playful. Some ushers had arrived at the arena, and were sitting in the stands watching, and Jordan hit another shot and teased Wennington again. Some of the ushers began to laugh, and a couple of them yelled mildly insulting comments in Wennington's direction.

And Jordan stopped in his tracks and turned toward them. No smile on his face, he stared at the ushers who had laughed, and said to them in cold, even tones: "You want to join in?"

It wasn't an invitation. It was a reminder—to them and to anyone else who was merely an observer of all this. The reminder was: You do not play this game. You are here only because you work in the arena. Do not do that to my teammate. I can kid with him because we have something in common. We play this game at this level in this league. You are not a part of this.

Jordan whispered something to Wennington, then took a jump shot that missed badly, bouncing off the backboard. I couldn't tell if he had missed the shot on purpose. He made the next one. "I like this building," he said again, and the ushers were quiet.

Jordan, in long red gym shorts and a black Bulls T-shirt, guarded

Wennington, in white shorts and a black sleeveless sweatshirt. He was all over Wennington, sticking his hands wherever Wennington tried to dribble, moving his body to the parts of the floor Wennington was trying to take over. "Oh, good defense, M.J.," Jordan called to himself; Wennington retrieved the ball, took it into the lane, hit a short jumper, and Jordan nodded at him and said, "Good shot."

Whatever those first few days with the team must have been like when Jordan came up from Florida, whatever awkwardness he and they may have felt, this had to be much different. The feeling-out period was over—Jordan and the Bulls were becoming a club now, and Wennington was smiling at the goofy incongruity of this little contest, Bill Wennington versus Michael Jordan; Wennington seemed pleased to be spending this time this way. Jordan missed a jump shot from the left side of the key and announced:

"I *stink*."

An out-of-the-ordinary thing to hear coming from his mouth— maybe spontaneous, or maybe something he was saying for Wennington's benefit, one more reaction to what the ushers had done. Apparently he had been keeping score in his head, because after Wennington dunked over him Jordan tossed a long line-drive of a shot into the net from over by the sidelines, called out "Game, set and match," and walked toward the tunnel that would take him to the locker room.

"Call if you want another one," he said over his shoulder to Wennington, and Wennington, laughing, waved Jordan off with an exaggerated motion of his right hand. Meaning: Get out of here. Meaning: That was fun. What a priceless thing for these men to possess: the good fortune to be able to spend their days and nights making their livings this way.

Jim Gray handed me a business card he had been given. The business card was Magic Johnson's.

On the back, Johnson had written various private telephone numbers where he could be reached.

"He's been trying to reach Michael," said Gray, a reporter for

NBC Sports. "He told me he hasn't gotten his calls returned, and he asked me to give the card to Michael and ask him to call."

Gray had interviewed Johnson for a story scheduled to run at halftime of the Chicago–Charlotte game. It would turn out to be a newsmaking piece: Johnson, in the interview, told Gray that he would be willing to come back to the Los Angeles Lakers for the play-offs—this year's playoffs.

Johnson had seen the excitement that surrounded Jordan's re-turn. Now he was questioning his own decision to retire, and was floating the possibility of rejoining the Lakers and the NBA in the next few weeks.

The Johnson interview with Gray would make all the papers the next day. In the weeks and months to come, the playoffs would begin and end without Johnson playing; then during the summer he would talk about coming back to the NBA in the fall, then later say that he didn't really want to, and in the end would announce that it wasn't going to happen. To me, though, the giving of his business card to Gray, hoping Gray would give it to Jordan—that said as much, in a different way, as the talk about playing basketball.

If Magic Johnson couldn't get through to Michael Jordan . . .

"He said that the number he had for Michael had been changed," Gray said.

Undoubtedly true—Jordan had the phone company change his number all the time. He would give it to his friends, and within weeks too many people would have it, and he'd get a new one. If the home phone number for Jordan you had was more than six weeks old, chances are it was no good.

"When he couldn't reach Michael, he left word with Michael's agent for Jordan to call him because he wanted to talk," Gray said. "But he hasn't gotten a call, and he knew I'd be doing an interview with Michael today, and asked me to pass the card along after the interview."

I had known for a long time how much distance Jordan tried to place between himself and the rest of the world. But there were some people, who had reached a certain level in the same heady strata in which Jordan traveled, who I assumed always could get through. I looked at the back of the card, where Magic Johnson had written his numbers in the hopes that Jordan would see them and pick up the phone and call.

Perhaps, once you are no longer a daily part of this, the nonstop attention you accept as standard goes away so quickly that you suffer withdrawal pangs. Perhaps once the phone stops ringing, once the voices stop cheering, you need to seek re-entry to that world. Many people had said that this was the real reason Jordan came back to basketball—that he realized how much he had missed the attention.

Whenever we talked about it, he dismissed that notion with a shake of his head.

"Please," he said. "Think about it."

There wasn't even a twinge of wanting to be at the center of everything again?

"That never went away, anyway," he said. "It's not like it stopped when I retired from basketball. Think about what things were like for me at baseball."

I asked him if the noise and the adulation inside the NBA arenas didn't play a bigger role in his decision than he was willing to admit—maybe even to himself.

"I like Phil," Jordan said. "I like Scottie. I like B.J. I like playing basketball in the city of Chicago. That's what I figured out I missed. And I missed winning—I missed the feeling I had when the Bulls were winning and playing at their best.

"But come back for the attention? The attention is one of the only things that made me think about *not* coming back. If I could do this—play on the Bulls and compete in the league without any attention being paid to me, play and be invisible—that would be the thing I'd like the best. But obviously that's an impossibility.

"Anyone who says that I'm doing this for the attention it brings me doesn't know me at all. I get enough attention as it is. I don't need to play basketball to find out what attention feels like. The less I get, the easier my life is. At this point in my life, I could live very happily with no attention at all."

There was a fleeting moment that captured, all at once, both the absurdity of sport and some of the enduring value of sport.

Just before the Bulls–Hornets game was to begin, public address announcer Ray Clay said: "Ladies and gentlemen, our nation suffered a tragedy this week with the senseless killings in Oklahoma City. Let us stand for a moment of silence."

The bombing of the federal building in Oklahoma City, with the horror of the deaths it caused, was still new in everyone's mind; the country was nervous, security was in full force at every mass gathering point in the U.S.—including the United Center—and every package left unattended, every car stalled in traffic, bore a meaning it might not have a week earlier. Today the more than twenty thousand people in the arena rose, and the huge room became silent . . . and Benny the Bull dipped and bobbed merrily overhead.

Benny the Bull—this was the airborne Benny; the landbound version with the human inside danced around on the court during games—was the team's mascot. The one floating over the court was made of red plastic, lighter-than-air and radio-controlled. It was a silly-looking thing, designed to make people laugh. On this day the fans in the arena, and the members of the two teams, stood at attention, somber and still—and directly over the bowed heads of the Charlotte Hornets the Benny the Bull blimp hovered and hissed and made mechanical buzzing noises, Jerry Lewis at a wake.

There it was: both the ridiculous side of sport and the serene side. The serenity was in the promise that days like this fulfill for the people who come to the contests—not only on days following a tragedy, but on common and uneventful days and nights at the ballpark and the stadium, too. The daily promise of sport is that it can provide a relief from the regular world for a couple of hours—the promise is that no matter how cold the real world seems, for those hours in the arena you can count on a little warmth, and the prospect of peace, and a sense of things being all right. You can count on sports to take you away to somewhere happy. At least that's the way it's supposed to be; at least that's the ideal.

Before the game, Steve Kerr had come out to take some warmup shots, and someone had said to him, "What do you hear from your brother?" Kerr's brother Andrew was on the staff of the National Security Council in Washington, and times like this, in the aftermath of something like Oklahoma City, were presumably busy ones for him.

"He always tells me that he can't tell me anything," Kerr said, bouncing the basketball. "And that if he did, he'd have to kill me."

It was a rim-shot punch line—the way Kerr said it, you could tell he'd used it many times before. But as he took his practice jump shots, I thought about his father.

Malcolm Kerr was president of American University of Beirut when, in 1984, he was assassinated with a bullet to the back of his head. A terrorist group claimed responsibility for the murder. Steve Kerr was a freshman in college at the time. Now, in this week of the Oklahoma City bombing, the Bulls prepared to tip off against the Hornets. *And that if he did, he'd have to kill me. . . .* Kerr went through a series of exercises, as he always did before a game. He had a bad knee.

"Thataway, Michael!"

The sound floated out of the stands with less than a minute remaining in the first quarter and the Bulls trailing. Jordan had just hustled to pick up a loose ball skittering across the floor; "Thataway, Michael!" the voice called with approval.

I have no idea whether he heard it. But that prosaic sports phrase, the "thataway!" heard at every playing field in the country, from Little League parks to domed stadiums, sounded just the slightest bit amiss with his name attached to it. The reason wasn't hard to figure out.

"Thataway!" is what the fan yells to an athlete who needs encouragement and urging on. The fan might be a father watching his son take an energetic swing at home plate; the fan might be a partisan in a college arena hoping his underachieving team can move up in the standings. It's the time-honored cry of the supporter, the person on the sidelines who believes and cares.

"Thataway, Michael!" sounded a little off because, for him, the rules had become something subtly different. People might come to stadiums to urge on other athletes, but the implicit assumption with Jordan was that he needed no urging on. The people who bought tickets to games in which he was playing came not so much to cheer him—at least not in the definition of *cheer* as to gladden, to raise spirits. He was the one who was there to cheer them.

Instead, they came to observe him. Rote ovations and adulation notwithstanding, the act of watching him had become something like going to a museum; the value of the exhibits was assumed before the trip was made, the reason for the trip was to acknowledge and pay homage to the artifacts. No "thataway" was needed. The thataway was taken on faith.

Which is why, on this day, the sound of that particular word coming from the stands was both jarring and right. Jordan—and everyone knew it—hadn't been playing like Jordan. He had had some great bursts, some memorable shots, but the Jordan who could walk onto the court and know he could take over a game at will—that Jordan was not here yet.

Yet everyone had been treating him like he was that Jordan. For all these weeks, it had been as if he were the distinguished gentleman—the statue come to life. But as much as he might have earned the status of the distinguished gentleman, the last thing he needed on the basketball court was for people to treat him like that. "Thataway, Michael!" had a better sound—it spoke of how the people who knew him best might have called to him back when all of this was new, of how those who wanted him to succeed might have phrased it when they were hoping he'd do well, and not counting on it. It was a tiny thing, something that came and went in the flash of a second. But the eager and bolstering sound of it—"Thataway, Michael!"—had the cadence and the pulse of something he needed to hear.

· · · · ·

John Bach, a man who used to have Jordan's ear, watched him in silence as the second half commenced.

Bach, a basketball coach for forty-four years—in 1950 he became the youngest college head coach in the country when he was selected to run the program at Fordham University—had been an assistant to Phil Jackson, and the Bulls' chief defensive specialist, during the three championship seasons. A sardonic, worldly fellow who had always had the air of a man much younger than his chronological age, and who favored cowboy boots and Western-style suits, Bach was a particular favorite of Jordan and Horace Grant. He referred to Jordan and Scottie Pippen as "my Dobermans"—he all but salivated at the sight of those two singular athletes, tall and quick and instinctive, sprinting down the court to swarm all over opponents trying to score against the Bulls on a fast break.

But Jordan had left, and Grant had left, and Bach himself had been beset with serious cardiac problems. His contract with the Bulls had not been renewed; Charlotte had hired him, in the hopes of making a physically talented but unrefined young team more disciplined on defense, and this season Bach sat to the side of Hornets head coach Allan Bristow every game.

As he did in the United Center today. This was his first visit to the building since Jordan's return. Jordan hit a long shot from behind the key, and Bach, looking inevitably older and more than a little fatigued, on the road with a team of youthful basketball players in the 1990s just as he had been in the 1950s, turned to Bristow on his right, said something, and on a clipboard diagrammed a play.

It could be assumed that the play was a defensive move intended to stop Jordan. But Bach, in his years on the Bulls' bench, had lived through so many nights when coaches on the other bench had drawn up just such plays, when those coaches had struggled to devise ways to do what could not be done. Now it was Bach's job to do it; having been sent away from the Bulls, he spoke to Bristow, and when the brief conversation was over, his clipboard in his hand, he stared out at the court, at Jordan, at Pippen, his Dobermans. If Jordan was to be stopped, it would be by the passage of time, the accumulation of the years, not by a play anyone might draw up. And it would happen, later if not sooner. The world changes; the only question is how rapidly, and that is not for a basketball coach or a basketball player to determine. Bach, on the enemy bench, watched.

"*Three*-point basket by *Steve Kerr*!" Ray Clay shouted into the public address microphone, and the crowd exploded into cheers. The Bulls were on a run, heading toward a 116–110 victory over the Hornets.

Kerr, having seen his shot go through the net, turned to get back downcourt on defense. Hitting a three-pointer on any court is a task that demands great talent; hitting one under the pressure of an NBA game, against defenses designed to make such a feat even more difficult, is something worthy of respect and praise. To accomplish just such a thing, on a consistent basis, was what Kerr was paid for. It was his job.

He never celebrated much on the court, even after his most spectacular shots. There are difficult jobs, and then there are difficult jobs. If anyone knew that, Kerr did. I thought about his brother; I thought about his father. At the far end of the basketball court a game was going on, and Kerr was in it.

Allan Bristow, standing in the hallway after the game, was being asked questions about his team's loss to the Bulls. He was aware the contest had meant little; the first round of the playoffs, beginning in a week, when the two teams would meet in a best-of-five series, was all that counted.

He and the Hornets had played the Bulls earlier in the year in Jordan's absence; now they would be playing the Bulls with something important on the line, and Jordan would be on the court. Someone asked him how Jordan's presence had affected the Chicago team. Perhaps the questioner was expecting an answer that touched on offensive production or defensive matchups, but Bristow's reply, apparently impulsive and unrehearsed, was from another precinct of the human experience. What impact on Chicago and the Bulls was Jordan having?

"It's almost like healing," Bristow said.

· · · · ·

"I think I've figured out what the difference is," Jordan said.

We were talking about the United Center. The rest of the world could dwell on the philosophic and metaphysical meanings of Jordan's return; to him the most pressing concern was still the unfriendly building, and how he might finally make it his ally.

"See, it's open, real open," he said. "It feels like an *arena*, not a *stadium*."

"But you've played in other places just like it," I said.

"I know," Jordan said. "The old Stadium didn't feel like any other place in the league. So when we were on the road, we'd play in a lot of places that feel just like our new building does. But those buildings weren't ours. When we came home, it was to a place that we knew was home. We had one of the only stadiums, and everyone else had arenas. Now we have an arena too. It's going to take some getting used to—home feeling like the road. And I think that for me, a lot of it's psychological, too."

"What do you mean?" I said.

"For so long, I made up my mind that I would not play in the new building," he said. "I just knew that I'd never play a game in there. I condemned it before it even opened, I told everyone that I couldn't play in it and that I wouldn't play in it.

"And now I'm playing in it. I had decided that I was going to hate it, and I kept saying that I was going to hate it, so it's almost like I have to hate it because I'm supposed to hate it. But that's not doing me any good. I have to get over that, and deal with it."

"So you think it's all in your head?" I said.

"Well, a lot of it," Jordan said. "But there's something that really is different—something I couldn't figure out at first, but now I know what it is."

"What's that?" I said.

"The warmth," Jordan said. "In the new place, you don't have to run for five minutes just to get yourself warm. The old Stadium, it was so freezing in there that as soon as you put your uniform on you had to run just to make your body warm.

"The new place, the building's temperature is already warm. So when you put your uniform on, you feel different than you did across the street. It's like you're thinking you ought to be doing something, but there's no need to do it. I hadn't figured this out at first, but that's it. In the old place, you'd feel like jumping around as soon as you were in your shorts, just to beat the cold. Now there's no need to. And you know it even if you don't really know why you know it."

"So you think the new place is eventually going to feel like home?" I said.

"Oh, yeah," he said.

"How long do you think it will take?" I asked.

Jordan grinned.

"Not long," he said. "Maybe thirty years."

"Schedule Next Week."

The handwritten note had been taped to a board inside the Bulls' locker room, for the players to see before they left the United Center. This would be the last time they were here before the playoffs; the coaching staff was letting them know when they were supposed to be at the practice facility in suburban Deerfield.

"Monday Eve—Pizza Nite—7:00 p.m."

The playoffs and NBA Finals would be telecast around the world; this was the sports industry at its most sophisticated and business-driven, with the stakes enormous, the revenues astronomical, the audience—tens of millions in the United States alone—all but un-fathomable.

And for the twelve men on the Bulls, it came down to "pizza nite" in Deerfield. Like a high school squad being enticed by the coach to give up a free evening for the good of the team, the Bulls were being told to come to practice at night instead of during the usual daytime workout hours. But there would be pizza provided—yes, you have to practice after dark, but it's a pizza party, too.

Were life's pleasures and pressures only able to remain so simple. Jordan and his teammates read the notice, then drove out of the new arena and past the old one, now almost leveled, on their way home.

CHAPTER 17

In the midst of the first round of the playoffs, Bill Smith arrived at the arena five hours before tipoff, as he had for much of Jordan's career in Chicago. Smith, the Bulls' official photographer, began linking his cameras via a series of wires to strobe lights mounted up by the ceiling.

A tall, quiet man, Smith had to his credit fifteen covers of *Sports Illustrated*. Down here on the floor in the silence of the nearly empty building, he pushed the button on his camera that tripped the shutter, and all the way up at the top of the soaring structure his lights flashed. Push, trip, flash; push, trip, flash; Smith kept running tests to make sure that when the game began, every time Jordan shot he would shoot too, and every time he shot the strobes would ignite.

"In the old Stadium, I went up and adjusted the lights so they were positioned just in the right way to light Michael's face when he was dunking," Smith said. "He was dunking a lot more back then, and he got higher over the basket than most players. Unless he was lit exactly, you would see shadows on his face in the pictures. So I would go up on the catwalks and angle the ceiling strobes at both ends of the court so they would illuminate his face in just the right way as he was putting the ball into the hoop."

"Did Jordan know that?" I asked. "That the lights had been set up specifically to shine on his face?"

"I'm sure he didn't," Smith said.

He clicked the camera again. Way up there, the strobes answered him.

"And if he did know, he wouldn't care anyway," Smith said.

Jordan, a man who went through life always assuming he was being lit, had not yet arrived for the day.

The Chicago–Charlotte series began on the Hornets' home court in North Carolina. Jordan, in his public comments before the game, tried to portray as a potential benefit the fact that he and his teammates were still getting to know each other: "There's an advantage we have because no one really knows what to expect from the Chicago Bulls. I like that. We may not be favored. We may not be the team of two years ago. We may not need to be the team of two years ago. Our play is going to dictate what we need and what's going to happen." When reporters asked him if he thought the Bulls really had a chance in the playoffs, he said, "I believe we can win, or else I never would have come back."

In that first game the Charlotte team appeared giddy and too young, celebrating every time they went ahead, leaping into the air as if they had just won the NBA Finals whenever they scored a basket that put them a point or two up on Chicago. Pippen was playing poorly—he attempted no shots at all in the first half, had three fouls before the second quarter was over, and missed much of the fourth quarter because he had picked up his fifth foul midway through the third. The lead changed hands eleven times in the final quarter, and regulation ended in a 92–92 tie. In overtime Jordan took over, scoring 10 of the Bulls' 16 points—he had also scored 10 in the fourth quarter—to finish the game with 48 points and lead Chicago to a 108–100 victory.

The win deprived Charlotte of the home-court advantage over the Bulls it had worked all season to achieve, and after the game, asked by the press why he had chosen to personally dominate the overtime period, Jordan said, "I felt like a shark in the water that saw blood. I just had to attack and hope I'd bite the right person." Asked what the world could expect next, Jordan said: "Tonight was a scrap game. Find a way to win. Get the first game out of the way and now go back, tune things up, and play the way we're capable of playing. Now we're at the point where we're going to get greedy."

Although circumstances called for Jordan to make those kinds of public comments, he understood that—at least for him—the outcome of this series, or the playoffs themselves, would constitute only a small and barely significant chapter in an ongoing story. Regardless of how far the Bulls advanced in the playoffs, a series of questions would be waiting for him afterward—not the least of which would be whether he wished to play on the United States Olympic basketball team in 1996.

For most players, being asked to join the Olympic team was an enormous honor, and for them such an invitation was far from a certainty. Jordan had won a gold medal while a collegian in 1984, and in 1992—the first year NBA players were allowed to compete in the Olympics—he had wavered before accepting a position on the team. At first he had said he didn't want to play—he'd already played in the Olympics, and preferred to let someone else take his spot—but then, faced with criticism about the message refusing to play in the Olympics sent, he agreed to compete. In Barcelona he spent much of his time in his hotel room, and did not march in the opening ceremonies. He knew that he would be mobbed if he marched—and he was castigated in the press for not being a part of the evening.

He and the rest of the U.S. team easily won the gold medal—but the whole question of the Olympics, and his role as an Olympian, was something that plainly annoyed Jordan. Any time we talked about it, he didn't attempt to hide his feelings.

"Look, I knew that if I went to the opening ceremonies, I couldn't enjoy it," he said. "I had marched in opening ceremonies—I had done it the first time I went. So it wasn't going to be a new experience for me."

"But people thought that you were snubbing the rest of the Olympic teams from other countries by not going," I said.

"I was there in Barcelona, wasn't I?" he said. "How could I be snubbing the Olympics? I was playing in the Olympics. I watched the opening ceremonies on TV, from the hotel. I saw them better on TV than if I'd been in the middle of them. I saw Scottie marching. I saw Magic marching. For them, it was new—they should have been there. For me, it would have been something I'd done back when I was in college."

"Did you enjoy the Olympics at all?" I said.

"In Barcelona?" he said. "It was so commercialized—that was the whole point of sending us over there. It was a sales trip. We were salesmen."

"For what?" I said.

"For the NBA," Jordan said. "Our whole purpose there wasn't to win a gold medal for the United States—everyone knew we were going to do that. Our purpose was to sell NBA basketball, so that it could expand into a worldwide business. Every one of us on the Olympic team knew that. It started as soon as the NBA Finals ended that year, with the practices and the games that we played leading up to the Olympics. It was one long sales call, and we were the salesmen."

"Some business trips can be fun," I said.

"Our own practices were fun," Jordan said. "Playing against the other guys on the team—that was great camaraderie and great competition. But I was in a Catch-22 the whole time, and it never left my mind. I would have preferred not to go, to have some time between basketball seasons for myself and my family, and to let people who had never competed in the Olympics have the experience. I probably should have stuck by my guns and not gone. But if I didn't go—well, I could see what the reaction was going to be. It seemed like less trouble to just go and play."

For him, there was a logic to this. For many other people, it made no sense. Here was a man who would get up before the sun every morning to take batting practice, with no one there, knowing that his chances of becoming a good baseball player were dim—yet he would spend endless hours at it. But he was reluctant to devote time to playing a sport he was great at in front of a global television audience on every continent?

"That makes perfect sense to me," he said. "The one, I had done, and there was no real challenge to it—I knew how it was going to come out. It wasn't a new experience. The other, I had no idea if I could succeed. It was up to me to do the work and find out. And that provided me with great enjoyment and fulfillment."

He was well aware that, in 1996, the decision was going to be his to make again. He didn't want to play in the Atlanta Olympics—but he knew that as the time grew closer, there would be pressure from the NBA, pressure from the public, pressure from companies whose products he endorsed, all of them telling him that, for his own good, he ought to play. If he decided not to play, he would be called unpatriotic, and unappreciative of what the United States had given him. It was a powerful argument—one he had mistakenly thought he could walk away from back in 1992.

"I had thought it was something I could make up my own mind to do or not to do, and it would be no big deal, just a personal decision based on personal reasons," he said. "But it didn't work out that way. It wasn't a question of helping the team to win—you know they were going to win whether I played or not. But the NBA needed the whole sales team to be there, and I was one of the salesmen they wanted. That's what it was about."

Pippen had scored only 8 points in the Game 1 win over Charlotte. Sometimes it was easy to overlook that Pippen, a brooding man who had complained all during the season that he felt underappreciated by the Bulls, and that he wanted to be traded, was at the absolute top of his profession—he owned three world championship rings, he had been a member of the NBA All-Star team five times, he had won his Olympic gold medal and would be invited to play on the '96 U.S. Olympic team, too.

Yet it was never clear how he truly responded to his career-long role in Jordan's shadow. After Jordan had led the Bulls to the overtime victory in Charlotte, he told the sportswriters, "The reason I took more responsibility was because Pippen wasn't in the game. I felt I had to show my leadership. I felt I had to do something. In doing so, I may have taken some people out of the game, but they have to learn to be more aggressive."

There were times when it seemed Pippen felt pleased to have Jordan back, and to be relieved of the responsibility of being the Bulls' main focus, and other times when he seemed frustrated to have been moved back a notch again with Jordan's return. Mostly it was complicated in the way all human questions are complicated. To me the most telling scene in the Jordan–Pippen tale came during a road trip before the regular season had ended.

A seven-year-old girl in a wheelchair, obviously very ill, had been taken before the game to a dim hallway back near the locker rooms, and had been waiting for more than an hour for the teams to come out. She suffered from Werdnig-Hoffmann disease, a deadly disorder that causes spinal-muscular atrophy. She was at this arena as a beneficiary of the Make-a-Wish Foundation, an organization that tries to brighten the lives of children affected by the severest life-threatening sicknesses. The idea is to give the children one special memory, of their own choosing, while they are here to savor it.

One of the Make-a-Wish representatives told me that this little girl had said her wish was to meet Pippen. Arrangements had been made—Pippen had agreed to do it. The child's mother was with her; Tom Smithburg, a young front-office staff member for the Bulls who was traveling with the team, had gone to the visitors' locker room to tell Pippen the child was here, and after the girl had waited a few more minutes Pippen came out, in his uniform, smiling, and approached her.

He knelt to shake her hand, and she was visibly excited. Pippen is not a person who is entirely at ease in public situations, and can be curt when he is in an irritable mood, but on this evening he clearly recognized the importance of the meeting, and was going out of his way to be gracious to the girl. He touched her hair, and softly said "Pretty hair" to her, and she beamed, her eyes wet. He had some pictures and Bulls souvenirs that he wanted to autograph for her; he saw me a few feet away, and came over to ask if he could borrow my pen. Seeing that it was a regular ballpoint, and knowing that he should sign for her in something more permanent, he said, "I'd better find a marking pen," and waited until someone had located a black felt-tip pen for him.

Although the visit was a short one, he spent more time with the child than he needed to, and when he left to go back to the locker room he seemed as moved as she was. I was moved, too; it was a lovely moment. I asked one of the adults who had brought the child to the game whether she had chosen Pippen on her own—whether it had been the little girl's idea to make him her wish.

"Yes," the adult said.

And then added:

"Of course, that was before Michael Jordan came back."

It was said without irony or intended bite; it was said simply as a fact. Pippen didn't hear it—he was already on his way into the Bulls' locker room. *Of course, that was before Michael Jordan came back.* Nine words that spoke to the basic imbalances on life's playing field, even life at these exalted levels. Nothing Pippen could ever do, either on the court or off, could change his role in relation to Jordan. It was not his to determine.

And when the Bulls came out of the locker room prior to taking the court, and gathered in their pre-game huddle before running into the arena, Jordan saw the little girl sitting there, walked over to her without having to be asked, signed some things for her, talked to her, saw her just about melt with joy. Pippen saw this, too. He saw Jordan, at the last minute, become the child's most vivid and happy memory of the evening. That was all right; Pippen's knowing smile said that it didn't matter to him. It was good for the girl. And Pippen was used to it.

Of the 42 shots from the field the Bulls attempted in the second half of Game 2 against Charlotte, only 12 went into the basket. Jordan, the North Carolina crowd heckling him, led Chicago with 32 points, seven rebounds and seven assists. But Charlotte won easily, 106–89, sending the series to Chicago tied at a game each. Allan Bristow vowed that his Hornets were now on their way to eliminating the Bulls in the best-of-five series: "We're going up there to win two games. We're going to go up like we're going to take the series up there."

That might or might not happen. But the merchandising arm of the NBA, indifferent to who might win a given game or a given series—realizing that such things were hardly the point—had devised a new bit of commerce by the time the Bulls and the Hornets arrived at the United Center for Game 3. A company had been authorized to sell the seats. Not tickets—the seats themselves.

On the cushions of the courtside seats in Chicago, when the fans showed up for the game, were notifications that, for $175, they could take home "one of these same courtside Authentic Collectible Playoff Chairs that you sat on and cheered on as your 1995 Chicago Bulls playoff memories were made." Seven hundred fifty of these close-in seats were available. The fans, who had paid to sit on them and watch the games, now could pay more to take them home and sit on them again.

"Where's my seat?" Toni Kukoc said to Tom Smithburg.

Kukoc wasn't referring to the take-one-home-for-posterity seats. He had just arrived in the arena, and had seen Smithburg setting up the press tables under the basket. Smithburg was taping cards bearing the names of the sportswriters onto their assigned spots at the tables; Kukoc said he wanted a place.

"You don't feel like playing today?" Smithburg said.

"Maybe not," Kukoc said. "Maybe I'll sit here."

Six-feet-eleven, from Split, Croatia, Kukoc had an endearing quality to him—a stranger in a strange land (two strange lands, actually: the United States and the NBA), there were times when, with his halting English and his sunny but bewildered expressions, he seemed a character out of poignant sports fiction, a cross between *The Harder They Fall* and *Requiem for a Heavyweight*.

Several years back, when Bulls general manager Jerry Krause had first recruited Kukoc, Jordan had made no secret of the fact that he was less than agog over the idea of Kukoc joining the team. During these Charlotte playoffs, though, Jordan had told the press, "He's my project. . . . He's really, really trying hard to learn this style of basketball. He has a lot of potential. There are just a lot of expectations on him and I'm trying to make him understand that it's really simple. Just play. I laugh because he's a kid who's really trying, but he's lost sometimes."

Unlike the befuddled athlete-characters of novels, Kukoc did not have to worry about how he might pay for bed and board after his days in the arena were over. The Bulls had signed him to a six-year contract worth $26 million. In a blue pin-striped suit, a grin on his face, a fellow far from home, he gazed around the arena.

"I don't think Phil would appreciate it if you watched the game from the press table," Smithburg said to him.

"All right, then," Kukoc said affably, and went in to put on his shorts and his basketball shoes.

I went up to the Fandemonium gift shop, the one that had been locked on the day I'd first seen its employees stacking the Jordan jerseys on the counters.

It was open now, and packed. The most instructive sight was not the array of Bulls merchandise that covered every flat surface of the store, and most of the walls. That was to be expected. But over in a corner, behind glass, was Jordan's old locker from the Chicago Stadium.

It was a cubicle, really—the cubicle where he had sat as he had dressed and undressed on all those Stadium nights. The public had seen it thousands of times; he had sat in front of it after virtually every game at the old Stadium, answering questions while the television cameras recorded it all. Someone had once joked that Jordan ought to sell advertising space on the cubicle wall behind his head—it was the most-seen wall in Chicago, and if a company had purchased the rights to display its logo on it, that logo would have been on every channel, on every game night, for those many years.

The idea had been a fanciful one—but if the person who had come up with it had thought he was being ludicrous, then he wouldn't have believed this. No one could have made it up. On the glass that enclosed the Jordan cubicle was a placard of the kind found in art museums. It said: "Michael Jordan's Original Chicago Stadium Locker." And people were lined up so they could file past it.

Their voices were hushed, as if this were, indeed, a museum exhibit of priceless and ancient artifacts—or a house of worship. They whispered rather than talk at full volume. "Look," a man said softly to his wife. "His shoes."

Jordan's shoes were, to be sure, on the floor of the exhibit, right next to the chair upon which he used to sit. A pair of his white socks were hanging out of the locked compartment at the top of the cubicle—whatever curator had arranged this display was a stickler for authentic period detail, the socks couldn't have looked any more right had Jordan tossed them in there himself after a game.

There was no admission price to see this. It was a way to attract more customers into the gift shop. The line grew longer, as more people waited their turns. They passed his chair, they passed his socks, and when they were finished some returned to the end of the line to walk past the locker again.

Jordan always seemed like a man who could not bear to be in one place. When he had departed the Bulls, he had felt the irresistible urge to be somewhere else: The reasons he expressed for needing to go to baseball made sense, but the real drive seemed not so much to go to a baseball diamond as to just go somewhere, anywhere other than where he was. Then, when he left spring training in such a hurry, he had his explanations for why he felt he must. Again, though, he was in such a rush to get out—it seemed like a more dramatic version of how he would always speed away from every building he ever left, as if he were being chased.

And there was something else. Every time he'd get to the next place, the place he'd left behind would look suddenly better to him. He had fled because he'd felt it was necessary—but wherever he alighted, it was as if he immediately blocked out the bad parts, and yearned for the good.

So it was with his memories of baseball. Now that he was a basketball player again, he loved to think about those baseball days and nights. One in particular—one that meant the most to him.

"The home run," Jordan said. "The first home run."

I asked him why it had signified so much for him. The world had heard about him pointing to the sky, a symbolic gesture to the father who wasn't there. Was that the whole reason?

"No," he said. "It was a lot of things. I'll never forget that night.

"I was thinking about my dad, of course. But my mother was in the stands that night, and so was my sister. They'd come to see me play. So for me to do it in front of them . . . what a feeling. What a night."

I asked him what he was thinking as he rounded the bases.

"I was just so happy," he said. "Because after all the talk about how I didn't have a chance, and then all the talk about how if I was sent to the minor leagues I wouldn't have the patience to stick around—and then the ball was going over the fence, and my mom was watching, and I knew that this was something no one would ever be able to take away from me.

"It wasn't that I was mad at people for saying I couldn't do it. It was just that at that moment, those people stopped mattering to me. It didn't matter what they had said—it was a real game, and the pitcher was trying to get me out, and I hit that ball and no one would ever be able to tell me that I hadn't done it. Because I had done it. The ball was gone.

"When I say I had done it, I don't just mean hit the home run. The home run, to me, stood for a lot of things. It stood for staying with it even when I was feeling my lowest, when I was feeling that I'd never make it. It stood for not listening to anyone who told me I was stupid to try to be a baseball player. It stood for believing in myself and shutting everyone else out. It wasn't just the home run.

"All the things I've ever done, all the things I've ever hoped for— I'll never forget the feeling that night. The feel of the bat hitting the ball, and watching the ball go over the fence, and I was out there, running the bases, and I'd done it. I'd gotten it done."

But that was over now, which was why he could linger on the particulars of it with such pleasure.

Now he was somewhere else, with something else to accomplish. In Game 3, the first playoff game ever in the United Center, he and the Bulls showed themselves at their very best, and for those forty-eight minutes the Hornets never had a scrap of a chance. Pippen and Kukoc, for the first time in the series, had their games turned up at the same time. Kukoc made 9 of his 10 shots from the field for 22 points, and dished off five assists to his teammates; Pippen shot 6-for-10, good for 14 points, found his fellow Bulls for nine assists, pulled down five rebounds, stole the ball from the Hornets twice—he looked like the smoothest and most selfless player anyone could ever want on his team.

That anyone was Jordan, who scored 25 himself, grabbed six rebounds, stole the ball four times. On the floor, he had the look of someone who had somehow wandered into a motion picture, decided he liked the plot and the actors, and joined in the performance. That's the way it appeared—as if he were observing the game and playing in it at the same time, as if he were watching the show as an approving fan, and also choosing to star in it. You could see it the whole game: his unhidden happiness at seeing the other Bulls on the floor playing so well (sometimes, for an instant, he seemed to hold back for a beat, just so he could take it all in), mixed with his determination to add to the script himself. It's the kind of thing you only witness on a basketball court once in a while—this inebriating mix of studied appreciation and delirious spontaneity—and when it happens, it's as if the scoreboard clock has no alliance with real time, as if the events on the floor exist in their own universe, and that no one on the court, and no one beholding, has any choice but to ride the joy. He may still have been remembering that home run, but tonight it was Bulls 103, Hornets 80, and he left the court with the gait of a rhapsodic and contented child.

. . . . .

Which he was not, and could never be again. The real rhapsodic and contented children—he could see them on his way from the locker room onto the floor, on his way from the floor into the locker room—were leaning over the railings, stretching their hands toward him, many of them (at some moments it seemed like most of them) wearing the jerseys with the number 45 on the fronts and backs.

It was, as it had been at the arena on the road against the Nets, a little unsettling, all those 45s. Jordan seemed to have spawned these youngsters, it was as if he were some kind of space creature and they were his miniature offspring, multiplying faster than anyone could control. Yet on him (if not on them), the 45 still looked wrong, felt wrong.

From the moment he had put it on on a basketball court, it had the crass feel of a less-than-subtle commercial. Like the Nike logo on the shoes he wore, like the Gatorade emblem on the cups he drank from, the 45 seemed like a contrivance baldly intended to move a product, in a way that 23 never had. Not that 23 hadn't moved millions of products—but 23 was the number he had been assigned when he had first become a Bull, while 45 was something he had devised. The 45 had worked in baseball—in a way, it had been right for baseball, it had been his signal that he recognized the different world he was stepping into.

Here, regardless of his intentions, whenever he put on the 45 it was as if he were a high-fashion runway model, showing off the new spring line. If the glamorous and highly paid model can wear it and make it look good, then so can the folks in the mall, in the community-center gyms, in the parking lots, as long as they are willing to make the purchase. So can the children leaning over the railing, reaching out to touch him as if he had the answer.

Just as the series with Charlotte had started, news services had carried the story that Larry Martin Demery, one of the men charged with the murder of Jordan's father, had entered a guilty plea.

Asked for a reaction by reporters covering the playoffs, Jordan said that he had "no thoughts" about the court proceedings. "It doesn't really make a difference for me in terms of where my life goes right now," he said. "I'm committed to letting that thing take its course and let the judicial system take over. . . . But in terms of the impact on my life, it really doesn't make a difference."

He had said before that the court proceedings involving the accused killers were of little interest to him, because regardless of what happened to those men, his father wasn't coming back. Yet without question the news about Demery was a reminder to Jordan of how little control he had over outside events—and not just the terrible events surrounding his father's death.

"I suppose I'd better prepare to start feeling like a criminal again," he had said, resignation in his voice, as we talked one afternoon after he'd decided to come back to the NBA. "Because I'm sure I'm going to be treated like one."

The bedrooms, the bank accounts, the family troubles of successful and famous men and women had become fair game for anyone who wished to profit from their frailties. People in the public eye usually accepted this with some version of the "It-comes-with-the-territory" sentiment. But some people were less hardened to this phenomenon than others. Jordan many times seemed not hardened at all.

"When you're a kid and you first dream of achieving something, this is the part no one tells you about," he said.

He had been mortified when his gambling excesses had been made public during his first basketball career. He had almost frantically apologized to the public, his family, his friends. It was as if he had somehow failed to discern, up to that juncture in his life, the ravenousness of the public appetite for hurtful news about people who have risen to the top.

"I know you're supposed to take the bad along with the good," he said. "But people who envy people who are in a position like mine—I don't think they have any idea what it feels like. You're supposed to pretend not to care, but how can you not care?"

The murder of his father had put much of this in perspective; that hurt so overwhelmed any pain he had felt before that everything else became insignificant. Yet even in his grief after the murder, he was deeply wounded by speculation that appeared some places in the press before the arrests were made, speculation that James Jordan had somehow been killed as punishment for his son's gambling debts. The people who printed and broadcast those rumors had no basis for what they wrote and said—they were playing guessing games, filling space, as if there was no one on the other end who might suffer at hearing such things.

But there was. In the wake of his father's murder, Jordan was in effect being accused of being responsible for it. That is just about the worst thing you can say to a grieving son—that he brought on the death of his parent—yet because Michael Jordan was a public figure, it was said with impunity, and without apology.

"I can forgive a lot of things," he said. "But I can never forgive that."

Jordan said something into Pippen's ear as the Bulls came onto the court for the beginning of Game 4; Pippen nodded. The Bulls had been here before—on the floor against a nervous team that knew, with one more loss, its season would be over. During the championship years this was a situation in which Chicago had proved itself adroit and coolly efficient: taking advantage of the other team's fear, making sure the opponents never forgot that any sloppiness, any slip in concentration, would send them home until the autumn.

The ball went up, the sneakers squeaked against the wood, the crowd stood and roared, and the clock started to tick down, as in any other game during any NBA season, but different at this time of year, on this kind of night. Jordan darted toward the basket, raised one arm to draw Pippen's attention. The Hornets converged in the lane, water filling a vacuum.

"Michael was looking for the ball. . . ."

John Paxson's voice came out of the ceiling. He and his radio partner, Neil Funk, were broadcasting from courtside; the national sports press was in town, packing not only the press tables beneath the basket but also the long, multi-tiered press boxes high in the United Center, up by the roof.

The Bulls radio broadcast was piped loudly into these upper press boxes, not exactly like a laugh track on a situation comedy, but a distracting sensation anyway—to watch the game in person and listen to the true sound of the crowd, and at the same time hear the game through the radio speakers as if it were taking place in some other city, the game and the radio version of the game, the crowd and the radio version of the crowd, noise on noise, information on information, and down below a rubber ball kept smacking against a wooden floor.

That one of the voices was Paxson's made it seem all the more removed. Like a reminder of triumphant Bulls moments gone, of the way now turns suddenly into then, his voice told the story of the game, and so recently he was not the teller but the told-about, his name the name on others' lips. There was a television version of the game inside the new arena, too, big screens on the scoreboard, tempting all the eyes in all the seats, those eyes conditioned in a video age to reject the game played by little men on the floor and instead watch the parallel game played by giant versions of those men on the color screen.

The chairs—the chairs that were for sale—were all occupied by their potential buyers down near the contest, and somewhere in the building the Jordan locker/museum was open for whatever visitors might wish to walk away from the game. Toni Kukoc ran up the floor, and Paxson's voice, spoken into a microphone near the court, sent by wires to his radio station's studio, transmitted across the Midwest from a steel tower, arriving back in this building within milliseconds of Paxson's committing his thoughts to voice—Paxson's voice came out of the ceiling, and on the scoreboard screen Kukoc wiped big drops of sweat from his forehead. From his position under the basket Bill Smith pushed a button on his camera, and in the rafters a strobe light blazed, casting even light on Jordan's face so far below.

. . . . .

The Bulls did everything they could to lose, but Charlotte seemed afraid of winning, so Chicago moved on to the next round.

Scoring only 11 points in the third period—including no points at all in the first five minutes and twenty-two seconds—the Bulls set a new franchise record for lowest production in a quarter. Jordan removed himself from the contest and sat on the bench for a couple of minutes in the third—"They kept throwing the ball to me, and they had to realize they have to walk on their own two feet if we're to succeed," he would say after the game—and the team's cold streak continued into the fourth quarter.

But Charlotte was tentative, and Jordan—on his way to a 24-point game—helped keep the contest close. He hit two free throws with 1:07 left, putting the Bulls ahead 85–84. Chicago did not score again, and Charlotte had plenty of opportunities to win—Larry Johnson missed a jump shot with three seconds remaining, and then Hersey Hawkins missed a close-in shot of his own. The Hornets shouted that Hawkins was fouled on that last shot at the buzzer, and should have been sent to the free-throw line with a chance to win for his team. They said that the NBA didn't wish Charlotte to advance in the playoffs—that the league wanted the better TV ratings that would be earned if the Bulls advanced to the next round, so the referees knew not the call the foul. "If that's what they're crying about in the other locker room, so be it," Jordan said after the game. "That wasn't the only call missed tonight."

Asked by a reporter whether he had touched Hawkins on that last play, Jordan, having been through these kinds of one-day controversies too many times before, said, "Yeah, I probably got his whole arm." Meaning: Forget about it. Meaning the game was over and the playoffs were moving on. Happens every year.

Except that it had been two years since he had been a part of this. I wondered whether there was anything he knew about basketball now that he hadn't known two years ago. It had seemed that there was nothing more he could discover about his sport.

"But that's wrong," he said. "I do know something about basket-ball that I didn't before."

"What's that?" I said.

"The game is just the game to me now," he said. "It had become something else—I had let it get too complicated. But now I know that it's just the game."

"You didn't know that the last time you were in the playoffs?" I said.

"I think I probably knew it a long time ago," he said. "When I was a kid. But I'd forgotten. You just have to let the game be a game, and enjoy it as that. To play a game and have some fun. It's why you started doing this in the first place."

CHAPTER 18

On the day before the Bulls were scheduled to begin their playoff series against the Orlando Magic, I was supposed to meet some people for a business appointment at Michael Jordan's Restaurant. I had never been there.

The meeting had nothing to do with Jordan. The restaurant to which he lent his name was merely the site that had been selected. When I arrived early, one of the managers asked me if I would like to wait "in the boss' room."

We climbed a concrete back stairway used by employees. When we arrived on the second floor, the manager led me through the big dining room, where patrons were having lunch, until we got to a room-within-the-room, its windows blocked by venetian blinds. He unlocked the door.

Ever since Jordan's restaurant had opened in downtown Chicago, it had been a phenomenal moneymaker. For tourists, for people staying downtown after work for a drink, for suburban children planning birthday and bar mitzvah celebrations in its party rooms, the name of the place was all the sell that was needed. Any time there was an important Bulls game, or a piece of news involving Jordan, all the local TV stations would assign their reporters to do live dispatches from the bar or the sidewalk. The restaurant, like the statue, had become a destination.

And there was much talk of Jordan's private dining room. That was part of the tease—the management company consistently mentioned that Jordan liked to have dinner here, or to come in after games, and that he and his friends gathered until late at night in his private room. The private room was never shown on television or photographed—it was left to the imagination, a luxurious spa where the man whose name was on the building could stretch out and have his meals in the splendor he had earned. Of course, all the diners at the restaurant each night were spurred to wonder whether he was behind those drawn blinds—maybe he was present, having the kind of party the rest of the world could only hope to be invited to.

The restaurant was sort of the culinary equivalent of a Michael Jordan rookie trading card, or an Air Jordan shoe, and it had never occurred to me to have a meal there. Now, though, the manager opened the door to Jordan's private room, and said that I was free to wait inside.

The room was tiny. There was a dinner table with six chairs, and a couch, and those venetian blinds blocking the view into the main restaurant. Claustrophobic and overheated, his private dining room seemed that it would feel like a jammed-to-discomfort elevator if more than twelve people tried to get inside. It was difficult for me to imagine Jordan unwinding here, or wanting to, especially knowing that outside the room hundreds of eyes were staring at the windows; the room had the aura of a nicely decorated minimum-security prison, with guards standing sentry at all hours. Except in the case of Jordan's little dining room, the guards were his fans.

The room was a clever and efficient piece of marketing—it was there to add a kick to the customers' evenings, to give them the tantalizing questions to ask themselves as they ate, and to talk about when they returned home: Was Jordan in there? Were the lights on behind the blinds? Was that a shadow—was someone moving inside the box?

I sat alone at the dinner table. On one wall was a framed portrait of Jordan's late father, wearing a sport shirt; on another wall, a second piece of James Jordan artwork, this one a painting showing him wearing a golf cap, overlaid with a depiction of Michael playing basketball.

It had the feel of an item from a poster shop, and I wondered whether Jordan had been the one to choose to have it here.

There was a phone with a button indicating that his private extension was Line 23; menus with his name on the front, the same menus the customers out in the main room used, were placed atop the table. I went over to one of the windows that faced the public room and tilted a slat on the blinds; I looked out at people looking in. One man had his face pressed to the glass. It would be hard to conceive of a setting designed to make Jordan feel less at ease. I sat there for a while, waiting until the time to meet the people who had arranged our appointment. The manager knocked on the door and came back in. I had noticed that there was no bathroom in Jordan's dining room.

"We have a security person take him down the hall," the manager said. "Security stands outside the regular men's room and keeps people out while Michael is in there. And we have him carry this."

He showed me a small electronic device.

"He carries it with him to the bathroom, and he knows to press the button if anything happens where he needs help," the manager said. "We can have someone in there within seconds."

There was something that seemed more than a little unfortunate and sobering about all of this, the thought of the man in the box. He had reached the apex of what America has to offer its most favored, and had made it to here: a custom-designed cell where he could eat in solitude surrounded by unseen strangers trying to look in, where he could feel secure in the knowledge that there were protectors outside the bathroom door, and a button in his hands to bring them running. When it was time for my appointment I left his dining room, passing people who were standing a foot or two away and gazing at the glass. Downstairs, in the gift shop, the merchandise was being stacked up, just like at the United Center. There was a line of people waiting to get into the bar.

"There won't be any farewell tour," Jordan said. "When it's over this time, it will be over for good. It's been one long tour, anyway."

He had always said that it made him sad when a great sports star—Kareem Abdul-Jabbar was one he frequently named—announced the end of his career one year before retirement, and then turned the final year into a grand and nostalgic tour. Gifts presented at center court before each road game, tributes read by the P.A. announcers in all the opponents' arenas—it had the half-dolesome, half-droll feel of the crowned head of a small royal principality saying goodbye to his subjects before he stepped down.

"First of all, I can't think of many people who need gifts given to them less than me," he said. "I've never understood that whole thing.

"If the purpose of a farewell tour is to make the person know he was appreciated, I've been lucky enough to know that for a long time now. There's no need to organize it. I've felt it."

Toward the end of his first time through the league he had consistently said that when he decided to leave it would happen so quickly that "people's heads will spin." He had lived up to his word on that one. Now, though, back for a second career the duration of which no one knew, had he changed his mind? When it came time to stop once and for all, would he give a year's notice?

"No," he said. "All that does is stir things up. And right now I'm hoping for the opposite. The best thing for me now would be if everything just died down, and I became a basketball player playing basketball games every night. This event thing has already gone too far as it is.

"When you think about it, I've had my farewell tours, year after year. And baseball felt that way last year, and this spring, coming back to the Bulls, has felt that way, too. There's nothing that could be organized that would ever top it. I've felt everything from the stands that there is to feel.

"For me to go out with a big final tour—look, I wouldn't blame people if they got real tired of seeing my face on TV. I've been on TV so much that I'm tired of seeing my face on TV. This has all happened as it's happened—there's no need to make a show of it at the end. The show will just stop some day."

· · · · ·

The National Broadcasting Company had planned a big Sunday evening around the Bulls' first playoff game against the Magic. This would be Jordan versus Shaquille O'Neal, and the viewership numbers were expected to be staggering. To make the night the kind of blockbuster that would most help the network in the May ratings sweeps, NBC had scheduled its first-ever airing of the motion picture *Jurassic Park* for after the game.

The network's graphic designers had come up with an electronic version of the *Jurassic Park* dinosaur logo to show on the screen during the game, to remind the viewers to stay with NBC. So the nation saw Jordan getting ready to shoot a free throw, saw him twirling the ball in his hands, and at the same moment saw the *Jurassic Park* logo, too. They were both logos—Jordan and the movie dinosaur, both of them logos and merchandise and corporate profit centers. Both recognizable in an instant around the world, both brands backed by teams of sales experts poised to exploit every business opportunity, they were logos that had become more effective and lucrative than anyone could ever have dreamed. The only difference was that one logo was a piece of artwork that never existed in real life, and the other logo—perhaps even more widely recognizable than the silhouette of the dinosaur—was a thirty-two-year-old human being. The dinosaur remained on the screen; the man shot the ball.

"I feel personally responsible."

With those words to reporters after Game 1 in Orlando, Jordan acknowledged the inescapable: The Bulls had had the game won, and were about to take home-court advantage from the Magic. And Jordan lost it.

There wasn't much anyone could, or would, say to him about it. Jordan had made a career of saving games for his teammates, covering for their errors. No one was going to be too critical on a day when he was the one to err.

But the way it happened was puzzling. With the Bulls leading 91–90 with 18.1 seconds left, all they had to do to secure their victory was hold on to the basketball. Jordan got the ball in the backcourt, worked it past Orlando's Nick Anderson, and dribbled across the half-court line to find Anfernee Hardaway waiting for him. While Jordan was concentrating on Hardaway, Anderson came up from behind, knocked the ball away from Jordan and toward Hardaway, who threw it to former Bull Horace Grant for a dunk. Orlando led 92–91 with 6.2 seconds remaining.

But there was still plenty of time left for the Bulls to come back. Jordan, getting the ball, dribbled into the lane past Donald Royal of the Magic. Just as he seemed ready to go up for the game-winning shot—or to draw a foul that would put him at the free-throw line with a chance to win that way—he threw the ball to his left, toward Pippen, who wasn't looking for it. The ball bounced off Pippen's right hand, and the Bulls were losers.

To see Jordan play that poorly with the game on the line baffled many people, and emboldened others. The Las Vegas jokes began immediately—the implication being that the only way Jordan could perform that badly was if he chose to. Nothing was destined to insult and infuriate him more than that kind of talk—unless it was a postgame comment by the Magic's Nick Anderson: "Number 45 doesn't explode like number 23. Number 23, he could just blow by you. He took off like a space shuttle. Number 45, he revs up, but he doesn't really take off." Jordan stopped talking to the press. And when he came onto the court for the next game against the Magic, he was wearing number 23. He had asked no one's permission—he had just gotten rid of 45.

It immediately became a national story—every aspect of it was massaged in the press and on television and radio, starting with the human interest tale of equipment manager John Ligmanowski's coming up with the idea for him to switch, and escalating into news reports of the NBA's issuing heavy fines against Jordan and the Bulls for changing the number, and threatening more punishment if he didn't change back.

In the first Orlando game Jordan had scored only 19 points, and had turned the ball over eight times in the Bulls' loss. Wearing the new/old number 23 in the second game, he scored 38, leading Chicago to a 104–94 win. Buried in all the clamorous talk about the number change was an obvious but salient point:

A uniform number exists for a single reason: to identify a player. With Jordan—the *Jurassic Park* phenomenon again—the number is superfluous. He has to wear one, but it's not as if any person in the seats or any player or referee on the floor needs to look at his uniform to figure out who he is. The can't-tell-the-players-without-a-program tradition doesn't apply. Jordan wearing a number—whatever number—serves the same purpose as would, say, President Clinton wearing a nametag at a cocktail party. He might wear it to show everyone else that he doesn't feel he's any better than they are, but he doesn't need the tag.

Yet the 45-to-23 story would dominate the sports news for days. With all that, the most interesting public comment in reaction to Jordan's terrible finish in Game 1 came from Phil Jackson, who said, "I came back and checked the lunar charts, the celestial stations of the stars, and figured that something must have been awry. That's all you can figure. It's not going to happen very often. We just felt like it was a mirage we saw, rather than reality."

Reality it was, though, and at times like those the idea of Jordan's walking away from basketball again sooner rather than later—farewell tour or no farewell tour—seemed not only conceivable, but likely. In private moments, when he talked about how it would end this time around, he seemed relaxed and reflective.

"For the whole time in minor-league baseball, I was reminded that if you really love playing a sport, you don't have to do it in the biggest stadiums and at the highest level," he said. "A lot of the guys I played baseball with, that was as high as they were ever going to get.

"But, boy, they loved to play. For a lot of them, the fact that they'd made it past their high school teams and were now playing professionally, even though it was in the minors—they considered that a great thing. And it was, they were right.

"A lot of us in the NBA, we take it for granted that this is the only place we can play basketball, because we've made it to here. We forget about what it felt like when we were playing in high school, when it was so exciting just to put on the uniform and go onto the court for a game. Or what it felt like to play at the YMCA or something. Those days felt just as good as a lot of days in the NBA feel—maybe better, because we didn't take it for granted.

"So when I don't do this anymore, that won't mean that I'll stop playing basketball. The YMCAs are still there—I don't have to stop being a basketball player just because I stop being an NBA basketball player. There are other courts, and I'm sure I'll be on them for a long time after I stop being on these courts. I want to keep in my mind the enthusiasm for playing that I saw in the minor leagues. It was the greatest lesson I learned down there. Those guys just loved to play— they woke up full of energy because they were going to get to play that day. I hope I never forget that."

"He's going to wear 23 and black shoes," the radio reporter, having rushed to the phone, announced breathlessly into the receiver.

Indeed Jordan would. Two hours before Game 3, which would be played in the United Center, Jordan had walked onto the court to take some practice shots. His timing was interesting; he arrived on the floor at exactly 4:59 p.m., a minute before the local five o'clock television newscasts would go on the air. And for his warmup shooting, he chose the end of the court where all the Chicago TV reporters were standing in front of their cameras for their live shots back to the newsrooms. So as the newscasts began, the producers could show Jordan, close up, on the court at that very instant.

The Bulls had announced that he would wear number 23, although the league had asked him not to—and that he would wear solid-black basketball shoes, in accordance with the league's wish that he stop wearing his new white ones trimmed with black patent leather (the rest of the Bulls were wearing black shoes for the playoffs; the league required all of a team's players to wear the same color shoes during a given game). So this was a compromise of sorts—no to the league's request to wear number 45, yes to the league's request to wear black shoes.

If it was all very silly—if the radio correspondent's exhortative report from the front lines about the shirt and the shoes seemed a little comical—maybe it was just another example of what sports are for, of the salutary purpose that sports serve: to make things that aren't very important seem, for a few minutes, important; to carry out the quite legitimate function of taking the world's mind off matters that are truly troubling, and to replace those matters, at least for a while, with things that only seem to be troubling—things that can be easily solved by morning. It's therapy of a sort, restorative solace in an anxious world that can use all the escape it can get.

And Jordan, on this day, was playing along with it to the hilt. He still wasn't speaking to the press before or after the games. But, mute, he stood there shooting as the cameras focused on his chest and his feet. Without Jordan's words to feature on their newscasts, the stations were reporting what kind of music he listened to before the games began, what kind of food he consumed for his pre-game meals. It was sort of like China-watching in the old world of foreign-correspondent journalism. The reporters had known that China was there, but since they couldn't get any information out of China, they had to interpret the little things they were able to discern. Same with Jordan. There he was—like China, he existed—but everything else tonight was conjecture.

One of the great sights on this China-watching evening was on display across the court, in the bench seats where the Orlando team would sit during the game. Seated next to each other, watching Jordan warm up, were two people who, if not for Jordan, would probably never in a hundred thousand years meet or speak. One of them was Jerry Reinsdorf. The multimillionaire owner of the Bulls had let it be known that whatever the NBA wanted to fine him for Jordan's insistence on wearing number 23, he would be happy to write a check. He was making a show of a rare pre-game appearance at courtside, in full range of the cameras, watching Jordan warm up, to send a wordless signal of support in the great numeral controversy. And sitting next to him—they were chatting like two old friends in front of the stock-market ticker at an exclusive old-line men's club—was George Koehler. Jerry Reinsdorf and Michael Jordan's driver. What a picture. What a symbol. What a world.

An NBA moment:

In the Orlando locker room, as Shaquille O'Neal, Horace Grant, Anfernee Hardaway and the other Magic stars got dressed for the game, Tree Rollins sat in his cubicle.

Not in front of it. In it. Rollins—seven-foot-one, thirty-nine years old, eighteen years in the NBA, a player-coach for the Magic, wearing his full game uniform—had pulled his chair inside the cubicle, had done his best to fold his body into the three-sided structure, and was talking in muted tones into a cellular phone.

He had turned the cubicle into a phone booth. Like a kid afraid that his brothers and sisters will hear him asking a girl out on a date and make fun of him, Rollins drew his arms and legs into the cubicle and, with the assistance of whatever satellite was conveying his conversation, sent his voice out of the Magic locker room toward destinations unknown.

Although he could simply have been trying to get in on disseminating the scoop: Number 23. Black shoes.

In the first quarter the Bulls took an early lead on Orlando, and just for a moment as I watched Jordan it was as if all the days and nights since the murder of his father had been compressed into one, as if I were seeing all those sunrise mornings of batting practice in Sarasota, and all the frustrating minor-league innings in the South, the cloudless afternoons in Arizona, the short and vexing return to spring training, hearing all the words, listening to all the expressions of hopeful longing and all the expressions of self-doubt—it was as if all that were coming together right here. I thought about where he would be tonight had he not taken this last chance, I tried to envision the bright nighttime lights of whatever small-town baseball park whose outfield grass he would be walking across right now, and everything that had happened, everything I had seen, seemed, if not impossible, then from some far and elusory time and place.

It had all happened so fast, and it wasn't over, and down there, wearing the same white uniform with the same red number as when he had left, Jordan cut hard for the basket. With 4:17 left in the first quarter and the Bulls leading 26–19, Pippen took the ball to the top of the key, went into the air, hit a swift, straight and even jump shot, and this was it, the crowd rose and roared and he and Jordan nodded toward each other on the way back on defense. This was the electrified feeling of those championship nights, and even though it would turn out to be a false surge of optimism, even though this was destined not to last even through this series of games, the anticipatory delight was in the air, the people in the immense room were believing, and I looked at Jordan and thought of all those unlikely months in between.

Tom Smithburg, who had been flying on the charter with the Bulls and, as one of the team's front-office spokesmen, had had to answer all the questions from the national sports press about why Jordan had stopped talking at the arenas, said that when he was with his teammates there was no sign that he was embittered or on edge.

"The thing I've noticed is that he's just completely focused," Smithburg said. "It's like he decided to turn on that switch that brings the curtain down and shuts everything out but basketball. He thought he had a bad first half in Game 2 in Orlando, and he came into the locker room and he kicked the garbage can, he was so upset with himself. He's just in this tunnel of his, and he doesn't want to be out of it.

"He's the same guy he always is at practice, the same guy with his teammates. Nothing has changed, except that he's put himself in that tunnel, and I think he sees the end of the tunnel as the last game of the playoffs. It's like he's built the tunnel to get him through this, and to keep every other distraction in the world away."

This was Smithburg's first time through a playoffs with Jordan— he had come to work for the team after Jordan's departure—and I asked him whether, seeing it from such close range, he was surprised by anything.

"The intensity of how he does this," Smithburg said. "When I put it into words, it doesn't really do justice to just how incredibly intense he is. The tunnel's invisible, but he's built it on purpose, and even when he's smiling and talking to his teammates, or walking through a crowd, you know he's in there, looking toward the end."

The Magic were up 52–51 with 5:07 left in the first half, and the ball came out of a crowd beneath the basket and drifted up onto the backboard glass. Kukoc, Pippen and Luc Longley moved toward it as one person, rising toward the thick glass pane in their white home Bulls uniforms, banging up against the board as the ball kept missing the hoop, until finally, all their fingers flailing, Kukoc tipped it in. The sheer effort of it, the sense of exuberant gladness amid the professional purpose, the explicit faith among the three of them that they could do it—those were not the kinds of things that wound up on the final statistics sheet, but they surely counted for something, they were part of what makes the game what it is. Kukoc's tip fell through the net, and the scoreboard changed to 53–52 Bulls, as if that were the only way to record what had just transpired.

And:

With 17.3 seconds remaining in the half, Jordan was standing with the ball, positioned straight-up above the key, his feet motionless on the light wooden planks of the court. The clock was speeding down in tenths of seconds, and everyone in the building—the fans in the seats, the broadcasters behind their microphones, the other Bulls and Magic players on the floor, the coaches and reserves on the two benches—every person was watching him.

When I was first getting to know Jordan, this was one of the things about which I had been most curious. The feeling at a moment like this one—the feeling as he stood there, knowing that whatever was about to occur, whatever was about to be seen in millions of homes around the world, would not take place until he made up his mind what to do—was it a frightening feeling? Did the pressure and the responsibility of that feeling weigh heavily on him, alone out there?

"I'm not nervous at all in that situation," he had said. "Because I feel like I'm in total control. Whatever's going to happen out there, it's not going to happen until I start it. And everyone in the building knows it. Moments like that make me happy. . . . It's fun."

Fun?

"Doesn't that sound like fun to you?" he had said. "Everyone in the building knowing you have to do something, and everyone on the other team not wanting you to do it? And then you have to do it in spite of all that?"

Tonight, before the game, when I had been standing on the edge of the court talking with Tom Smithburg, he had brought up a variation of the same thought.

"Sometimes I lose sight of the fact that he has to actually come out here and do this," Smithburg said. "Sitting around talking to him in the locker room or on the plane, watching him go through all the things he goes through every day, I don't usually stop to think about what he has to do once the games begin.

"The rest of us watch it, but every night he has to step out here onto this floor and do it again, with everyone trying to stop him. I know that's obvious—but when you stand right here where it happens, and you think about it, you wonder how he can always stay so calm."

And now it was that time again. Clock running down, every eye on him, defense converging. "It's fun," he had said. There are experiences in this life the rest of us will never taste, feelings we can never know.

"The best moment?" Jordan said. "That's easy."

I had asked him what was his single happiest moment since he had decided to come back to the Bulls. Was it the shot in Atlanta that won the game? The 55 points in New York?

"It was coming into the arena at home for the first time," he said.

"That regular-season game against Orlando—the first time I played in this building."

"That was the best?" I said. "You had such a bad game."

"Yeah, the game, I was terrible," he said. "I wanted so badly to do well. You have no idea how much it meant to me to have a good game. And I had a terrible game."

"Do you know why?" I said.

"Maybe I wasn't ready to do well yet, and I didn't know it," Jordan said. "I knew my skills were there—that wasn't it. So maybe for some reason I just wasn't ready for it to happen."

"So why do you say that was the best moment?" I said.

"It was the sound," he said. "The sound of the crowd when I came onto the court. I had put my uniform on, and I was in the hallway back there waiting to come in. And then I came in, and that sound I was hearing in my ears, I can't even tell you. . . ."

"You've always said that you don't need the cheers," I said.

"It wasn't that—it wasn't that I needed the cheers," he said. "It's not like I had gone around missing the cheers. But what I was hearing in those cheers that night, it was like they were saying something to me. It made me think that all those people were saying to me, 'It's good to see you.' Like they were saying, 'We're happy you're here. We want you to be here.' Whatever questions I still might have been having about whether I should have come back, the questions went away that night.

"I wish I would have played better. But I'll never forget the night."

Game 3 ended with a Bulls collapse, and after the game Shaquille O'Neal, whose team walked off the floor with a 110–101 victory, held court as if the series were already over. The Bulls–Magic matchup had been promoted on the nation's business pages almost as heavily as on the sports pages; Jordan and O'Neal were the two biggest names in basketball, between them they endorsed just about every top-of-the-line product an athlete's agent could desire, and marketing experts were saying that the Jordan–O'Neal corporate battle was even more important than the games between their two teams.

So O'Neal, loose and informal, talked with the sportswriters in a conference area down the hallway from the Magic's locker room. Still in his jersey—Jordan was invariably in a suit and tie by the time he met the press—O'Neal said all the right things. Asked about the relative appeal to children of Jordan and himself, O'Neal went into his by-now-well-rehearsed response, the one destined to make Jordan chafe: "It's an honor just to be mentioned in the same breath with a legend."

This time, he added a winking postscript:

"He's Superman. I'm Superboy."

Which is exactly what O'Neal's advisers would have wanted him to say, with the emphasis placed on his youth. He kept it up; someone asked him what the differences were between the two men, and O'Neal said, "We both have nice smiles. He's been in the league ten years, I've been in three . . ."

While this was going on, Jordan emerged from a side door of the Bulls' locker room, his off-duty police officers around him. Not only had his team lost, but once again he had looked weak down the stretch. He had scored 40 points during the game, but Horace Grant—his former teammate—knocked the ball out of Jordan's hands as Jordan was trying to make the tying basket with less than two minutes left; the Magic took control and the Bulls never scored again.

So his expression was glum and he looked straight ahead as his guards walked him out of the building. The contrast was stark: O'Neal, insouciant and laughing, joking with the press in his untucked-in basketball jersey, while Jordan, like a man going into surgery, marched stiffly past in his business suit.

A reporter asked O'Neal if he planned to change his uniform number, like Jordan had.

"My mother won't let me," he said, to more laughter. Jordan was gone from the building.

. . . . .

So often through the years, in situations like that, the emotions he showed were very much like those of a dejected youngster coming home from school after a bad day, upset because everything has gone unhappily, believing everything and everyone has turned against him—certain he's never going to have an ounce of energy again. And then the child is back early the next day, bright-eyed and eager, first one there, ready to try.

The analogy would seem to be too easy—except that with him, some of the most important parts of his life had happened just that way. Were he not so constitutionally unable to quit—were he somehow not the kind of person who can't give up for more than a day before deciding that giving up isn't acceptable—then none of the rest of us would ever have heard his name. On that watershed day he was cut from his high school basketball team at fifteen, was told he wasn't good enough, he had hurried home to cry by himself behind closed doors—and then, instead of walking away from the game, he had refused to accept the evaluation, and had merely made himself into the best player who ever lived. He had never forgotten the details of that day—in a lot of ways, that boy was always still inside him. Sometimes I found myself thinking that if he hadn't been cut from the team—if he hadn't been sent away—he might never have become who he was.

Now the long coming-back was from a hurt much more profound; now the rebound was from the murder of the man he loved the most. All of the things that had taken place since the day of the killing were Jordan's instinctive answer to his pain. Everything that he had done in the time since then, every day and every night, was part of his lifelong pattern, now being tested. Each move he made was part of his effort to keep moving forward, to not let anything or anyone slow him down. If he kept moving, things would work out all right. They always had.

For Game 4, he showed up early to shoot by himself. The despondency he had shown after the previous loss had disappeared; he was smiling as he shot, wisecracking with people on the sidelines, kidding around with some hockey players from the Chicago Blackhawks who were in the arena. The sun had come up; it always did.

The Bulls would win the game, 106–95. What stuck in my mind, though, was one small moment, not an important one in the flow of the game.

Late in the first quarter, Jordan was sitting on the bench. Phil Jackson had taken him out to give him some rest.

Then, with the Bulls ahead 31–20, and 28.6 seconds left in the quarter, Jackson decided that he wanted to bring Jordan back in for the team's final possession. Jordan, as was his custom, was sitting down at the far end of the bench.

Jackson, standing on the sidelines wearing a dark suit, pointed his left arm in Jordan's direction, signaling to him.

And Jordan, seeing that he was wanted in the contest, got up and came *running* down the length of the bench toward the game. *Running*, like a kid afraid of being left behind, like a boy who is finally getting the chance to play in his first game. Thirty-two years old, with nothing to prove to anyone, and it was like he was afraid that if he were to be late, the game would go on without him; it was like he thought he had to run or he would not get to be a part of this. Like this was his first and only chance, and he was not going to let anyone or anything make him miss it.

After the win that day Jordan and the Bulls lost their next two games against the Magic, and were eliminated from the playoffs.

When he got to Orlando for Game 5, he began talking to the sportswriters again. Of the uniform-number switch, he said, "That's me. Twenty-three is me. So why try to be something else?" He acknowledged that he was wrong in not letting the NBA know in advance that he was going to go back to his old number: "The biggest thing is that I kind of forgot about that rule that you have to notify the league, and I'll pay the fine." He said he had been critical of his own play, which had led to his decision to stay to himself and not talk publicly about his game: "Whatever I have to say, I'm basically going to do on the basketball court anyway. . . . Sometimes I set higher expectations than what I can produce at times. It isn't that I can't do it. I know I can do it."

He had 39 points in Game 5, and did his best to take over in the final quarter, after Chicago wasted a 7-point halftime lead by falling apart in the third. Horace Grant, with his championship experience from his Bulls years, again was the hero for Orlando, scoring 24 points on 10-for-13 shooting, pulling down eleven rebounds, and declining to let his teammates throw the game away. "Horace has been their MVP," Jordan said to the sportswriters after the game, knowing that Grant could just as well have been wearing a Chicago uniform in these playoffs, had the Bulls' management made an effort to keep him in town. With the 103–95 loss, the Bulls headed home trailing 3–2 in the best-of-seven series, and needing a Game 6 win in Chicago to stay in the post-season tournament.

They didn't get it. The Bulls led the Magic at the end of the first quarter, at the end of the second quarter, at the end of the third quarter, and were still ahead by 8 points—102–94—with 3:24 remaining. But Orlando would score the next 14 points—the Bulls would score none for the rest of the game—and Jordan would fail in his attempts to save it for his team. He completely missed the basket on one shot, missed again, and passed off two other times when he had the ball— once to Luc Longley, who missed the ensuing shot, and once to no one for a turnover. The final score was 108–102 Orlando. The Magic players were celebrating on the Chicago floor—Grant most demonstratively—and the Bulls were finished.

Yet Jordan, rather than hiding out or sulking, was in remarkably good spirits after the game. He sat and talked with the sportswriters until they were out of questions, his voice lively, his comments mixed with grins and laughter—it seemed that he didn't want to leave the arena. Those nights of walking out in gloom, those days of making no comments at all about the games—and now, faced with a situation that might have been expected to devastate him, it seemed that he'd stay in the building forever if he could make an excuse for doing it.

"I came back with a dream," he told the sportswriters and broadcasters gathered around his locker. "Was that unrealistic? Maybe, if you look at it right now. . . . Yeah, now, since we lost. But when I came back, no."

Over the summer ahead, he would keep moving, as always. The motion picture offer that had been his for taking—the live-action/cartoon feature with Bugs Bunny and the other characters—was still there, and he decided to do it. In August he went to Hollywood to begin his film career. He had planned his shooting schedule so that the movie would be completed in time for him to report to Bulls training camp in October.

But—one more move in a career full of moves that surprised and perplexed people—he, Patrick Ewing, and a group of other NBA players led the movement to try to decertify the players' union, which they felt was poorly representing the athletes. The action cast uncertainty into negotiations between the owners and the players, and by late summer NBA commissioner David Stern was saying that the new season itself was in jeopardy, and was trying to strike a last-minute bargain with a coalition of the union's members. ("The kind of money they're giving up, they're never going to see again," Jordan had said of the striking baseball players back at spring training.) Stern was especially upset at Jordan—the two had never been close—for being a part of the splinter movement. But Jordan was on a California soundstage, talking to those imaginary cartoon characters who would be drawn in later, after he had left Hollywood. As always, he was everywhere and nowhere.

On that night the Bulls lost their final game in the playoffs, though, he appeared to be in no hurry at all.

"I'm looking forward to starting over and getting to know everybody in a season," he said to the people around his locker.

". . . Maybe that was part of this team's downfall, just trying to rush getting to know each other and understand each other. . . .

"I'm not afraid to go back and go through the basics to see where it will lead me down the stretch."

· · · · ·

Even with those words about the future, there was a sense that something had just ended—this time in his life that had been defined by the tragedy that had changed everything. What he had done in the wake of that was now finished. What would happen next was still very much to be determined.

I asked him one day what was the most important thing he had discovered during this time since the death of his father.

"That I should never stop learning," he said.

"About what?" I said.

"Everything," he said.

"Basketball?" I said.

"Well, yes, basketball," he said. "But not that so much. I sort of know basketball."

"Then what?" I said.

"I just want to keep learning about everything I can," he said. "About life, and about my family, and about me. It can all end so quickly. You don't know when. So you've got to give yourself every experience, because if you don't, you may never get the chance."

CHAPTER 19

During the summer I received a telephone call from a woman by the name of Marcia Bogolub. She said that she lived in the same suburb north of Chicago where Jordan lived. She had seen something, and was surprised by how moved she was by it.

Her seven-year-old son was on a youth baseball team, in a local beginner's league. She and her husband went to watch him practice one evening, and there, off to the side, was Jordan, watching his own son practice.

"He was just by himself, his eyes on his boy," she said. "Obviously everyone there—all of the parents, all of the children—had noticed. I mean, this was Michael Jordan at a kids' ballfield.

"But no one walked up and bothered him. All of the parents told their own sons not to go up for autographs—that this was Mr. Jordan's time to be with his family. He was pitching balls to his son. Just like a regular dad would do—standing on the grass near the diamond, and tossing the ball to his son, teaching him how to catch. It was such a lovely moment—seeing him trying to just be a father. A person."

That was one part of Jordan—a part he seemed to regret he had so missed out on during all the years on the road. "My children love it that I'm not going to be playing in the minor leagues this summer," he told me. "When I first came back to the Bulls, I'd get up every morning and drive my son to school, and it was already a great day for me before anything else happened. That was enough to make the day, right there—waking up in the morning and being in my own house, with my own family."

I asked him what part of that gave him so much satisfaction.

"Being on the ground," he said. "Just feeling that I'm standing on the ground."

He had spent so much of his life in the air—both literally, in his perpetual jet commutes across the world of American sports, and metaphorically, in the extravagant language that was so often used to describe his playing style. Now he was saying that being up there no longer had the same appeal for him.

"I'm on the ground now," he said. "It feels right."

And yet that was only one portion of him, and he seemed to know it. Whatever attraction the idea of being grounded in a quietly satisfying and standard life held for him, every action he ever took showed that he was yearning for something different—always had, always would. Among all the reasons for his frenetic changes and nonstop motion during these recent years, there was one connective theme: the theme of a man who seems always to be striving for a life in which there are no seasons, or at least in which there is one never-ending season—a seamless season of the heart in which there is no need ever to pause, no reason ever to stop.

That fantasy he had told me about back when the baseball quest was new—the fantasy about what would happen the first time he came to bat—stayed in my mind. The most telling part of that fantasy was not the home run he imagined hitting—any would-be baseball player hopes for that. The part of the story that lingered was what he fantasized about doing once the home run had cleared the fence, and he had crossed home plate and run through the stadium tunnel. "I just keep on running," he had said. "Keep on running forever."

So which was it? The man who said how much he valued the idea of staying in one place, remaining tethered to the ground, being constant? Or the other man, the one whose deepest longing was that the trip would never cease, the finish line would never appear, the miles and years of running would never have to end?

"Sometimes I wonder what it will be like to look back on all of this," he once said to me. "Whether it will even seem real." But there's no looking back while you're still running. That's the blessing and the bane. As long as the race is on, the world passing by you is a blur, and will stay that way until you finally declare the contest over.

"There's only one person who can tell you whether you've won or lost," he said, seeming to mean it.

"And that's you."

ABOUT THE AUTHOR

Bob Greene, author of the national bestseller *Hang Time: Days and Dreams with Michael Jordan*, is a syndicated columnist for the *Chicago Tribune*. His column appears in more than two hundred newspapers in the United States, Canada and Japan. For nine years his "American Beat" was the lead column in *Esquire* magazine; as a broadcast journalist he has served as contributing correspondent for "ABC News Nightline." In 1995, for his reporting on how the courts fail children in need, he was named Illinois Journalist of the Year, and also was honored with the Peter Lisagor Award for Public Service Journalism.

Greene is the author of fourteen previous books, most recently his first novel, *All Summer Long*. In addition to *Hang Time*, his nationally bestselling works of nonfiction include *Be True to Your School*; *Good Morning, Merry Sunshine*; and, with his sister, journalist D. G. Fulford, *To Our Children's Children: Preserving Family Histories for Generations to Come*. His next book, *Chevrolet Summers, Dairy Queen Nights*, will be published by Viking in 1996.